Embedding Spiritualit
Religion in Social Work Practice

Blending material from social work with religious and spiritual sources, this book makes explicit that engaging with spirituality in its broadest sense is an essential aspect of socially just social work practice. Gardner connects shared understandings of spiritual/religious traditions, critically reflective social work, First Nations relational world views, green and relational approaches.

Through multiple unique case studies, *Embedding Spirituality and Religion in Social Work Practice: A Socially Just Approach* outlines the theoretical framework of critical spirituality, which is explored as a way of workers' understanding their own and others' sense of meaning, whether it is spiritual and/or religious, and to encourage workers to be mindful, open, humble and energised as workers.

Combining the theoretical and practical, this book outlines strategies and processes to ensure social workers embed spirituality in their practice constructively and inclusively across all areas of practice. This book will be of interest to those engaged in the wider field of social work, from direct service to policy development.

Fiona Gardner practised as a social worker for twenty years and now teaches and coordinates social work at La Trobe University's Rural Health School. Fiona has run workshops on spirituality, supervision and critical reflection and researched and written widely on critical reflection and critical spirituality.

Embedding Spirituality and Religion in Social Work Practice

A Socially Just Approach

Fiona Gardner

Routledge
Taylor & Francis Group

LONDON AND NEW YORK

Cover image: Drew Lawson, 'Iona Bench'

First published 2022
by Routledge
4 Park Square, Milton Park, Abingdon, Oxon OX14 4RN

and by Routledge
605 Third Avenue, New York, NY 10158

Routledge is an imprint of the Taylor & Francis Group, an informa business

British Library Cataloguing-in-Publication Data
A catalogue record for this book is available from the British Library

Library of Congress Cataloguing-in-Publication Data
Names: Gardner, Fiona, author.
Title: Embedding spirituality and religion in social work practice : a socially just approach / Fiona Gardner.
Description: Abingdon, Oxon ; New York, NY : Routledge, 2022. | Includes bibliographical references. |
Identifiers: LCCN 2021046525 (print) | LCCN 2021046526 (ebook) | ISBN 9780367677541 (paperback) | ISBN 9780367677558 (hardback) | ISBN 9781003132677 (ebook)
Subjects: LCSH: Social service--Religious aspects. | Social service--Practice.
Classification: LCC HV40 .G3659 2022 (print) | LCC HV40 (ebook) | DDC 361.3/2--dc23/eng/20211104
LC record available at https://lccn.loc.gov/2021046525
LC ebook record available at https://lccn.loc.gov/2021046526

ISBN: 978-0-367-67755-8 (hbk)
ISBN: 978-0-367-67754-1 (pbk)
ISBN: 978-1-003-13267-7 (ebk)

DOI: 10.4324/9781003132677

Typeset in Bembo
by MPS Limited, Dehradun

To Drew as always, a constant source of spiritual knowledge and inspiration.

Contents

**Application to practice: how to include spirituality and
religion in ethical social work practice**   111

7   Embedding spirituality and religion in practice: working
    with individuals and families   113

8   Spirituality, religion and the broader context:
    organisational, community and policy practice   134

9   Socially just spirituality – engaging ethically   149

    Conclusion   162

    Appendix: Further reading about religious and spiritual traditions   165
    References   166
    Index   177

Figures

Acknowledgements

Acknowledgement of country:

I want to start by acknowledging that I live and work on the land of the Dja Dja Wurrung People who are the traditional owners of this land and pay my respects to their Elders past, present and emerging. I express my gratitude for the sharing of this land and sorrow for the personal, spiritual and cultural costs of that sharing.

This land, particularly the forest next to where I live was constantly inspiring in the writing of this book. As I finish writing, bright yellow wattle is out in the ironbark forest and kookaburras are laughing in the distance.

General Acknowledgement:

I also want to acknowledge the many people who knowingly or unknowingly have contributed to the development of this book. Students, workshop participants, colleagues and managers, friends and family have shared examples and experiences which have influenced what has been included here.

Some people have also read and commented on this and related writing that has clarified and expanded my understanding. Particular thanks to Drew Lawson, who contributed the book cover and a poem, and to Jill Hanlon, who contributed several of the case studies. Thanks also to Jenny Mitchell, Cheryl Hunt and Robin Sinclair.

Introduction

It is often some kind of crisis in our personal lives that encourages thinking about what really matters. Significant illness, death in the family or of someone close, financial stress or a significant change in relationships prompts us to be more conscious of questions of meaning. Alternatively, the significance of war, climate-related bushfires or floods, leads to asking some of these fundamental questions of life. Our recent, global experience of the COVID-19 virus had a more universal influence for many in generating sudden, sharp, painful questioning of what really matters in their lives. Being suddenly removed from most of the things that have seemed to be essential has encouraged asking what really is important? For some people this included matters of life and death, having people in their families who are significantly ill or dying. For others it was loss of work, the ability to relate to others, lack of connection to family and friends, regret about the absence of all sorts of things – from informal catch-ups to being able to travel or simply to go to the beach or a park when they want to.

Such events as the COVID-19 virus seem to bring out the best and worst of us. Sad tales of hoarding, competing for toilet paper in supermarkets or for various kinds of food, people disregarding ways to safeguard their own and the health of others have frequently been in the media. However, these have been more than balanced by other stories. Many have noticed and appreciated smaller and larger acts of kindness, the altruism of those who have worked in ways that risked their own lives, who have adapted what they do to meet the needs of those who are more vulnerable. We have become conscious of those who are often not noticed: the person who delivers what you need, truck drivers working long hours to replenish supplies, those volunteering to sew masks or protective clothing at home. It was truly a time for thinking about values, contemplating what it is that you really miss and what you would like to have restored. It was also a time for some people at least to contemplate what is it that sustains them in times of trouble, what underlying beliefs and values, what connections are fundamental to living in a way that has meaning.

These questions are ones that, in my experience as a social worker and now social work academic, we return to, usually in times of crisis. Often it is the crisis that jolts us out of our normal routine that becomes then an opportunity

DOI: 10.4324/9781003132677-1

if we choose to see it that way. We ask why is this happening to me, how do I create and live with a sense of meaning about this so that it doesn't overwhelm me completely? This experience is connected to deeper, fundamental questions of who am I? if I am not simply the roles that I carry out, who am I at a deeper level? What is it that underlies these roles that creates meaning for me? What can I trust when life feels unpredictable? How do I live my life based on what really matters to me? Some people of course, do ask these questions more constantly, seeking to live from a spiritual or religious way of looking at the world that engages fundamentally with these questions.

I am writing this book because it seems to me that these questions are ones that social workers must be able to engage in, with those they work with. While they are questions that are more often articulated in a crisis or a time of significant change, they are also questions that underpin much of the work we do. They may be more likely to be asked when people are terminally ill or have had a serious accident. However, they can be equally useful when you are working with families in child protection, refugee communities experiencing dislocation or those who have offended. These questions are also vital to help you understand more fully where people are coming from: what beliefs influence their perspective on life and their struggles? Do these include spiritual and/or religious beliefs and, if so, what is their influence? Alternatively, are there unconscious values and beliefs influenced by past religious practices or simply from family expectations that are significant? We also need to ask these questions of ourselves as workers, personally and professionally.

Why does this matter? For those we work with, including the spiritual means connecting with what restores and enables them and it follows that if we recognise this for ourselves and others, there will be mutual benefits. For me, reflecting on my own work experience, I have found that being aware of and actively connecting to my spiritual self and paying attention to those times of transcendence and wonder helps me be both more grounded and more open, able to recognise my own beliefs and values about what really matters and what keeps me 'flourishing' but also more able to sit with the different experience of others. I am more likely to respond constructively and creatively to conflict and in engaging with all aspects of my life and work. It follows that this is likely to be the case for you and those you work with: also to be more restored, life live more fully and manage the inevitable challenges of life more positively.

While social work's beginnings were influenced by religious beliefs and related organisations, for many years in many countries there has been an emphasis on secular social work which has meant that religion and spirituality have been relatively ignored. This means that we have not paid sufficient attention to the centrality of spirituality and religion in the lives of many of our clients. We have also tended to underplay the importance of religion in many of the factors that affect the societies, communities and individuals that we work with. However, this has started to change with the increase of writing and research in social work generally and specifically related to including religion and spirituality in social work education. When we pay attention to it, religion and spirituality is everywhere: I decided I would identify everything that connected in the media to religion and spirituality one day when I was writing this book simply reading the daily news and listening to whatever happened to be on the car radio:

My breakfast reading included:

The costs for the Catholic church in paying compensation for people who had been sexually abused by those employed by the church.

The experiences of Uighur Muslims in China related to their religion.

On my way to work:

A radio program where the director of Corrymeala Institute was being interviewed about their work in reconciling people of different religious faiths – and incidentally how poetry encourages religious ways of thinking.

On my way home from work:

A discussion with a worker from a Catholic health care agency about what it was like for secular workers to work there and his reaction to the Pope's writings about the need to care for the Earth. A second radio program where an avowed atheist quoted from religious writers about how to manage conflict.

The aim of this book then is to make explicit how engaging with spirituality in its broadest sense is an essential aspect of social work practice. What I mean by spirituality will be explored in more detail in Chapter 1, but essentially is what gives life meaning including the experience of the transcendent: a sense of something greater than the self which might be a sense of interconnection and belonging to the universe. This is expressed in a multitude of ways and will be described differently depending on personal and group preferences as spiritual and/or religious. Meaning of life questions are ones we can all relate to and social workers need to be able to engage with these: questions of what really matters, what meaning does life have for me, who am I? This is not a value-free approach. I am also affirming the value of *critical* spirituality which "elicits, or is a way of naming, a desire to work with what is meaningful in the context of enabling a socially just, diverse and inclusive society" (Gardner, 2011, p. 77).

What I am advocating here is a holistic approach to social work practice that includes the spiritual, underpinned by understanding the theoretical connections particularly between religion/spirituality, critically reflective social work, First Nations relational world views, green social work and psychodynamic relational approaches. What these have in common is making more explicit what would generally be seen as an expectation of social work practice: working with all of a person with at least an awareness of the connections between them and all of their environment. Each of these theoretical connections informs this awareness more deeply and adds vital complexity. From this perspective spirituality may be an aspect of working with an individual, a family or a community, be part of political, social and policy change and of program development and research. Including spirituality and religion will add a significant dimension that is often implicit in practice, that needs to be made more explicit. Canda, Furman and Canda (2020, p. 236) affirm that while spiritual and religious perspectives have significant differences "they also have a remarkable similarity in the core of their values with regard for service. The commonalities imply possibilities for finding common ground. The differences provide many insights for various helping strategies in social work."

Part of what I will argue is that as workers we need to be aware of our own assumptions and beliefs related to spirituality and to understand how our social context and history has influenced us. First Nations wisdom also prompts acknowledgement of who we are in relation to family and community. So some background of my own: I was born into a family of Scottish Presbyterians, with my grandfather and an uncle on my mother's side being ministers in that church. We emigrated to Australia when I was 9 and my parents continued the same tradition of church attendance, with all my family regularly attending services on Sundays and seeing ourselves as part of the community there. My parents had different perceptions of the value of this: for my mother the essence of the religious tradition was more important, the power of prayer. My father relished the community aspect of church and especially the singing. As an adolescent growing up in this community, the Friday night youth group, Sunday bible study/discussion evenings became important ways of exploring who I was, developing confidence socially and in contributing to organising activities. It was also an environment that fostered asking and exploring meaning of life questions. My Celtic background may also have influenced my connection to nature with significant early experiences as a child of feeling interconnected to and transcending all of the natural world. Indigenous Celtic spirituality was also what Duncan (2015, p. 1) describes as "an earthy religion based on a close and intimate relationship with the environment."

As an adult, I became interested in the more silent worship of Quakers, and their commitment to social justice also appealed to me. Quakers, like any other faith tradition have different ways in which this is expressed. I would fit with what are called universalist Quakers: engaging with what is shared across religious traditions. My experience is with those Quaker Meetings that don't have paid religious leaders, but rather expect all members to share this responsibility. In this form of Quakers, we have what is essentially a silent form of worship, what you might think of as shared meditation or shared seeking of the spirit for an hour. My experience of this silent time – with someone occasionally speaking if moved to – was that it was for the most part, deeply regenerating and encouraged me to live from my fundamental values. Much of what is essential to Quakers' beliefs was congruent with my social work values and reinforced them: for example believing that "there is that of God in every one" – or spirit or goodness – reflected my social work values of respecting each person I worked with. Taking this seriously meant paying attention to all those I met, seeking to find their perspective or the validity of where they were coming from. Valuing each person's spiritual experience also fitted with social work's respecting of each person's perspective combined with an expectation of acting "justly." I found that my spiritual experience supported and sometimes actively challenged me to be a better social worker.

Given my background, I was somewhat surprised coming into the social work course in the 1970s in my late teens to find that there was almost no mention of religion or spirituality. It was as if my personal life remained attuned to the spiritual, but my work life strictly secular. I was even more surprised when I started teaching social work twenty years later to find not much had changed. As I have written elsewhere (Gardner, 2020) I was challenged first by students raising this as an issue. Several students in my early years of teaching felt uncomfortable about being explicit about their religious beliefs, including how these influenced their desire to do social work. A nun chose not to reveal her vocation because she believed she would be judged, and students would be reluctant to befriend her. Around the same time, I worked in a Catholic agency for half a day a week and found many clients, including those not identifying as Catholic, saw it as legitimate to raise spiritual and religious issues. This was significantly different to my experience in secular agencies where these issues weren't named. Now, in my regional community, the issues of acceptance of religious diversity have become particularly relevant, as they are in many other communities. Students themselves recognise this and are somewhat more likely to raise issues related to acceptance of spiritual and perhaps more religious diversity.

Having seen and experienced the negative impact of no time for reflection in practice, I was also interested in critical reflection being part of social work education. Critical reflection in unearthing underlying meaning can provide the link with spirituality. While these may seem externally quite different, they have much in common. Asking about meaning implies acknowledging the spiritual world. It encourages asking how do I see life, my own and others? How do I want to live my life? What beliefs and values underpin what I do and why I do it? How does the spiritual realm influence me? Taking spirituality seriously means stopping and being still, taking time to sit with the larger questions of life's meaning, allowing transcendence of the immediate for connection with that which is greater and beyond the self. Critical reflection fosters this process: it provides a way of understanding my reactions to experiences, the deeper meaning that comes from connecting to fundamental values and seeing how these can be transformative, changing perceptions and interactions with the world.

This book explores all of these questions to encourage fully and holistically engaging with individuals and communities about their perspectives on what matters and what sustains and nurtures their spirit. I am emphasizing here the broad theoretical and practice knowledge and processes that foster this. Rather than providing specific in-depth information about specific religious and spiritual traditions, this book focuses on how to include spirituality and seeing what difference this can make.

I am assuming here that spirituality in the sense of paying attention to what is meaningful is a significant aspect of life for everyone in some way. One of the implications is that for you as a worker to be sustained in your practice as well as in working with others, including spirituality allows and enables asking about meaning and the deeper questions of life. It encourages seeking inner awareness of self/values and asking how you can live/act according to life-affirming values. The history of religion/spirituality teaches useful practices whether or not you would see yourself as religious, that will be explored in later chapters.

The book divides into three parts

Part One: Context and theoretical framework

This part outlines background ideas to understand how to include spirituality and religion: exploring how spirituality and religion can be understood, the context and history that has influenced social work attitudes to these and proposing a critical spirituality framework integrating learning from comparing theories and worldviews. More specifically the chapters include:

Chapter One: Understanding spirituality and religion

There are many descriptions of spirituality which reflects how difficult it is to define. People also disagree about whether to define the spiritual or not; some see it as problematic to try to define what is essentially subjective, beyond words, but others find being more explicit helpful. Religion is relatively easy to define in terms of shared beliefs and activities across religious traditions. Four separate groups of people are identified: those who do not see themselves as spiritual or religious (but for whom meaning is important), those who see themselves as having spiritual practices but are not religious, those who identify as religious but not limited to one religious tradition and those who identify with one religious tradition. Finally, the implications for practice with all four groups are named briefly.

Chapter Two: Spirituality, religion and social work – history and context

This chapter explores where spirituality/religion has been located in social work practice and how has this changed over time. Historically, social work had close connections to religious institutions, but with the development of more secular expectations, social work in most Western countries disengaged from these. How this is changing, both in the social context and in social work is explored and the implications for social work training.

Chapter Three: Building a theoretical framework for critical spirituality

Including spirituality means working towards more socially just, critically aware and inclusive way of practicing. What I am advocating here is the development of a critical spiritually framework that encourages integration of social work practice and spiritual understanding firmly based on a socially just and actively inclusive approach. As the basis for this, the chapter explores a number of theoretical approaches and First Nations worldviews that can foster this and to identify how connecting these can provide the complexity needed for an underlying framework. These are: First Nations worldviews, critical and postmodern, green social work and relational approaches combined with learning from spiritual and religious traditions.

Part Two: Capacities and processes for embedding spirituality and religion in social work

The second part of the book first explores the capacities or qualities that foster how to put all these ideas into practice – many of which will be familiar. Next, it outlines two key processes: being critically reflective and engaging with how spiritual journeys change over time. More specifically:

Chapter Four: Qualities of critical spirituality

This chapter will focus on the kinds of qualities, capacities and attitudes integral to spiritually inclusive and sensitive practice. These are a combination of those that are more internally focused and those more externally. The inner qualities or capacities include openness, humility and vulnerability, the ability to sit patiently and lovingly particularly with uncertainty and 'not knowing,' to listen deeply and in the process of listening being attuned to the other person's experience of what is meaningful. More externally focused capacities include understanding the influence of history and social context and connection to place and space. These are complemented by spiritual and cultural responsiveness and the commitment to a socially just approach: to be actively inclusive in advocating for celebration of diverse spiritual and religious perspectives in communities and society generally. While I will explore each of these separately, in practice they interact with each other to form the complexity of engaging holistically with each person or community.

Chapter Five: Embedding critical reflection

Understanding your own spiritual preferences and how these are influenced by your personal and social history and context is a key aspect of being able to work effectively with others in this area. This chapter outlines how workers can use critically reflective processes to identify their own, often deeply unconscious assumptions and values in relation to spirituality and religion, tapping into the underlying meaning that influences how they engage with practice. The resulting awareness means workers are less likely to be unconsciously and unhelpfully biased in how they listen to their client's experiences and beliefs.

Critical reflection does take an ideological position, is not neutral in advocating for social justice and social change. The process though is one that encourages unearthing your own position and understanding it more deeply. Critical reflection also encourages stopping and asking the important questions of spirituality: what is the meaning of this for me? Why is it important? How does it connect with what is deeper in my life?

Chapter Six: Understanding the spiritual journey

Writers from spiritual and religious traditions often use the language of a spiritual journey to help people identify how their beliefs and experiences have changed over time. This chapter gives an overview of ideas about stages and other aspects of the spiritual journey. I suggest that it is more helpful to use these ideas to think about aspects or ways of being in the spiritual journey rather than expecting a linear trajectory. This provides ways of thinking about these so that workers can see how these apply to their own journey and those they work with. This might include, for example, understanding the relative simplicity of beliefs of a new convert to a religion compared to the more nuanced experience of someone towards the end of their life.

Part Three: Application to practice: how to include spirituality and religion in ethical social work practice

Here the focus is on how to apply all that has been covered in engaging with practice: initially with individuals and families and then in organisations, communities and in policy development. Finally, how to manage the ethical issues that arise is included. More specifically:

Chapter Seven: Embedding spirituality and religion in practice with individuals and families

This chapter reinforces and extends existing social work knowledge and skills to including spirituality and religion. The critical spirituality theoretical framework identified in Chapter 3 underpins this, complemented by narrative and strengths approaches. The kinds of question that can help you engage where appropriate as you engage with others, work together on assessment and seeking change are outlined. Finally, the chapter suggests a number of spiritual practices that can help with embedding the spiritual, paying attention to what is meaningful for both workers and the individuals and families they work with. Examples include meditation or prayer, the use of silence, paying attention to what nurtures you spiritually and recognising the value of integrating spiritual practices into life. Such practices can foster the self-care benefits of embedding spirituality for practitioners as well as those they work with.

Chapter Eight: Spirituality, religion and the broader context: organisational, community and policy practice

Here, I move to engaging with how the organisational, community and policy contexts can all influence how spirituality is considered and how they are included – or not in practice. It may be that in order to build spiritually critical practice, the emphasis for change needs to be on one or all of these contexts rather than individual change. Each will have implicit or explicit assumptions related to spirituality and religion that may need to be articulated, reinforced or challenged. This chapter takes each context and uses examples to explore how to build spiritually inclusive practice.

Chapter Nine: Socially just spirituality: engaging ethically

This follows from the previous chapters: how can we engage with the dilemmas that arise related to spiritual and religious beliefs. How do we ensure that we are allowing each other to be spiritually celebrating in our own way including balancing rights and responsibilities? What are the ethical dilemmas of this and what frameworks for engaging ethically open up possibilities for practice? I use a number of case examples here to illustrate how this has been achieved in different parts of the world including in policy development, community building and organisational change.

I have used many scenarios and case studies throughout the book. Apart from my own examples, each of these has the essence of an experience of someone I have known and/or worked with, but each has been either combined with others or significantly changed to ensure anonymity.

Finally, it is important to say something here about the language of spirituality and religion. This is an issue that people often feel strongly about, related to past experience. When I worked with some palliative care teams, for example, some people were irritated by the word spirituality suggesting it was too vague and general; others didn't like the use of any specifically religious language including pastoral care, saying it had too many negative connotations. How language is used will be explored further in this book, but I ask you to be conscious of your reaction to language about spirituality and religion and where it comes from and interpret what is written accordingly.

Part I

Context and theoretical framework

1 Understanding spirituality and religion

A significant classroom experience for me was the discussion that emerged after two Muslim women described their faith tradition in a subject called Introduction to Diversity. After their presentation, a First Nations student who was also Christian started to ask them more detailed questions about their faith and to make explicit the links to her own Christian beliefs. For many in the class, the theological concepts were beyond their knowledge and understanding, but what was clear was that all three were enjoying making these links and feeling more deeply connected because of them. Religious beliefs that students thought would be opposed to each other had much in common – dialogue was clearly possible. It was also clear that their religious faith was important to all three and influenced how they lived and worked. Many of the other students described this as an eye-opening experience. First, they came to understand Muslim beliefs in a way not conveyed by often judgemental media and questioned the assumptions they had made about what Islam meant. Secondly, they recognised that if religion was such a key aspect of people's lives, for all three students involved, then this needed to be included in their practice.

This experience illustrates my own assumption, given my own experiences personally and professionally, that if social workers are to work holistically, we need to understand fully where people are coming from, as well as understanding ourselves and what fundamentally influences who we are. Social workers generally do aim to see the world from the perspective of those they work with including experiences of disability, culture or gender that are significantly different from theirs. We need to also include ways of being 'spiritual' or seeking meaning in our lives, which for some would include a religious tradition. This is not to suggest this is easy: the challenges of including spirituality and religion in social work reflect the tensions about how these are perceived in the broader social context. The broader culture tends to emphasise conflicts and differences related to spiritual and religious experience, rather than valuing the rich diversity of this aspect of life. However, as my classroom example illustrates it can help to seek common ground, to identity what is shared as well as being interested in what is different. This chapter explores how spirituality and religion are explained and experienced, how understandings of spirituality have developed and how spirituality relates to religion. I will also explore perceived benefits of religious traditions, as well as the need to manage the

DOI: 10.4324/9781003132677-3

tensions and challenges of how the essence of a religion will be expressed differently by individuals and groups. Four separate groups of people are identified: those who do not see themselves as spiritual or religious (but for whom meaning is still important), those who see themselves as having spiritual practices but not as religious, those who identify as religious/spiritual but not limited to one spiritual orientation or religious tradition and those who identify with one religious tradition. The implications for practice with all four groups are considered briefly and will be explored in more detail in the third part of the book.

What is spirituality?

One of the reasons social workers and others may be reluctant to explore spirituality and religious is that they are perceived as both personal and difficult to define and explain. In some ways, by their very nature you would expect this. However, I want to start by suggesting that there can be common ground for most of us here: that the experiential nature of the spiritual can provide a useful bridge in understanding what is shared across the spiritual and religious. What people mean by the spiritual generally encompasses a sense of transcendence, something that is inherently mysterious. Some name this as awe: a feeling of wonder, awareness of the interconnectedness of all things or the deep connections between the self and others or a deep longing for something else, something more in our lives. What I mean by transcendence is that sense of something greater, deeper or beyond our selves, but that also includes us. This is not separate from what we do and who we are, but rather can give us a deeper, more grounded sense of meaning, if we are aware of it. For many people this combines a connection between their inner lives and the external world. Some possible examples of this:

- Walking through a forest or up a hill to see a broader view of the landscape and feeling part of and in awe of the wonder of the physical universe
- Being creative in some way and feeling connected to others who create and the wonder of this process.
- Having a conversation at work about a painful experience that resonates with you so deeply that there is a depth of understanding between you and perhaps beyond you to the sadness or experience of others that transcends explanation.
- Taking part in a religious ceremony or form of worship and feeling connected to and transcending the immediate.
- Being present at significant life changing moments for yourself or others: the birth of a child, the death of someone close, a traumatic event that harms yourself or others; all of which can shock you into awareness of what really matters; sometimes a mutuality of joy and sadness; a consciousness of life and its fundamental meaning,
- Meeting with family or friends and suddenly noticing the warmth and mutual nurture that envelopes you and which fosters a sense of generating that warmth to the world

- Praying or meditating and feeling moved by awareness of your inter-connectedness to the universe and all the beings within it
- The experience of love, receiving and giving it.
- Being filled with a sense of purpose and belief in the value of what you are doing and how it contributes to a fairer, more caring, more inclusive world
- Gathering with others to share experiences of the spiritual.

What is key here is finding what this means for yourself, as Sue Wilson (2014) writes:

The red-flashing wren dances before me
a few marvellous minutes.

Experts interrogate me:

Was it black with scarlet back
or the crimson variety?
Do you know the wren responds to certain calls that we could teach you?

What I know is this:

My bird lives among the rocks, roots and growth at my ground of being, following its own rhythm.

I want to stand with a steady heart when it comes blazing out.

Naming spirituality as experiential can build connectedness: spirituality in this sense is something experienced by those who are religious as well as those who are not. Johnson (2017, p. 123) suggests that "If we pause to recognise that as professionals we share the same sky and the same earth as those who seek our help, then we would come to understand that our experiences of spirituality are also intrinsically interlinked." People do vary in their awareness of this idea of spirituality, but often this is more about paying attention rather than not having this kind of experience at all. Very few people would say they had never felt awe or wonder or felt deeply moved in a way that is beyond their rational experience. Affirming the aspects of life that are beyond the rational can take us to a place of more fundamental values, a place where we can embrace an underlying common humanity and shared sense of what really matters. This can happen as part of our work: "the *practice* of reflective practice offers keys to personal and social transformation in ways that encompass both the pragmatic and the transcendental" (Hunt, 2021, p. 57).

Moving beyond the duality of religion and spirituality

Thinking about spirituality as experience of the transcendent also helps move beyond the unhelpful duality of religion and spirituality. Hunt (2011, p. 6) says an underlying premise for the *Journal for the Study of Spirituality* is that many people seek guidance and resolution for such [meaning and value] questions within religious traditions and teachings while others prefer to do so within a humanist framework, often shaped by principles of social justice; and that some may reject the language of spirituality altogether but espouse what might be called 'spiritual values' in their lives and work. It also recognises that there are dimensions of spirituality to which predominantly cognitive answers about 'meaning and value' cannot easily be found, including lived experiences of awe and wonder.

Many people who are religious would also name spirituality as important. Hodge (2015) gives an example of this from a 2012 US national survey which found that approximately two thirds of the population considered themselves to be at least moderately spiritual and nearly 60% at least moderately religious with a strong correlation between these two. While this may vary depending on culture and country, it suggests that there can be significant common ground. A more specific example of this is my experience of two students who were initially perplexed about the meaning of spirituality: one described herself as religious, but not spiritual and the other as having no idea about religion or spirituality. We were using a First Nations framework to explore a holistic way of working which included the spiritual. Through discussion with the student who was religious, the second student came to understand that she too had her own spiritual self: the part of herself that was deeply regenerated by the wonder of the natural world. Similarly, the student who thought of herself as religious but not spiritual, could see that what she experienced both as part of her religious tradition and more generally could be called spiritual.

When we look for such connections, we do surprisingly often find them. Taylor (2010, pp. 7–8) who writes about 'dark green religion,' suggests that both traditionally religious people and those who see themselves as spiritual speak

> of the sacred importance of everyday life. Thus, spirituality can also be understood as a quest to deepen, renew, or tap into the most profound insights of traditional religions, as well as a word that consecrates otherwise secular endeavors such as psychotherapy, political and environmental activism, and one's lifestyle and vocational choices.

Because such activism can influence a person's beliefs and values, how they live these out and provide a mutually supportive community, Taylor suggests that "Unless one considers belief in divine beings or forces to be essential to a definition of religion, most contemporary spirituality can easily be considered religious." From this perspective, spirituality refers to the individual's longing for a sense of meaning by "means of morally responsible relationships between individuals, families, societies, cultures, religions and the natural environment within which people must live" (Ferreira, 2010, p. 14).

Clearly, there are many different perceptions and experiences of both spirituality as well as religion and it is important to be aware of these. Swinton

(2014, p. 172) for example takes the view that given how hard it is to define spirituality, it makes more sense to see how it manifests, to ask what spirituality does rather than what it is: "in all of its diverse forms, spirituality helps us to pay a different kind of attention to the world" – the kind of attention that draws "our gaze towards aspects of being human and caring humanly that is vital, but often overlooked" (Swinton, 2014, p. 168). Avoiding definitions can have a positive aspect given spirituality "rejoices in ambiguity and by avoiding simple resolutions maintain[s] the elusive qualities of the human condition" (Cobb, Rumbold and Puchalski, 2012, p. 487).

However, particularly for those not familiar with these ideas, it does help to try to explain what is meant. A definition that I like to use, partly because it is broad and inclusive, was developed by palliative care organisations seeking international consensus. They name spirituality as "the aspect of humanity that refers to the way individuals seek and express meaning and purpose, and the way they experience their connectedness to the moment, to self, to others, to nature and to the significant or sacred" (Puchalski et al, 2014, p. 642). This way of looking at spirituality reinforces the need for meaning and the varieties of ways people experience the spiritual. Similarly, Canda and Furman (2010, p. 5) name spirituality as "a universal quality of human beings and their cultures related to the quest for meaning, purpose, plurality, transcendence, well-being, and profound relationships with ourselves, others, and ultimate reality." Implict in this is the transformative aspect of the spiritual, the potential for understanding life differently and for healing and wellbeing, reaching greater clarity and purpose.

Some communities would describe spirituality as integral to who they are, that it is so much a part of the person and their way of life that there is no choice about including it. From a First Nations perspective for example, spirituality is central to life and to well-being: Grieves (2009, p. 52) says "Spirituality" is a feeling, with a base in connectedness to the past, ancestors, and the values that they represent, for example, respect for elders, a moral/ethical path. It is about being in an Aboriginal cultural space, experiencing community and connectedness with land and nature including proper nutrition and shelter. Feeling good about oneself, proud of being an Aboriginal person. It is a state of being that includes knowledge, calmness, acceptance and tolerance, balance and focus, inner strength, cleansing and inner peace, feeling whole, an understanding of cultural roots and "deep wellbeing"." For others, the loss of focus on inner spirit has resulted from various combinations of cultural change, the busyness of life, the pressure to focus on the material and outwardly successful. These discourage finding times of stillness or silence from which to become attuned to our inner selves, our inner spirit, to whatever spiritualities make sense for us.

What is distinctive about religion?

So what then is distinctive about religion and in what ways do we need to recognise religion as distinct from spirituality? Those who identify as religious are generally more explicit that their religion is part of how they live, which may also include the spiritual. Given the numbers of people who identify as religious, religion is an important part of life for most people on the planet (Brunn, 2015). Canda and Furman (2010, p. 76) define religion as "an in-stitutionalised (i.e. systematic and organised) pattern of values, beliefs, symbols, behaviors, and experiences that involves spirituality, a community of ad-herents, transmission of traditions over time and community support func-tions." Note that they are explicit about seeing spirituality as part of religion. Firth (1999 p. 174) writing about Hindus, Sikhs and Muslims affirms religion is an integral part of life: "Religion is not a part-time activity but a way of life, set in the context of a living belief in the divine, the importance of the scriptures as authoritative guides, and life after death which demands preparation and readiness at all times."

This makes explicit the first key aspect that social workers need to be aware of: that being part of a religious tradition is generally a way of approaching all aspects of life; the beliefs and values of the religion are expressed in how the person lives, influencing their expectations and assumptions of family, work, health and wellbeing and indeed all of their lives and interactions with their environment. Degrees of commitment will vary depending on the person and their situation, but this is the underlying expectation. This has implications for how illness and healing are perceived, for example, Sorajjakool, Carr and Nam (2010, p. 166) found that increasingly health care providers understand that religious beliefs can affect how people respond to illness and healing: "We have learned the possible variations in the way people may interpret cancer, kidney disease, heart failure and many other diseases and the way belief systems impact health and the treatment process." This also makes explicit that in most religious traditions there is an expectation of inner values being matched by how the person lives, their expression of these values in the external world which may be explicit or implicit. These are not necessarily the same for everyone in the religion although they may be. For Muslims for example, there are quite specific and universal expectations – for example about giving money to charity. For Christians, this varies more depending on denomination with some expected to give a proportion of their income to the church. The expectation to live from your values may mean people living in harmony with the culture they live in but conversely may mean expecting to challenge the existing culture.

Secondly, Firth makes explicit belief in the divine. Most religious traditions would name the divine using the language of God as creator who is both transcendent – beyond the world and also part of the world. However, each has specific language that they use for this and once you start to explore more detailed understandings, there are significant differences. These differences will be individual as well as in how they are expressed in the religious tradition. For example, in the Christian tradition, some people would use the word God to mean ultimate mystery, a sense of the other, universal spirit; others would relate to a personal God, a being they experience as a person, that they talk to, feel they receive loving care from and who influences how they live. Some would see Christ as God's expression in the world and would relate to Christ as a person, who is a source of comfort and/or challenge or an expression of God's mystery. Others might relate to Christ as a historical figure with teachings that remain relevant to how they live, but feel a deeper emotional connection to saints or to Mary as the mother of Christ.

Third, religious traditions have a set of beliefs and suggested related actions about how to live your life which are expressed in sacred texts: the Torah for Jews, the Quoran for Muslims, the Bible for Christians and so on. For some people, the written word is strongly influential in determining how they live. How these are interpreted will vary and be influenced by the culture of the time, but they will generally be seen as key sources of wisdom for how to live. Again, how individuals understand and interpret these will vary depending on the culture and context – which is partly why within each major religious tradition you will find a variety of groups. In the Christian tradition, for example, Protestants and Catholics would interpret aspects of the bible and related teaching differently. Within each of these, some people, often seen as more fundamentalists, would read the bible more literally, seeking a more factual understanding, clear answers to specific questions. This would influence discussions about gender and the place of women in the church and, for some, in the community. Others would interpret the bible more metaphorically so that biblical stories are read for an underlying message of a principle rather than a specific answer, perhaps requiring more socially just action. For example, one of the parables in the Bible is that Jesus was able to feed a crowd of five thousand in a matter of minutes. If you understand this literally, Jesus was able to create a miracle of food appearing; if you read it metaphorically, you might interpret this as Jesus created an atmosphere of caring for each other that meant everyone shared their food and everyone was fed.

Generally, within each religious tradition, there are what Hunt (2021, p. 218) calls "intermediaries [who] are appointed with varying roles and degrees of authority to control and/or to guide others through the doctrines and practices." How these are named varies: even with Christian traditions, there could be ministers, clergy, priests, nuns and so on. Many traditions have people who are paid, but also have others who carry out some of these roles voluntarily. For some people, having the rituals of their religious tradition supported and organised is vital, particularly the form of, usually, collective worship: the Mass for Catholics, the five daily prayer times for Muslims, weekly Shabbat for Jews or more individual puja for Hindus and meditation for Buddhists. However, within each of these traditions, people would sometimes worship together and might also worship separately. There are likely to be other rituals or traditions around welcoming children, recognising when adolescents or adults are making their own choice to be active members of the religious community, marriage, ceremonial times such as Christmas and Easter for Christians, Ramadan for Muslims or Hannukah for Jews and so on.

More informally, most religious traditions would have other ways of joining together to foster social connection and mutual support. There might be specific social activities for children or young people, shared meals, discussion groups or fundraising events, for example. All of these contribute to providing a rich community life.

This is the final distinctive aspect of religion – the communities in which it is usually situated. How religion and spirituality are experienced and expressed is influenced by those who share their particular religious expression. From a positive perspective, such communities can provide deeply nurturing, mutual support in life in general, through significant celebratory or challenging events and in living life from underlying values. When they work well, people feel very sustained and inspired by them to help each other and to be a source for benefitting the wider community. A religious community may be quite explicit in setting up charitable organisations to seek changes in what it sees as inadequacies in structural issues: liberation theologists who can be from any religious tradition would seek to bring socially just and/or environmentally just actions.

It does have to be acknowledged though that there are very obvious examples of how such communities can also act to repress difference, to isolate or actively undermine those seen to be not living up to the expectations of the religious tradition. This may be on an individual level – a woman being counselled by a priest to stay in a violent marriage or someone who interprets religious writing to judge and censure others. On a larger scale, we know religious communities can contribute to war, acts of terrorism, policies that exclude vulnerable groups of people from accessing human rights and abuse of many kinds. Media coverage of religion tends to focus on these so we are well aware of such examples as the abuses of children in church communities, the pressure to conform to dominating sexual norms, how religious extremism of various kinds causes tragic deaths across the world.

Note that some groups that would see themselves as spiritual rather than religious might also have aspects of these religious traditions. An online meditation group might meet at set times for meditation, but also have time for exploration of meditation practices or social times to encourage mutual support. A Wiccan group would have particular ceremonies often related to the moon and to seasonal changes, but would also be likely to have social gatherings, times of teaching and recommended texts to read.

It can feel overwhelming to try to grasp the variety of religious and spiritual experiences. What is more important, as Ragsdale (2018, p. 61) points out from a chaplaincy perspective, is to recognise that "we know a brief description of a major world religion's beliefs do not tell clinicians what an individual family's application of that belief system will be." What is vital then is to be aware that there are many ways that any form of spirituality and/or religion tradition can be expressed and to ask individuals about their beliefs and how these are expressed: to ask and explore rather than making assumptions. How to do this will be explored more later. Just as it is true that individuals may experience their religion differently, this is also true of religious communities: some may take the sacred teachings more literally, others more metaphorically; some believe there is only one way to express religious beliefs, others that there are many ways for these to be expressed. It is therefore vital as a worker to remember to make the distinction between the ideals of religious traditions, their desire to create a better world and how these are expressed in practice. However, we also know that many destructive acts have been done and continue to be done across the world in the name of religion, often to justify non-religious imperatives, for resources and land, for power or influence. All too human preferences and perspectives get in the way. When you look at the deep-seated beliefs shared across religious traditions there are strong connecting threads of being loving to all, seeking charitable ways of acting, seeking peaceful ways to resolve conflict and differences. As Brunn (2015, p. 4) says

> After all, the quest for a meaning to life, a hope to improve the human condition and the role that humans play in their associations and interactions with others and their spiritual links to environmental worlds around them have been topics of interest from the earliest humans in local setting those living in global cultures today.

How religious beliefs are expressed by individuals and communities is influenced by the particular culture they live in. Whether to wear explicitly religious symbols or what kind of symbols to wear will vary between communities and even within them depending on culture, history and individual preferences. If you have ever taken part in a group discussion about a novel or a film, you will know that people will have experienced it differently, been amused or frustrated by characters in conflicting ways and seen the overall message in sometimes opposing directions. Similarly, in religious traditions, people wrestle with their different interpretations of sacred texts and other writings, with how to live out what they see as their key beliefs including how these fit with the prevailing culture. Part of the challenge for social workers is when to accept that an individual or a family have a religious preference that is their right to express in their particular way and when it is important to discern it is a damaging and ethically unacceptable way of being. This will be explored more in Chapter 9.

How people think about faith may help with separating the essence of a religious life from how it is expressed. Tim Costello (2016, p. 7) says

> There are three great imponderables: the universe, the self and the other. Faith opens up the possibilities to speak of these mysteries. We all need a faith story that makes sense of all three mysteries to understand why we are here and what it all means.

Faith has traditionally been seen as religious, having faith in God or Gods, but you can more broadly see faith as believing in values that transcend cultures and religions; a person who is secular might have faith in humanity or in political structures. Alex Miller (2020, p. 170) remembers his friend Max, who at one stage was in training to be a Rabbi and who also at another time was an active member of the Communist Party in Germany suggesting that both Judaism and communism can be seen as faith-based. Trelfa (2005, p. 207) a youth and community work lecturer, finds some students come with what in Christian language is a calling to this kind of work based on religious values. She argues that "practitioners need faith in something that has intrinsic worth" to "provide focus, coherence, meaning and order," but that you can have faith without being religious; you have faith in what you see as meaningful. Similarly, Fowler (1981, p. 4) says faith is a way a person can "see themselves in relation of a background of shared meaning and purpose" an active expectation of seeking transcendence in a way that is relational. For Trelfa (2005, p. 207) reflective practice is "the window through which we aim students to develop their faith."

This provides another way of thinking about crossing what are often artificial boundaries between spirituality and religion including where being secular or actively identifying as not being religious fits. My view is that the inclusive, experientially focused view of spirituality the chapter begins with, is one that most people could identify with including from a secular perspective. To use the metaphor of a vegetable soup, spirituality is the broth, the rich connecting fluid that flavours the many vegetables in it, some of which represent religions. Most of the vegetables keep their essential shape and flavour, but become a bit blurred at the edges; as they all continually bump into each other, they subtly alter each other. Some vegetables lose their distinct shape and change over time contributing to the increased richness of the broth. My sense is that we all contribute to the broth, but some also to the distinct vegetables: to particular religious groups or particular ways of seeing the world.

It is also helpful to think about how this has changed over time in many contexts: If we think back to what it was like to live in the 13th century, in a Western European context, for example, most people would have been living in small villages and would have been part of the same religious tradition. Everyone would have expected to attend the same religious services, to be operating from at least similar religious beliefs and to carry out the same kinds of related practices. These are very clear when you think about death and dying. When death occurred or when someone was seriously ill, the priest, as the religious representative of the church, would have been expected to come and say prayers and perform other related rituals. Those gathered around the bedside or in the graveside would have understood and shared the intent of those prayers and rituals. It is likely that the people in the village, including the family would have found these religious practices to be helpful at least to some degree. The village would also have offered practical and emotional support, that was interconnected to their mutual relationships in their community. There would be no separation in perception between the village as community and their religious expression of community. Shared beliefs about life and death and life after death would have sustained individuals, families and communities through the inevitable crises of life. Of course, for those who challenged these, life wouldn't have been easy.

As life changed in a more industrial era, many people left their villages and moved to larger cities losing their close connection to their local church and its interdependence with community. With the advent of printing presses people became able to read religious writings such as the Bible for themselves, and began to challenge some of the views of the established church. Some would have become disenchanted with the ways that the church operated and perhaps what they saw as the hypocrisy of some of the church leaders. Science in modernity also meant that people began to see that there were other explanations for why things happened. A death might be related to lack of hygiene rather than the will of God. Increasingly, people questioned the centrality of the church and its knowledge about how things were and how things should be. Gradually more people turned away from the church and looked to other sources of information and knowledge. Some found their own ways of being supported, others struggled. In terms of death and dying, people gradually came to believe that it was better the people who were ill or dying to go to hospital to be cared for by professionals rather than in their own homes. Questioning of religious values meant it became less common for religious rituals to be used.

By the early 2000s there was clearly a much wider understanding of what spirituality could mean and how religion and spirituality might be expressed. Heelas and Woodman's research in the UK (2005) identified a change from most people seeing the church as the authority for how to live life to a more 'subjective life-as' focus on the inner authority of the self along with interest in holistic healing and practices like yoga and tai chi. Forman (2004), from the United States, and Kavanagh (2007), from the UK, both carried out research in the early 2000s on how people were expressing their spiritual and religious selves. What they found was that people were increasingly exploring how to develop their own spiritual understanding, which for some people was connected to a religious tradition, but for other people was not. Individuals have continued to wrestle with what this means for them. Julia Baird's (2019) book Phosphorescence, for example, explores her strong connection to the mysterious experienced in swimming, while also naming explicitly her continuing connection to a religious tradition. Rowson (2017, p. 13) says "When pushed to describe where my appreciation of the spiritual comes from I describe myself as culturally Christian, psychologically Buddhist, domestically Hindu and temperamentally sceptical."

What I think is happening now in many countries is that all of these ways continue to operate in some ways: there are still many people who would identify with a religious community and others who would feel sceptical about what religions have to offer. However, we have moved beyond this apparent dualism so that there are now also a variety of other ways in which people connect to the spiritual. While there are many ways to think about how people experience spirituality and religion, J am going to explore how you could think about these as four separate groups, always keeping in mind that it is the person's perception of their experience that matters. In doing this, I don't want to suggest that these groups are totally and neatly separate from each other or that within each group people experience spirituality or religion in the same way; there will be significant differences within each group. Dividing people up in this way is to some degree artificial but I think it's helpful to trying to tease out the different kinds of experiences of spirituality and religion that social workers are likely to engage with. This is a way of prompting you to remember always to wonder what are the variety of ways in which people might explore their spiritual and religious selves and how does that connect to community for them. This might of course also apply to you. I have certainly moved groups over time and this sense of possible movement is also important here.

How people identify their spiritual or religious selves

Group one: identifying as not spiritual or religious

The first group I have identified as those who do not see themselves as spiritual or religious. I do assume that this group still wrestles with some of the meaning of life questions that are an inevitable part of religion and spirituality. Depending on your particular context, there may be significant numbers of people who have never had contact with any kind of formal spiritual or religious tradition and would not see themselves as having had any kind of spiritual experience. This may be because they see religion/spirituality in a particular way that doesn't include what we have explored here as a more general sense of transcendence that can be grounded in everyday experience or in paying attention to the essence of a person. It may be that at an earlier time in their family history, the family made a conscious choice to withdraw from religious tradition. This kind of reaction might come from the experience of trauma such as war, a significant external crisis such as fire or flood or a more personal experience of loss that has led family members to reject the idea of any kind of religious meaning or might simply be that it didn't seem relevant to that generation of the family. Those with close experience of how people have been killed or tortured in war, for example, sometimes link this with a loss of faith: how can a loving God allow this to happen? Some might see themselves as humanists who focus on the capacity to be fully human taking into account the ability to articulate thought through values and actions, which is generally secular but may also be part of a religious understanding (Payne, 2011).

This group is likely to include people who would call themselves atheists or agnostics: those who have actively rejected religion seeing it as perhaps not being scientific or being the cause of wars and other forms of conflict, although some of these might see themselves as having some spiritual practices.

However, this isn't always as straightforward as it seems. Schneider (2014, p. 71) is a good example of crossing spiritual and religious understandings. He embraces enchanted agnosticism as an approach to life saying

> I take mystery seriously ... with a kind of holy reverence once reserved only for the devout. Far from mere uncertainty, mystery arouses in me both the spiritual sense of "wholeness" (fulfillment) and the secular sense of unknowing (discovery). The combination of the two I find exhilarating.

Enchanted agnosticism leads him to states he sees as similar to religious states of awe and wonder, in all sorts of places, both religious and not, related to people and place. Vernon, while crossing what some might see as barriers of atheism and agnosticism, has a contrasting view of saying the agnostic spirit of not knowing is also important in religion (Vernon, 2007, p16). He suggests the key aspects of being an agnostic are to have practices of questioning, of love, of negation (saying what God is not as well as what is), of waiting and of wonder (Vernon, 2011, pp. 226–8). Some atheists would say they don't believe in a God of any kind, but do believe in such transcendent values as altruism, harmony, love. Hodge (2015) points out the need to not see this group in a way that they would not see themselves, i.e. if people do not see themselves as spiritual, it is important not to use this kind of language in talking to them.

Marina described her family as simply not interested in religion or spirituality. Her first experience of a religious tradition was in her early 20s when a work colleague she had become friendly with invited her to her Catholic wedding which included a Mass. She was bemused by the ceremony, describing it as like being part of a different culture, except it wasn't. She had also been invited to a Wiccan ceremony by a friend, which she enjoyed, but didn't feel was really her. This made her interested in why her family were not religious; her mother explained that her grandparents had become disillusioned with their Protestant faith tradition when an unmarried mother had been rejected from their church. Her father wasn't sure why, but said his family worked too hard to spend time in churches and that he believed people helped themselves without needing a God to get in the way. She recognised that these implicit beliefs had influenced her too: the assumption it's better to stand on your own two feet. As a social worker though she could see that some clients valued their religion and that her lack of knowledge and different attitude might well get in the way. She also recognised that part of her had been moved by the Mass in ways she found it hard to articulate, that perhaps something was missing that would be restoring in her life.

Group two: spiritual but not religious

The second group is those people for whom spiritual practices or an under-lying belief in spirituality is significant, but who would not see themselves as religious. They often have a consciousness of this and will often describe themselves in this way, so that the 'spiritual but not religious' has become a familiar way of talking about this group. This group may include people who have previously identified with a religious tradition, but who no longer do. Alternatively, it might simply be that people have drifted away from belonging to a religious tradition given the pressures of other aspects of their lives. If you are exhausted from life demands including the expectations of others, it may be that you simply don't have the energy to be involved in more formal organisations. Western culture encourages focusing on what works for you individually. This combined with questioning of the beliefs and practices of religious traditions means that gradually over time there has been an erosion of expectation that people belong to these. However, some people in this group would still describe themselves as interested, perhaps even regretful that they no longer have a way of expressing themselves in this domain.

It also includes those who have become interested in spirituality and related practices often for a particular reason that relates to their life experience. For some, it might be a life event or crisis, either personally or as part of a community and perhaps being offered some kind of spiritual practice as a way of managing that. How to learn spiritual practices might be offered through social workers or psychologists suggesting mindfulness as a way of managing distress and anxiety, for example. Alternatively, some people at a particular stage of life, become more interested in asking about meaning, values, wanting to think about and sit with the development of the inner life. Adult education centres or neighbourhood houses or the internet can also be places where people are offered some kind of short course in meditation and mindfulness that can be a pathway into valuing spiritual experience.

Ben had always been vaguely interested in spiritual practices. His father had regularly gone to Buddhist retreats before he had children and continued to meditate daily when possible. Ben and his brother went through phases when they liked to sit with him when he was meditating. This felt like a peaceful time when they could be close to their father. He had a close friend in high school who was Hindu and he was intrigued by his religious practices but they seemed like too much hard work. In his late twenties his partner Mark became severely depressed after causing a car accident where a child was severely injured. Mark's social worker suggested mindfulness meditation to still his mind from his negative and undermining thoughts and Ben started to meditate with him for support. The experience also led to both Ben and Mark wanting to explore more deeply what really mattered to them, to change from what they felt in retrospect had been living from other people's and society's expectations rather than from what they felt was worth while. The social worker helped them describe their initially conflicting hopes for what this might mean and to identify what they felt was a more meaningful way of living.

Group three: actively interested in spirituality and religion

The third group is those who identify as being religious and might well in-clude spirituality in that, but don't necessarily relate only to one form of spirituality or religious tradition. This group, like the first two tends to be more individual and subjective in how people express their religious and spiritual selves. Each person wants to develop their own sense of what religion and spirituality means for them. To varying degrees, they might still value some connection to a religious tradition for a sense of community, but not see themselves as limited to that community as people would have historically. An Anglican might go to a Buddhist retreat annually for a more intensive form of meditation. It might be that someone who identifies essentially as Protestant, also values attending a Catholic retreat centre on a regular basis, but sees her bushwalking group as another source of spirituality. Practising yoga as a meditative practice might complement Buddhist or Christian meditation practices.

Mavi is Jewish and describes herself as moderately practising. Some of the rituals, particularly the ones that represent different times of the year are important to her and she does go to the local synagogue when she can, perhaps once a month. She also has a close friend who goes to a Christian meditation group weekly and she often goes with her, finding meditating with a group works better than meditating on her own. They also went to a Buddhist retreat for a week last year and agreed that it fostered their capacity to meditate in the weekly groups, although Mavi found it physically tiring, and they are thinking of doing this again. Mavi has a very mentally demanding job and she says her religious beliefs and the meditations really help keep her grounded.

Group four: identifying with a religious tradition

Finally the fourth group is those who would identify with one religious tradition and who actively participate in that tradition to some degree. It is important to acknowledge here that this is a significant group of people. A major demographic study across 230 countries and territories found that 84% (5.8 billion people) identified with a religious group; with the main religious groups being Christians, Muslims and Hindus, but with significant numbers also of Buddhists, Jews, Sikhs and many other traditional and smaller religious groups (Pew Research Center, 2012). Interestingly, they found that nearly all Hindus and Christians live in countries where they are in the majority, and a significant proportion of Muslims and religiously unaffiliated people. For those who leave their own country and move to where another religion is in the majority, this can be add to a sense of cultural and religious dislocation. While exactly how many people identify as religious will vary depending on which country you are in, these figures confirm that a significant number of people still fit into this group.

If you are also part of this group, you are more likely to be able to understand why people relate to a religious tradition and what they see as the benefits and possible challenges. For many people belonging to a religious tradition provides a place of community, where people actively and mutually support each other. Sharing values and beliefs provides a degree of comfort and support and reinforces living life from a particular perspective. Knowing that there are such solid foundations for mutual understanding fosters confidence and well-being. This does not mean that there are no challenges in living life with such connections. Even within a religious tradition, as described above, there will be significant differences in how to translate those values and beliefs into specific practices for life. Many people who are part of a religious tradition will have been born into it; it is a significant aspect of their family history. Wanting to become less involved or change religious traditions can have implications for family relationships as well as community connectedness. It is also important to recognise that some people join a religious tradition as adults for a variety of reasons and may want explicit acceptance that this is a valid life choice. They may also want help in connecting to their chosen religious tradition, finding people who can help them learn the language and customs.

Sayeed is Muslim and works in a local business. He describes himself as an active Muslim and it is important for him to be able to pray at the set times of the day. His faith was what sustained him through many difficult years in detention and continues to do so now. When he came to Australia as a refugee, it was hard for him initially to find work where this was possible and he felt he had to compromise. Now, in the rural town that he lives in, there is a greater number of Muslim families and the local council has provided education to businesses about the importance of allowing for daily prayers. This has also helped reduce, but not eliminate the comments he gets still from other workers. He married several years ago and his first child will go to a secular school next year; he is hoping that she will be accepted as a Muslim.

Implications for practice

So what does this mean for you as a worker? I will explore this in detail in later chapters, but just briefly here:

Recognising these four different ways of thinking about spirituality and religion can help you be clearer that you need to be able to engage with each of these. In each group, people are seeking to make sense of their lives in some way, there are underpinning assumptions and values that relate to each of these. If people are experiencing some kind of life crisis, their fundamental beliefs about who they are and what is meaningful will significantly influence how they respond and what they want from those who are working with them. If we don't understand this, we can easily miss opportunities for connecting people in what is life affirming for them. Working in socially just ways means ensuring basic human rights such as expressing religious freedom as articulated and ratified in the United Nations Declaration of Human Rights provided people are also allowing others to express theirs. However, Hodge (2012) points out that religious persecution or discrimination remains a significant and increasing global issue and that social workers have a responsibility to promote religious freedom.

What makes this more challenging is when you are working across these four groups venturing into areas you don't feel familiar with. If you are from a family that has never had an experience of religion in a more formal way, it can feel particularly daunting to be expected to communicate in a meaningful way with those who have. It can take a significant degree of energy to comprehend what this can and clearly does mean for some of the people that you might be working with. On the other hand, if you take very seriously your own religious beliefs and see them as fundamental in your life, you may struggle to accept people who seem to you to be ignoring paying attention to what really matters. It may also be that you have a number of assumptions about how religion is expressed or the 'better' ways to express religion that it will be important to make conscious.

It is also important to work across groups in seeing how what is meaningful connects to all of the person which may be a combination of ways of seeing and being in the world. An individual might describe themselves as a mystical, feminist Muslim or a Catholic liberation theology activist who relishes church rituals. The expectation is not that you can know all of how every spiritual and religious tradition is expressed. The danger of thinking you can simply learn about each is that you assume everyone from a religious tradition will have the same expectations. What is important is being respectful in this as all other areas of social work and engaging with the person 'where they are at'. This might mean using the language of their faith tradition as they explain it to you: God, Allah, Jehovah, seeing to understand what their beliefs and practices mean for them and how you can support them in carrying these out. Equally, it might mean putting to one side your own preference for 'God' language and listening for what is meaningful symbolically to this person, their love of nature, of connection to others. This will be explored in more depth in other chapters.

You could also think about this in terms of key themes emerging here (see Figure 1.1). If the experience of spirituality is common then you could also think about the four key aspects of spirituality as:

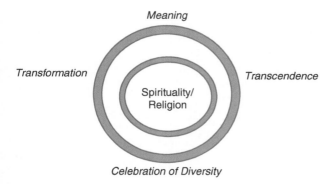

Figure 1.1 Spirituality themes.

meaning: what is the essence of what really matters for individuals and communities;

transcendence: how does the person experience transcendence, a wider connection to what might be something greater or deep links to others or to the natural world;

transformation: what is restoring, healing and enabling, even if challenging about the spiritual experience;

celebrating diversity: recognising the richness of spiritual experience and the many ways in which it can be expressed.

2 Spirituality, religion and social work – history and context

Social work has had at best an uneasy relationship with spirituality and religion in its history, particularly in the West. Part of my interest in writing this book came from my own experience of the exclusion of spirituality from social work education and practice. As someone who had been interested in the issues of spirituality and religion all my life, I am somewhat surprised in retrospect that when I trained as a social worker in Victoria, Australia, I simply accepted that social work education didn't address this issue at all. I was vaguely conscious that there was really no mention of spirituality or religion, in spite of at least some of my fellow students being actively involved in religion themselves. My own experience came from a Christian background, shared by many other students including a Catholic nun, and there were several students who were Jewish. However, I don't remember any of us commenting on or discussing the fact that we talked about almost every other aspect of what it meant to be human, but excluded the spiritual or religious.

My own experience of being a social worker has mirrored some changes in attitudes to the inclusion of spirituality in social work since my training. In the first 20 years of my social work practice, I worked across many fields, but generally in government departments or not-for-profit organisations where there was still little or no inclusion of spirituality, in spite of one of these being auspiced by a religious tradition. At this stage, I joined a university and was surprised to find that there was still very little mention of anything to do with religion or spirituality in the curriculum. What there was, was introduced by individuals who thought this was an important issue rather than being embedded in the curriculum. As I said in the introduction, I gradually found that this issue was raised by students who were concerned that other students would perceive them negatively if they were honest about their religious background. This came up in a variety of ways, often related to asking students to share their motivations for social work. For those students who had a religious background this was inextricably connected to their religious tradition; usually from a Christian perspective of feeling led to be loving and giving to others, often combined with creating a more socially just world. Consistently, these students feared assumptions from other students that Christianity equalled patriarchal and judgemental attitudes. The students were not

DOI: 10.4324/9781003132677-4

unrealistic about the complexity of their Christian background. Most of them were critical of some of the attitudes and values in their religious tradition. What they wanted recognised was that there were other affirming and life enhancing aspects for them. This included a student who identified as a lesbian who felt judged by her church community and struggled to remain connected to it. Other students were astonished that she simply hadn't moved on and expressed this very directly and judgementally – the assumption was *you would have to be stupid to stay somewhere that isn't supporting you*. What she wanted was recognition that the community of the church was one that she had grown up with and felt very supported by. She didn't want to lose the range of re-lationships that she had there or the essence of the faith that she found very sustaining. What she would have found more helpful was an empathic ex-ploration of why this was important to her to clarify whether or not she wanted to stay, what would be lost as well is what would be gained and what her other options might be.

This experience was reinforced by working half a day week in a Catholic auspiced agency providing generalist counselling. I was surprised to find that many more clients raised religious or spiritual issues as an integral part of the background to what they wanted to talk about. Some also wanted to talk more specifically about something that related to their religious faith. For example, a couple planning on marrying wanted to explore the differences in their beliefs and what that might mean for them if they had children, the husband of a Catholic woman wanting to separate requested support to 'make' her remain in the relationship and a woman whose husband was dying wanted to name and explore her struggles with her faith, asking how can a loving God allow this to happen? From a more spiritual but not religious perspective, a couple struggling in their relationship used crystals to explore it, a woman explored her involvement with the Wiccan community that her family and friends were judgemental about and a parent wrestled with how to encourage his children to retain their sense of wonder in nature once they started school. I began to wonder why there seem to be such a difference in the naming of religious and spiritual issues in this agency compared to essentially secular agencies that I had worked in before? Was it that I had somehow missed this aspect of what people wanted to explore or did the agency auspice give people permission to raise these? Had I changed or did people now want to talk more about the religious and spiritual?

I think the answer is a combination of all of these. There has been a gradual shift both in Western society generally (religion has more generally been in-cluded in the global South) and in social work about the need to engage more with spirituality and religion. In Chapter 1, I identified the broad shifts in society in relation to religion and spirituality and the four different groups that have emerged that I think social workers now need to engage with in ex-ploring meaning. Social work's own history has perhaps made it slow to understand and reluctant to actively include these changes in how it operates, in spite of the religious and spiritual issues frequently presented in the media.

As Mathews (2009, p. ix) wrote: Social work "often seems to be oblivious to the debate which rages around it. A discussion of the role of religion or spiritualty rarely features within the profession and it could be argued that there is ambivalence, even hostility, towards such an engagement." He suggests that this continues in spite of social work seeking to be seen as profession that works holistically, and that it means "social work has often failed to engage with those core beliefs that shape who we are as people, which we choose to define in a shorthand way as religion and spirituality."

History of social work and religion

To explore this further it is useful to look at least briefly back at the origins of social work to see how intertwined they were with religion and how part of our history has reflected reactions to that initial engagement. This will vary of course depending on the particular social context and I am primarily exploring this from the perspective of a white, Western woman who has practiced social work briefly in the UK and mainly in Australia. However, I think there are parallels across much of social work practice, particularly, but not only in the Western world about the changing perceptions of and connections to religion and spirituality. Note that I am covering a complex history briefly. For more detailed reading about social work history see Dulmus and Sowers (2012) and/ or Pierson (2011).

The beginnings of social work were closely tied to religion and religious beliefs. Before there were trained social workers, religious bodies including local churches, mosques or synagogues were where people went to seek support, spiritual and practical. If you and your family had fallen on hard times, particularly if this was not seen as your 'fault', your religious community was likely to help you. The initial impetus for social work was partly a positive aspect of religious traditions, a desire to make things better for individuals and communities in which they lived. Religious traditions generally see it as a responsibility to offer what might be called loving kindness or giving of some kind. For social work in India, for example, Nadkami and Joseph (2014, p. 72) say that "[p]hilosophies of welfare and humanitarianism that arose from deep-rooted religious beliefs and practices of Hinduism, Buddhism, Jainism, Islam, Christianity and indigenous beliefs were at some point the driving forces behind education and practice of Social Work." Similarly, Leighninger (2012) identifies how Islam, Judaism and Christianity are all underpinned by a 'charitable tradition' and suggests that social welfare developed first in Middle Eastern and related countries then transferred to the US and Europe based on Judaeo-Christian and Muslim practices and beliefs. The religious institutions of a particular country then became the providers of early forms of social work, influenced to some degree by their particular culture and history.

As more countries become more industrialised, people began to move from the country to the city and lost the traditional communities that offered some form of usually mutual and informal social support. After the industrial revolution in England for example, it was primarily the church that was more formally seen as responsible for administering relief for those experiencing poverty (Pierson, 2011). The early charitable organisations were organised by people whose religious faith was a key aspect of their lives; some like Octavia Hill also considered themselves to be Christian socialists. However, they were often influenced by moral expectations of their time. While Octavia Hill, for example, recognised the undermining nature of inadequate housing and was highly empathic, she also believed in what she saw as a Christian morality of responsibility, a more individually focused expectation that people should be more active in managing their lives 'better.' Similarly, in the United States the national social work body was called the National Conference of Charities and Correction. Clearly, this linked to the still prevailing division between the deserving and undeserving poor, or what some writers called the helpable and unhelpable. Such organisations focused on providing volunteer visitors to encourage and support individuals – both by giving practical and emotional support, but also by fostering changes in behaviour.

However, some aspects of religious traditions also represented a different understanding of society that remains integral to social work practice: Judd (2013, p. 178) suggests that "social justice is a concept deeply embedded in both the professional mission of social work and religious doctrine" and that organised religions have often participated in advocacy for social justice. This relates to the Muslim practice of 'zakat,' for example, of expecting to give a certain amount of income to the poor as part of their annual fasting time, not seen as charity but "an act of social justice through the redistribution of wealth" (Leighninger, 2012, p. 2). In Chapter 3, I will talk more about liberation theology: the aspect of religious traditions that actively seeks to "think from the situation and standpoint of the oppressed and its commitment to social change on the institutional level" (Petrella, 2017, p. 236). This way of thinking fitted with social work practice and gradually there was a shift in social work from an individual focus with the 'friendly visitor' role to "concerns related to structural problems of society such as housing, health care, sanitation, poverty, and employment" (Judd, 2013, p. 179). Jane Addams, for example, founded Hull House in 1889 and worked to address social inequities and environmental issues including the impact of excessive rubbish on the health of surrounding communities (Kennedy, 2018, p. 411).

One of the tensions for social work was finding a balance in these roles: how much to focus on engaging with individuals with obviously urgent needs and how much to focus on trying to change the structural issues at least partly causing those needs. Another related issue was also seeking validity and legitimacy as a profession. One of the ways to gain that was seen as being more 'scientific,' based on reason and logic rather than morality and religion. Being scientific was also seen as being in opposition to the intuitive or creative, the 'art' of social work practice. This started early. For example, the first secretary of the Charity Organisation Society hoped that "such an organization could renew and discipline the life of the people by a nobler, more devoted, more scientific religious charity ... It could help us to realize in society the religion of charity without the sectarianism of religion" (Loch, 1904, p. 68). Sectarianism and evangelism were major concerns related to charitable practices: workers seeking to impose their own religious values on their clients and furthering division between religious communities. Loch sought to foster the COS as a neutral and unofficial 'church' that could encourage peaceful and united communities.

After the second world war, this division increased with some social workers seeking a more radical approach advocating the need for structural change in response to increased poverty; others focusing on the trauma caused by the war and the need for more intense therapeutic practice. As social work continued to seek more formal recognition as a profession, key social work academics in the 1950s such as Bisno (1952) called for separation of the new social work profession from its religious roots noting that Catholic or other religious social workers could have to oppose on moral grounds a client's request for abortion, contraception, divorce or gay and lesbian relationships. By this time the place of religion was more actively contested in society generally but the issue of some social workers consciously or unconsciously imposing religious views on others continued to be a concern. There was an expectation that a secular state could and should better provide services for all of the community: in Britain the introduction of the Welfare State influenced social work provision in other parts of the world. In the 1960s in the United States the War on Poverty increased the number of social work services particularly in public welfare. What prevailed was a view that: social work

> must apply the scientific method in its processes. This implies the possibility of rational processes; of the application of inductive principle to social work study; of quantitative research. Social work is not only empirical in its outlook, but almost by definition thoroughly pragmatic despite the fact that irreconcilable differences may exist between pragmatism as a philosophy and the religious and ethical tenets of many institutional sponsors of social work. (Bisno, 1952, p. 91)

Impact on social work practice

Overall, the result was that social worker educators, at least in the global North, as well as seeking scientific evidence rather than exploring the art of practice, became reluctant to discuss religious or spiritual issues at all. In relation to Christianity, for example, Bowpitt (1998, p. 676) suggests that for those "contributing to social work literature, the Christian legacy has been the skeleton in the cupboard, something best forgotten and preferably ignored." One of the ways of managing this was to assume that religion and to a lesser extent spirituality were part of culture, so didn't need to be considered separately. In this way, they were unlikely to appear specifically in the curriculum, except in a broad brush way: saying that culture included religion.

When she started teaching social work in 1979, Lindsay (2002, p. 4), comments "I unquestioningly adopted the unwritten philosophy of the School at that time: that social work was a secular profession within a secular society." Parsloe, Professor of Social Work at Bristol University, (1999, p. 140) interviewed forty students in 1996 and found that about 90% had discussed spiritual matters before starting the course and thought it was appropriate for social workers to talk with clients about spiritual matters, but that they had not discussed spiritual matters either on placement or with fellow students or staff. She questioned whether social workers' reluctance to ask spiritual questions meant clients felt unable to name them. She saw social work history as influencing this, particularly the influence of 19th century voluntary societies which as well as providing social services took part in evangelical activities. She concludes "Social workers today are at pains to reject this part of their history. In doing so they confuse spirituality, religion and evangelism and, to be on the safe side, avoid all three. Sadly, their professional training plays into this rejection." (Parsloe, 1999, pp. 140–1).

However, by the 1990s there were the beginnings of change, both in social work and in the community generally. Of course, some writers and researchers had continued to identify both the need to include religion and spirituality in social work education as well as the ethical dilemmas this would inevitably provoke. When I started teaching social work in the late 1990s, my concern that students felt uncomfortable in naming their religious values, meant that I began asking about how or whether this was included in social work education. When I started teaching at my university, religion was included as part of culture in the context of migration. David Cox who taught the subject, was however clear about his own belief that religion needs to be understood as an entity in its own right because "religious systems are almost always far broader than any cultural system' and 'religion is an important basis for stratification in many contexts" Cox (1987, p. 72).

When I looked for relevant literature, it was clear that there was more in other countries, particularly in the United States where the general population was more explicitly religious. Access to resources was more limited then, no internet! However, I did find Canda and Furman's book Spiritual Diversity in Social Work Practice: The Heart of Helping (1999) which used the language of the 'spiritual' in taking a comparative education approach to comparing different concepts of religion and spirituality. Their guiding principles were demonstrating value clarity, respecting spiritual diversity, being reflective, supporting strengths and empowerment, taking a holistic approach. This was a useful beginning in reinforcing a broad view of spirituality in social work, including religion and the value of stressing an actively reflective approach.

Processes bringing about change on social work attitudes to religion and spirituality

From the early 2000s, my sense is there were four inter-connected processes bringing about change in social work's attitudes to spirituality and religion.

First society generally was engaging more actively with ideas about spirituality and religion, a shift from expecting the world to become increasingly secular to realising that spirituality and religion continue to be major influences. Secondly, it was becoming clearer that some services users wanted social workers to understand the importance of religion and spirituality in their lives and also how these issues might be affecting their lives. This partly related to the global issues of climate change and migration which meant communities were becoming more multi-spiritual. In social work, those interested in spirituality and religious issues were becoming more active in researching and writing about them, possibly partly influenced by First Nations peoples. Fourth, critical and postmodern thinking was influencing all of these and being expressed in the developed of critically reflective approaches to social work practice.

Changing community attitudes

To take each of these in more detail: first a range of people were researching how people and communities experienced the spiritual and religious. I have identified here some I have found particularly useful. In Australia, Tacey's (2003, p. 12) book *The Spirituality Revolution* epitomised this change, suggesting that "what we are seeing in so-called 'secular' or worldly society is a return of the spiritual impulse," a historic reawakening of interest in the sacred, of exploring the questions of what makes life meaningful, with an emphasis on the inner life. More specifically, in a town in England, Heelas and Woodhead (2005, p. 5) found those they interviewed divided into essentially two groups: first those who remained more traditionally religious, valued 'congregational life,' common religious beliefs, with the 'higher' authority of transcendent meaning, goodness and truth' and a related sense of community that included shared activities, ways of being and doing. The second group described themselves as "spiritual, seeing the 'sacred in the cultivation of unique subjective life' with emphasis on personal growth and development, with the inner, subjective authority of the self, often taking part in activities like yoga or tai-chi. About the same time in the United States, Forman (2004, p. 8) was interested in what he called grassroots spirituality, people who "hold to some kind of a universal energy or infinite spirit." Similarly, Kavanagh (2007) in the UK interviewed people aiming to live their lives from a faith perspective, not necessarily connected to a religious tradition. Both found people living in the variety of ways explored in groups two to three in Chapter 1: finding ways to blend their own experience of the spiritual that might or might not include a religious tradition. Rowson (2017, p. 11) terms this as having 'spiritual sensibility' which involves "deepening our engagement with questions of being (death), belonging (love), becoming (self) and beyondness (soul)."

Related to this, First Nations ways of knowing and being were starting to influence more people who are concerned about their own lives but also how to care more for the natural world. While First Nations peoples vary, a common thread is valuing the spiritual and seeing this as a part of all of life, both animate and inanimate. Across the world it seems that First Nations people are starting to assert their ways of being and their knowledge of how to care for the world in ways reinforced by the Black Lives Matter movement. In Australia for example, Pascoe's (2018) book illustrates how Europeans had completely misunderstood how First Nations people cared for the land as part of their spiritual way of being. Now there is beginning interest in how seeing the world from the holistic First Nations perspective illuminates how to live in harmony with self and all other aspects of the world.

At least some social workers began to applying these ways of thinking to themselves, asking what it might mean if they ceased "to split off their spirituality from their professional persona and whether this is possible if one is to incorporate spiritual practices into work with service users" (Crisp, 2020, p. 967). Some started to more actively use spiritual practices as part of self care such as mindfulness, reporting the advantages of including spiritual practices in the workplace, partly in caring for their own well being and partly seeing how these enabled them to engage more effectively with others. McGarrigle and Walsh's (2011) research with 12 social workers who undertook an eight weekly 2 hour classes on meditation reported that participants thought that practicing mindfulness deepened their attentiveness to their clients. Others like Carrington (2017, p. 293) write about a paradigm shift: seeing her social work practice as "resolutely positioned within and informed by a spiritual perspective" not just by specific spiritual practices.

Service user perspectives

Secondly, there was the gradual recognition that these were important issues for those using social work services. My own experience fitted with this: finding that more of the people I saw at the Catholic agency I worked with asked about religious or spiritual issues and students also named these as important for them. More broadly this related to greater population movement, with the number of refugees and asylum seekers increasing related to wars and displacement – some of which was caused by religious differences. For some of them, their religious experience was a key aspect of their survival. Ni Raghallaigh's research (2011, p. 552) with 18 refugees who were unaccompanied minors found that religion "provided them with meaning, comfort and an increased sense of control in their new lives in Ireland". They came from countries where church or mosque attendance was a positive and integral aspect of life, so arrived with "a strong tradition of religious faith and practice, and with a worldview that held God at its centre." Part of what they had to navigate was a very different view of faith by their peers which needed to be recognised by their social workers. Similarly, Martin (2009) found that older Iranian migrants saw their spiritual health as integral to their physical and emotional health; if this wasn't recognised they became frustrated with their doctors and feared misdiagnosis.

Greater population movement also meant that communities were also becoming more diverse, so that in the United States, for example, there were growing "multicultural and multispiritual heritage populations" without social work educators understanding that the learning and therefore helping environment is not only European American" (Nagai, 2010, p. 436), but much more richly diverse. This change is reflected for me in my rural Australian city and in many other parts of the world. Such changes have issues not only for individuals, but also for communities needing to adjust to great diversity (Gardner, 2020). Communities have not always reacted well to becoming more multispiritual and this is also a challenge for social workers to embrace. It may be that what their individual clients need is not so much individual services, but community change with heightened awareness of how religion and spirituality can be expressed in ways that are life enhancing for the individuals engaged in them and providing richer community diversity.

From a service user perspective, trauma from child abuse within churches has become more publicly known and acknowledged, with legal challenges and government investigations. For at least some of those involved, their religious or spiritual values will be important. Harms (2010, p. 106) points out that religion or spirituality can help to foster resilience or act as 'protective' factors when people are experiencing stressful experiences. This happens through both their inner world of beliefs and values, past experience of religion and spirituality and/or related ability to forgive and the external world such as their participation in religious activities and supportive relationships with others. When we asked people in a regional hospital about what kept them going during their illness and for many an extended period of rehabilitation most were able to respond with examples; some of religious practices and the importance of remaining connected to their religious community. Others named the importance of family, the flexibility of vising hours so they could see those who mattered to them which fostered healing (Gardner, Tan and Rumbold, 2020). The global issue of climate change and related environmental issues for some has increasingly become a spiritual issue too. The climate change rallies, school strikes all demonstrate the concerns for many about the need to care for the environment spiritually as well as physically. Ferreira (2009, p. 13) for example, advocated for eco-spiritual social work or deep ecological social work that would actively recognise the connection between people and the natural environment and how this relates to individual and collective development and issues of social justice. The COVID-19 virus has shaken many people's expectation of a certain and prosperous world and fostered much soul searching about what really matters.

Growing interest within social work

Third, as society generally began to engage more with ideas about spirituality and the place of religion, social work as a discipline also started to question (slowly) the lack of inclusion in curriculum and practice. Changes in language fostered this with spirituality as something that anyone might engage with whether or not they were religious and by its very nature a diverse experience. Given that social work is a very contextual profession, it was perhaps inevitable that this changing context was also expressed in expanding interest in the spiritual and religious. Social work academics were more actively researching practitioner and academic attitudes to spirituality. A review of the number of journal articles related to religion and social work showed there were five times as many articles between 2000–2007 compared to 1970–1979 (Graham and Shier, 2009). In the UK, for example, Holloway (2007) compared spirituality in social work practice from a research project in 1990–1992 to another in 2003. Survey results from 99 social workers in the first study (social workers in teaching hospitals), found that while 86% thought spiritual pain was always present, only 4% thought they had a role in spiritual care. However, in the 2003 study of a random sample of practising social workers who were members of the British Association of Social Workers, 64% had a religious or spiritual affiliation and particularly on issues related to loss and death, over half agreed it was appropriate to raise spiritual issues. There had also been a significant shift with those in the first study not seeing religion as part of anti-discriminatory practice, whereas by 2003, taking a religious or spiritual history was seen as an essential aspect of culturally sensitive practice. Similarly, Gilligan and Furness (2006) surveyed students and social workers and found students were less likely than practising social workers to include spiritually or religiously sensitive interventions. Apart from Muslims, this didn't vary with having their own religious beliefs. Social workers across countries saw some topics as more related to religion/spirituality, particularly illness and death. Stirling et al (2010, p. 609) found at least 50% of UK and New Zealand workers saw terminal illness, foster parenting and bereavement as more appropriate for religious exploration whereas Canda and Furman in the US (2010) found a greater focus in their 2008 research on also including substance abuse and chronic mental health. Interestingly, most Christian social workers thought it was appropriate to raise spirituality for any issue, but not religion (Furman, Benson and Canda, 2011). Lindsay's Australian research found all practitioner participants agreed that spiritualty/religion should be addressed in social work education and seen as 'part of life and not a pathology' (Lindsay, 2002, p. 81). She also found most "educators acknowledged the relevance of this domain to the education of social work students" (Lindsay, 2002, p. 65).

Other changes at this time included the increased expectation that religion/spirituality would be included as part of assessment. Hodge (2001) started to write about this at the beginning of the 21st century advocating for both including a spiritual history similar to a family history and a way of identifying the person's spiritual strengths such as the use of rituals, participation in a faith-based community, having a deeper spiritual purpose in life. Since then there has been a huge increase in assessment tools including the FICA – Faith, Importance, Community and Action tool (Puchalksi and McSkimming, 2006), Generally, there is emphasis on a tool that encourages discussion and understanding rather than a quantitative or too narrow set of responses. Assessment tools will be discussed more in Chapter 7.

Gale, Bohan and McRae-McMahon's (2007) edited book while not only about social workers, demonstrated that 'helping professionals report a growing number of people bringing spiritual issues' and explored how professionals respond in practice. Some writers provided specific information about religious traditions such as Sorajjakook, Carr and Namm's book (2010) with a particular focus on illness and death. In the last ten years there has continued to be a significant growth in interest in the religious and spiritual in research and publications in social work. A major achievement was Crisp's (2017) edited book: the *Routledge Handbook of Religion, Spirituality and Social Work*, with 40 contributors representing many nationalities, religious and spiritual interests and fields of practice. Crisp (2020) also reviewed the international literature on social work and spirituality from January 2010 and also found a significant amount of writing on three key themes: a lack of consensus in the social work literature on what spirituality is, the need for models to encourage inclusion of spirituality in practice and seeing a variety of practices and voices that need to be understood, respected and valued.

Influence of changed societal thinking

A fourth thread here is how societal and social work change has been influenced by other ways of seeing the world. Part of general community change has been a shift to a postmodern way of thinking from a more traditional, modernist view that there is one 'right' way to experience the spiritual/religious to an acceptance that there are many ways. This fits with seeing the spiritual including the religious or spiritual as a personal, individual and subjective experience. From this perspective

> [o]ur meaning (and therefore our reality) is constructed out of the language or our (multiple) discourses about it. In this way, there is not one universal truth or reality, but instead 'reality' is constructed out of a multiplicity of diverse and fragmented stories. (Fook, 2016, pp. 12–3)

Postmodern thinking helps with articulating the 'dominant discourses' in society, the main ways of thinking: it is important to recognize that the dominating discourses in particular countries still tend to make assumptions based on often unconscious religious values and beliefs. The benefit and also the danger of postmodern thinking is that it can seem to value subjectivity at all costs – the right of each person to form their own way of being spiritual. However, from a social work perspective it is also important to include critical social theory: the affirming of 'universal truth' in the form of human rights to balance postmodern thinking. From a critical postmodern view, people have the right to express their spiritual and religious beliefs provided they are not harming others and are allowing them to have the same right of expression.

From a critical and human rights perspective, there are inevitably tensions between individuals' more subjective understanding of their religious and/or spiritual beliefs and the prevailing assumptions often embedded in law. An obvious example of this would include Christians or Muslims not able to publicly express being gay where this is illegal in their country.

These theories (which will be discussed in more detail in Chapter 3) have became increasingly part of social work education generally and also underpin the processes of critical reflection. Critical reflection, which will be explored in detail in Chapter 5, fosters social workers articulating their own assumptions and beliefs as well as being aware of those of others, including how these assumptions have been influenced by the historical and current social context. Understanding the history of the social work experience, suggests that at least part of the move away from religion and spirituality was fear of how workers might impose their values and beliefs on those they worked with. The active use of critical reflection can address some of these concerns providing a process that workers can use individually, including in individual and/or peer group supervision. Critical reflection also makes explicit the need to both value individual subjective experience and to affirm socially just approaches to practice: the balancing of postmodernism with critical theory.

From a critically reflective perspective, I can see that my experience both at the university and in the agency I described at the beginning of this chapter encouraged me to question the contextual assumption I had internalised: that religion should be separate from social work practice. One aspect of this was assuming that social work needed to be a secular profession because of the dangers of social workers imposing their religious values on others in spite of acknowledging that social workers have many other personal values and assumptions that they successful avoid imposing on others. I also questioned whether my practice had been disempowering by not including what was an important aspect of life for many people – including myself! This led to exploring for myself, then with others what I called 'critical spirituality' which seeks to bring together these theories, with an understanding of spirituality, in a critically reflective approach to working in practice. Critical spirituality from my perspective "is a way of naming a desire to work with what is meaningful in the context of enabling a socially just, actively inclusive society. It also implies working in a spirit of openness and the ability to manage uncertainty and work with contradictions" (Gardner, 2011, p. 180). My understanding of this has been expanded in this book to including what we can learn from First Nations wisdom and green social work and this will be explored in the next chapter.

However, it still seems to be a struggle to have these issues more firmly in the curriculum. Students and staff continue to experience negative judgements about their religious affiliations. When I asked for feedback in a subject called Introduction to Diversity recently, several students mentioned how difficult it was to talk about their religious affiliations – both Christian and Muslim. This largely came from anticipating that their fellow students would react negatively. This was influenced by their general knowledge of how spiritual and religious practice can be abusive reinforced by the results of Royal Commissions or similar investigations in many countries to identify and seek restitution for those abused in churches and related institutions. There is also still a tendency to see religious and spiritual issues as part of culture only, rather than as having separate significance.

What I am advocating is that we are at a point where social work needs to actively include religion and spirituality in education and practice, identifying these separately from, although interacting with culture. There are specific aspects of spirituality and religion that stand apart from culture: those in re-ligious traditions can name the common themes across cultures as well as what is influenced by the local context. As Holloway (2007, p. 267) says social work's concern with anti-oppressive practice requires it to rise to the challenge of pluralism of belief and belief practices." Religion and spirituality are so much part of the experience of many of those we work with (consciously or unconsciously), social workers can't claim to work holistically if they ignore these. We have theories and processes that we can use to ensure that we don't repeat the mistakes of the past, particularly in avoiding conscious or un-conscious imposition of religious and spiritual ideas on others. In Chapter 3 I will explore a number of theories that can work together to provide a basis for practice: the underlying theories of critical spirituality, particularly critical social theory and postmodernism as well as First Nations ways of being and doing, green social work and relational world views. The key aspects of these can fit well with a spiritual and/or religious understanding of the world: a focus on understanding the importance of context, values that enable all the aspects of the world, animate and inanimate, to flourish and commitment to socially just change. The processes of critical spirituality, particularly critical reflection can encourage individual workers to reflect deeply on their own spiritual and/or religious experience, their beliefs and values, how these in-fluence their actions and how to ensure that they act in ways that respect the values and beliefs of others. The 'critical' aspect encourages constructive questioning of meaning and how this has been influenced by the person's own social context.

Social workers already develop skills that help with this. Part of what we are used to as social workers is having to balance competing views. We do this with families struggling with conflicting attitudes to disability, ageing, gender and so on. What we need to do is remember the values and processes we use with these to help us find ways forward in including spirituality and religion. The question is partly what are we aiming to do? If we are encouraging people to think about what really matters in their lives, we need to be prepared to engage with such issues. If we know from our own experience or from hearing that of others that spirituality and/or religion can be life-enhancing the challenge is how to include this in social work practice in holistic and inclusive ways. The danger is that if we fail to do this we are inadvertently causing the feelings of alienation that we want to prevent. Rowkith and Bhagwan (2020, p. 12) make this explicit in bringing together religion, tribal or Indigenous ways of knowing and awareness of history and social context: "Decolonized social work cannot remain at a disjuncture from religion, as social workers who work with individuals, groups and communities must be respectful of related religious, caste, ethnic and cultural differences."

3 Building a theoretical framework for critical spirituality

Why write a chapter on theory in a book about spirituality and religion? Theoretical approaches are essentially ways of seeking to understanding the world, generating knowledge or ideas of ways of knowing, being and doing. These are implicit in how societies are organised, in how we relate to each other and other aspects of our worlds. We each have a world view influenced by our own history and context, and our personal and community preferences. We make assumptions about how the world is and how it can be based on our ideas about how things are and how we would like them to be. For some of us, and those we work with, those are influenced by specific spiritual and/or religious experiences and practices. Chapter 1 explored how spirituality is part of the underpinning theoretical structure for how people live, the values and beliefs that inform who they are and how they act in the world. This chapter focuses on how as social workers we need to connect these ideas to the social work and related theories we use to provide the underpinning theoretical structure that influences our practice.

Identifying common themes across theoretical approaches will also enable us to embed spirituality in our practice in ways that are life enhancing for the individuals and communities we work with. Embedding spirituality can mean working towards more socially just, critically aware and inclusive way of practising. This chapter focuses on the interconnections between broader meta-narratives or explanatory theories that underpin this way of working. My experience of developing a critical spirituality approach was that combining theoretical perspectives resulted in a richer and deeper base for practice. Here I am expanding its theoretical base making explicit connections between critically reflective social work, First Nations relational worldviews, green social work and relational approaches combined with common themes across spiritual/religious traditions. I will then briefly explore the implications for practice, assuming that from a practice perspective, spirituality is a significant aspect of life for everyone in some way, i.e. for workers to be sustained in their practice as well as in working ethically with others. I will more briefly link these ideas to practice theories such as a strengths and narrative approaches in Chapter 7.

DOI: 10.4324/9781003132677-5

I will take each of these approaches separately first and then look at how and where they connect; how they can complement and reinforce each other. My assumption here is that when you combine theoretical approaches in this way you gain a more nuanced understanding of the complexities of the world that fosters more holistic practice. While there are common threads across many of these, each also articulates a particular way of being more distinctly. While writers and advocates of each theory would not necessarily include spirituality or religion in any specific way, there are those who make active connections between each of these social work and related theories and their spiritual and/or religious tradition. I will use writings from these to make explicit how spiritual and religious ways of being are not as distant from social work practice as they might at first seem. However, with First Nations relational worldviews spirituality is always integral, although some First Nations people also engage with a religious tradition.

In social work, we still predominantly operate from Western paradigms where human beings are seen as dominant, with modernist views valuing the scientific and provable. A Western worldview is essentially hierarchical with humans at the top of the created world which "creates the attitude that other things and beings exist for our purpose, benefit and convenience. This gives rise to a situation in which beings are left to the grace of the spirit of human enterprise and subjected to our plans, exploitation and domination (Ferreira, 2010, p. 16). This creates different priorities from those in non-Western cultures: "the emphasis on rationality, dualism, individualization, individual self-determination and self-reliance, and therapy are frequently out of place in communal and traditional societies in which deference to the family and community is the priority" (Gray, Coates and Yellow Bird, 2008, p. 4). The tension between social work as an art or a science identified in Chapter 2 relates to this: a dualism between a view of social work as intuitive, responsive and creative as opposed to rational, causal and logical. A critical spirituality approach argues that these kinds of dualities are undermining to everyone. We need societies that value the intuitive as well as the logical, and to move beyond duality to valuing many ways of knowing and being and embrace interconnectedness. We also need to change the perceptions of the world order with humans at the top. McMahon (2017, p. 85) points out that "in Indigenous Relational ontology humans are not central nor alone in knowledge construction. Instead, knowledge construction is through the cyclical and equal relationship between Community, Country and the Ancestral Core." The predominance of Western or Eurocentric world views is also challenged by the other theories explored in the chapter: critical and postmodern, green social work and relational social work. Gradually there is more acceptance in social work education and practice that we need to be much more active in recognising that First Nations "ways of knowing, while different, have equal value and status as systems of knowledges and thus deserve epistemological equality" (Bessarab et al, 2014 p. 17).

First Nations knowledges

I am starting here with First Nations knowledges partly to affirm this equality of place and to seek to redress the balance of these so often being seen as an 'add on' rather than a fundamentally important way of seeing the world. I am particularly conscious of the dangers of writing about this as a white Scottish-Australian woman so have quoted from First Nations writers as much as possible. I am also conscious of the need not to over-generalise in seeking common themes. Canadians, Dylan and Smallboy (2017, p. 55), are explicit about the dangers of making assumptions that stereotype individual or groups and emphasise "the need to attend to particularities and context." Similarly, Bhodi (2011, p. 290) says "As far as the Indian context is concerned, there is a growing realisation among contemporary Social Work educators and practitioners alike that there cannot be one over-arching Indigenous Social Work knowledge base." On the other hand, Bhagwan (2017, p. 64) asserts that "African spirituality embraces not only the whole and unbridled humanity of all Africans, but of humankind the world over," while acknowledging that variation in "its characteristics, ritual and ceremonies, colour the African continent" (Bhagwan, 2017, p. 65). An Elder of the First Nations Kauma people in Australia, Lewis O'Brien (O'Brien and Watson, 2014, p. 457) says in Kauma language the word 'yara' means "to express the notion of individuality and reciprocity twice both one to another, difference." That means they are saying think about two things and not only think about it but also let's practise it." In that spirit, my sense is that it is possible and useful to identify what seem to be some common themes, while recognising that there will be many differences related to particular places and people. Because of this I have identified where each writer is from as specifically as possible.

Language is again an issue here, I have chosen to use First Nations, which is or is becoming the preferred language in Australia, in recognition that the many communities who have lived here for millennia were the First Peoples to be here. Other writers use Indigenous, Aboriginal, tribal, depending on their community preferences. I have aimed to be clear about what people mean when it isn't explicit in their quote.

The first theme is that First Nations worldviews emphasise interconnectedness or an interdependent view of life for all life animate and inanimate. Grieves, a Warraimaay woman from the mid north coast of NSW, Australia (2009, p. 7) says Aboriginal Spirituality for First Nations people in Australia derives from a

> philosophy that establishes the wholistic notion of the interconnectedness of the elements of the earth and the universe, animate and inanimate, whereby people, the plants and animals, landforms and celestial bodies are interrelated. These relations and the knowledge of how they are interconnected are expressed, and why it is important to keep all things in healthy interdependence is encoded, in sacred stories or myths.

Similarly, Graham, a Kombumerri and Waka Waka woman (2008, pp. 181–2) describes the two most important relationships in life as:

> The land, and how we treat it, is what determines our humanness. Because land is sacred and must be looked after, the relation between people and land becomes the template for society and social relations. Therefore, all meaning comes from land.

This also connects across time as Watson, from the Tanganekald, Meintangk Boandik First Nations Peoples in the south east of South Australia (2014, p. 511) affirms "We are part of the environment and in a particular relationship with the natural world. That relationship forms and informs all aspects of how we interact with the world and it is a relationship which continues; it's not just about the past, as the "Dreaming", or in my language, Kaldowinyeri, is often considered to be. It lives with us today. "Similarly, in India, Rowkith and Baghwan's (2020, p. 556) research with the Maharashtran Tribal people found." There appears to be a deep interconnectedness between themselves and elements of the earth and the universe, be it animate or inanimate, whereby the people, land-forms, trees, plants, water and celestial beings are in synergy with each other."

Grieves (2009, p. 11) affirms that this interconnectedness is a spiritual aspect to life.

> Aboriginal Australian Spirituality has been described as embodying a reverence for life as it is … a mixture of good and bad, of suffering and joy, and it is celebrated as sacred. Living itself is religion. The remarkable resilience of Aboriginal people is partly explained by the legacy of a Spirituality that demonstrates an enthusiasm for living, a readiness to celebrate it as it is.

Similarly, in Oceania, the atolls, islands and archipelagos across the Indian Ocean, health and wellbeing is associated with "the quality of our inter-connections with land, with sea, with sky, with family and other people and with spirit. It is not possible to leave out spirituality out of the health and well-being equation" (Mila, 2017, p. 61). Māori values significant to social work education in Aotearoa/New Zealand include "wairuatanga - spiritual well-being" and "atuatanga paying respect to divinity" as well as respecting a di-versity of beliefs and seeing the vital essence or life principle in all beings and objects (Ellis, Napan and O'Donoghue, 2018, p. 537).

The strength of the theme of interdependence or interconnectedness also relates to the importance of community and how communities provide mutual support for each other. In Africa, Bhagwan (2017, p. 66) says community is important for facilitating

> psychological growth and transformation … [p]sychological development is thus not an individual journey … Community then forms the realm for

the manifestation of Ubuntu or humaneness … It inculcates respect for the inherent dignity of all humankind and a deep reverence for interdependence … a spiritual as well as a practical resource to those facing difficulty.

This is a critical aspect of wellbeing for the individual and the community, often fostered by the wisdom of elders. In Australia too, Bessarab et al (2014, p. 28) name the centrality of community and the role of Elders:

> Through ceremony, practice and every day activities, people were taught and reminded of their ceremonial and spiritual responsibilities not only to the land but to each other to ensure the continuation of their spiritual and social connections and their mental, physical and emotional wellbeing and health.

Awareness of history and social context is important for First Nations people in two major ways: first positively: Grieves (2006 p. 53) "Thus, knowing about your peoples' history and culture enhances identity, gives strength and pride, a sense of belonging, it gives more grounding in life, a connection to the knowledge of ancestors and cultural activity including language, art, law/lore and dance." This knowing encourages empowerment and wellbeing in all aspects of people's lives including the spiritual. Lack of understanding of this history, culture and knowledge can be frustrating. Lewis O'Brien, an Elder from the Kauma people in Australia says "I find the approach by government and their agencies is limited in this country … we've got to take account of what our people have learnt over the centuries … they've not only talked about it, they've practised it and found it worked and so they're the only ones that really went about it and did things that provided a safe environment" (O'Brien and Watson, 2014, p. 453).

On the other hand, is it important to be aware of the impact of history as colonisation: Watson (2014, p. 516) says

> The colonial project of empire-building enabled European access to a large share of the world's energy and resources, but in that process of colonial expansion local Indigenous knowledges were diminished. European science … was used to increase human bondage and mortality rates amongst colonised peoples.

This reinforces why social workers need to understand the impact of history and how important communities are in generating their own ways forward. The Getting it Right document (a teaching and learning framework for integrating Aboriginal and Torres Strait Islander knowledges into social work education and practice) advocates the 'third way' or 'third cultural space' which is "the in-between space between the coloniser and the colonised … a contested space in which previous ways of knowing and doing are challenged and changed, where differences need to be understood in order that new understandings and ways of doing can emerge" (Bessarab et al, 2014, p. 18). For some First Nations people the third space includes being connected to a religious tradition. For example, Melissa Brickell a descendent of the Yorta Yorta and Wiradjeri peoples also sees her spirituality as living the values of a strong Aboriginal and Catholic woman. In expressing this through painting she gives an example of an image with a religious and cultural story.

> It has a plain cross with a twig of gum leave with gumnuts draped upon it … it is a Palm Sunday tradition to put your palm on the cross, for me as an Aboriginal person I put the gum leaves there, and these are an extensive part of the nature of this beautiful country, and used in tradition Aboriginal smoking ceremony for purification and in medicine to cure. The cross purified. (Brickell, 2011, p. 175)

This fits for me with recognising that for non-First Nations social workers integrating this as a worldview new to them is a major mind shift that requires commitment. First there is taking seriously that the land, the environment is not ours to use for our own convenience or even for those who are more environmentally attuned, only an object that we should be protecting. Instead, we need to see ourselves as simply another part of the universe, nurtured by the land, the birds, animals and in turn need to act in reciprocally nurturing ways. We also need to understand that when we look at the landscape, we are missing much of what First Nations people are seeing: trees, rocks, hills that are of sacred significance for the community and/or for the individual person. When I first heard a First Nations person explain this, I felt as if I was shifting internally to suddenly seeing my environment in a totally different way. I walked around seeing the land as having new meaning that I was also aware I didn't have the cultural background to understand. I can only manage to have this different perception intermittently but at least enough to understand what I am missing. In workshops with students, Mishel McMahon asks

> When making key decisions for your own life, do you include being still, sometimes pausing, deeply listening to those around you, including to the landscape you are on, 'the weather, animals, waterways, plants, sounds, your dreams or stories you hear to gain insight? (Townsend and McMahon, 2021, p. 1833)

Secondly, for those of us who are not First Nations people, as social workers, we need to make another shift from wanting to be helpful to First Nations people to understanding that we need to learn from them – about what is useful for them in enabling them to flourish, but also to see how their ways of being and doing would be better for all of us. An example of this for me is when I worked in a large Government Department that provided such services as foster care, residential care for children, juvenile justice, family support in a regional city. The local Aboriginal Cooperative wanted a representative to work with them on working together more effectively. One of the principles that emerged from this work (this was a long time ago) was that family is understood differently for First Nations communities compared to the standard Western nuclear family. If First Nations children could not live with their immediate nuclear family, their extended family and community should therefore first be asked if they could care for the children, rather than having them placed in foster care. What became clear is that this principle of prioritising kinship care should be applied more generally in the community: this was a question that should be asked first for everybody and led to significant changes in policy. You could extend this to recognising that those we work with are experts on their own lives and what is meaningful to them: identifying their own spirituality.

Critically reflective social work: critical theory and postmodernism

From a critical theory perspective, an individual's issues are always understood in the context of the society they live in, the political, economic and social systems that influence what is possible for them and what needs to be constantly negotiated or fought for. Understanding the context includes engaging with the history that has influenced it: what have been the events and circumstances that have led to these structures and the attitudes and values embedded in them. An obvious example of this is the impact of the Highland clearances in Scotland where wealthy landowners wanted land for sheep and dispossessed many small and just surviving farmers. These farming families then emigrated to the 'new' world of Canada and the United States, disrupting the cultures and ecologically sensitive lives of Indigenous peoples there in reproducing some of the social, political and legal structures that had caused their problems initially. "Modern critical social work is oriented towards understanding the structural conditions that impact on the genesis and maintenance of social problems and in which social work practitioners operate" (Healy, 2014, p. 184). To be able to engage with this, social workers must identify what these structural conditions are both in the sense of institutionalised policies and practices and in the broader community norms that influence these. For example, in Australia, when the COVID-19 virus affected employment, the Federal government increased what were effectively unemployment benefits: the assumption was that the 'deserving' unemployed could not survive on what the 'undeserving' unemployed had been receiving. Migration policy, particularly related to refugees can thinly disguise attitudes about which religious traditions are acceptable.

Adding to the complexity of this is how individuals and communities internalise the dominant ways of thinking in a culture that is embodied in its structures. "Dominant ideology ... refers to the set of beliefs and assumptions that are accepted as normal and commonsense ways of explaining the world"

(Brookfield, 2017, p. 10). This could include democratic values: what most people think must be 'right.' When you are surrounded by institutions that reinforce certain attitudes and values or that only allow these to be expressed, it is much harder to assert your own. Our community attitudes to religion and spirituality are often so much part of our thinking that we take them for granted – expecting that everyone will think being secular is better or that some religions, especially your own are better (or worse) than others. Families are also key places where community or social attitudes may prevail and so in turn be part of what is expected of children. Currently, in the West, even in explicitly or theoretically secular societies, there is often an implicit Christian influenced culture that is part of the dominant ways of thinking. This can mean that Christian religious traditions remain more acceptable and those from Christian backgrounds are more likely to be elected to positions of power than those from other religious traditions. Similarly, terrorism related to religion is more likely to be seen as problematic if the religion is not part of the dominant culture and to lead to policies that target those religions (Finch and McKendrick, 2019). After 9/11, Muslims felt increasingly othered, treated with suspicion in Western culture even when they were long standing citizens. Brookfield (2011, p. 6) points out that these kinds of assumptions are "particularly hard to uncover, precisely because these ideologies are everywhere, so common as to be thought blindingly obvious and therefore not worthy of sustained questioning." Therefore, he suggests "part of critical thinking is making sure that the actions that flow from our assumptions are justifiable according to some notion of goodness or desirability" including the spiritual.

Engaging actively in seeking socially just change is a key aspect of critical social theory: understanding the dynamics of power and inequality and the challenges of structural change are significant aspects of this approach. Critical theory is "based on the idea that the way the world *happens* to be (at this moment with all its oppressive divisions) is not the way it is *meant* to be, or could be if we acted (individually and collectively) to make it otherwise" to make "a more just, peaceful, convivial and caring society" (Morley, Macfarlane and Ablett, 2014, p. 156). Healy (2014, p. 184) suggests that critical social workers

> should seek to address injustice at every level of their practice, from direct engagement with clients through to work aimed at challenging the inequitable distribution of resources. Critical social workers identify injustice as stemming from differences in power and access to material resources.

Using critical theory encourages an attitude of checking how an organisation (including a religious tradition) or community's policies and practices might contribute to "a system of inequality and oppression" (Granter, 2019, p. 68). Inevitably this means understanding the dynamics of power and inequality, asking who has power in any situation and how power is built into existing systems and relationships as well as how who exercises power can change. The challenge then in professional practice is to be aware of the dominating ideologies and how we and those we work with are unconsciously influenced by these, make them conscious and choose actively the values we want to operate from that reinforce a 'good' and socially just approach.

Critical theory does incorporate a wide range of perspectives including the tensions of working across race, gender, age, abilities and cultures and contrasting environments and histories. I want to say something briefly here about a feminist critical theory particularly given that feminism is sometimes perceived as being inconsistent with religious traditions. However, Cree and Phillips (2019, p. 133) say "it is of course, important to acknowledge that feminism is a common reference point for women of different faiths to frame the resistance within their religion and from external attacks on their choice to follow specific religious practices." They point out that dominant Western views "construct Islam as oppressive of women and the idea of Islamic feminism as contradictory" but that writers like Eyadat (2013) point out that "as is the case in the global North, there is diversity within Arab feminism, including critical reactions towards Northern feminism, regarding it as a re- colonising force." This complements postcolonial feminist social work which "rejects colonial and development discourse that characterises women from the global South as passive victims of timeless, oppressive cultural and religious traditions in need of being rescued by White men, and sometimes women" (Deepak, 2019, p. 182).

These ideas also fit with what, from a religious perspective, is called liberation theology. This is also underpinned by critical theory with an expectation that workers have a structural understanding and seek to bring about broader political and social change (Bennett, 2007). Petrella (2017, pp. 237–8) sees liberation theology as challenging predominating Western and Christian worldviews, attempting to "think from the situation and standpoint of the oppressed and [with] commitment to change on the institutional level" and actively working with those who are disadvantaged to "imagine and build new, more radically egalitarian models of political, economic, and social possibility." Writing across religious traditions, Admirand (2018, p. 165) links Christian and Jewish liberation theologies and advocates for inter-faith liberation theology which "necessarily entails a humbled theology, one that does not contain all answers and truth and so needs and seeks the wisdom and partnership of others."

I have included postmodernism in this section because critical social theory and postmodernism provide a useful balance for each other. Postmodernism can be understood as a reaction to modernism: the expectation that scientific ways of knowing can provide a way of understanding all problems and generating solutions for them. A modernist way of seeing the world assumes there is one universalist theory that will explain everything, that knowing about Asian culture for example means you will understand anyone who is Asian, whereas an postmodern view is that this may be understood very differently if you are Indian rather than Indonesian or Buddhist rather than Hindu. Postmodernism can also question

> the usefulness of the feminist tendency to universalise women's experiences and position women as a disadvantaged or disempowered social category.... From this perspective, some of the grand narratives associated with feminism can be interpreted as unintentionally disempowering due to casting individuals as passive victims at the mercy of abstract structures. (Morley, 2014, p. 64)

Watson articulates that the modernist expectation of one right way or one truth "once flattened our world." She prefers "the 'many truths' approach of Kaurna elder Uncle Lewis O'Brien, that is, that there are many truths and there should be no difficulty with the co- existence, for example, of a creationist and evolutionist view of the world" (Watson, 2014, p. 513). Related to this, postmodernism encourages moving beyond apparently opposing dualities, seeing the world as either religious or not, for example. This can move you to a place that transcends either of these to a new possibility or new way of seeing the world. It might be moving to a new assumption: people understand and experience many equally valid ways of being religious. In Celtic spirituality the understanding is that in

> order to keep our balance, we need to hold the inner and exterior, visible and invisible, known and unknown, temporal and eternal, ancient and new together. No-one else can undertake this task for you. You are the one and only threshold of an inner world. (O'Donohue, 1999, p. 14)

In relation to spirituality and religion postmodernism has fostered the subjective valuing of the experiential, validating the individual's inner as well as outer experience as a way of being, respecting that an individual's' way of experiencing the spiritual is always individual even if part of a collective activity. Michener (2007, p. 168) a Christian theologian, for example, affirms the value of a "person-centered, dialogue-based apologetic in view of postmodern deconstructive thought." Postmodernism also encourages celebrating diversity: an assumption that there are many ways, many possibilities never only one. Grenz and Franke (2001, p. 51) see Christian beliefs as a "belief mosaic" with "a multi-patterned mosaic of interconnected pieces" and that we can't suppose another's person's mosaic will be like our own." For example, those

> who identify themselves as oppressed may interpret their experience of oppression through their religious faith. For instance, many African Americans support a meaning of Christianity that is radically different from the wider Anglo- American Christian community and reflects a religious response to the history of enslavement as a race. (Streets, 2014, pp. 68–9)

All of this affirms the value of a postmodern celebration of difference. However, postmodernism is sometimes critiqued for therefore being too accepting of difference, not being explicit enough that there are times and ways in which we need 'grand narratives,' particularly in terms of human rights and socially just approaches. Lartey (2003, p. 36) suggests there are three useful questions: "What of the universal experience of humanity is to be found here? … ….What is culturally determined about this way of thinking, feeling or behaving?.....What in the experience can be said to be uniquely attributable to this particular person?" This brings together the postmodern valuing of individual experience with understanding that there can be shared experience from belonging to a particular group – whether that is of women, those who are gay or those who are from a particular religious background – and that this can lead to seeking broader change.

Another aspect of postmodernism is developing the capacity to 'deconstruct' the meaning in language and in your own assumptions and values. Hodge (2012, p. 20) suggests that a key insight of postmodernism is understanding your own value influenced narrative, that "[p]ersonal experience provides 'inside cultural knowledge' that potentially yields deeper and more nuanced understanding of a phenomenon." Part of reaching a deeper understanding is being conscious of the subtleties of language and meaning that are individually and culturally influenced. Even for those using English as a first language, there are different meanings of the same word depending on the country. How people even from the same community understand each other can be significantly influenced by class, gender and cultural backgrounds. This has implications for how easily people inside or external to a particular group feel heard. Hodge (2012, p. 20) continues: "as religious cultural insiders, people of faith have an innate familiarity with the concerns of persecuted believers in other parts of the world." This means that "Christians and other people of faith are uniquely positioned to make a consequential and distinctive contribution to the critical struggle for religious freedom" in partnership with secular people.

Critical social theory and postmodernism do share several ways of looking at the world: both encourage asking what are the dominating discourses in our culture/communities: what are the taken for granted ways of being that we need to question. Both are conscious of issues of power, both see the interconnections between individuals and social structures. Fook (2016, p. 19) for example, says that social work practice that includes both "is primarily concerned with practising in ways which further society without domination, exploitation and oppression. It will focus both on how structures dominate, but also in how people construct and are constructed by changing social structures and relations, recognising that there may be multiple and diverse constructions of ostensibly similar situations." This can be fostered by combining critical values of advocating human rights and social justice with "the humility of postmodernism's capacity to entertain multiple realities and multiple truths" (Morley, Macfarlane and Ablett, 2014, p. 167). From a religious perspective, while (Michener, 2007, p. 231) affirms the value of a "coherence of beliefs [which] involves the willingness to test, reinterpret and recontextualise certain beliefs in the process of critical dialogue and appropriation," he also asserts that there is no one way of knowing and understanding; what is key is dialogue in a spirit of humility and openness. Similarly Ford (2003, p. 282) says this combination would mean recognising the benefits and limitations of modernity … taking responsibility for serving the mending, healing, and joy of human beings and all creation [encouraging] always to engage across one's boundaries with others, paying special attention to their suffering, joys, and wisdom in the midst of the contingencies of history and creation."

Green social work

A newer theme in social work is 'green social work' prompted by ever-growing concerns about the environment, partly, but not only related to climate change. How these concerns have been named over time has included ecological social work, eco-social and environmental social work all of which have explored the impact on or interaction between environmental issues on individuals and families and what to do about them. This often encourages moving to a more critical and postmodern understanding of the world. From an environmental social work perspective Gray, Coates and Hetherington (2012, p. 17) say that

> Environmental realities have played a significant role in pulling social work to re-evaluate its modernist foundations, and to shift from the primacy of therapy and rehabilitation to recognize humans' essential connection to all of nature, including all people and all life on the planet.

Green social work is explicitly political "as a theory and a practice [which] seeks to transform the socio-political and economic forces that have a deleterious impact upon the quality of life of poor and marginalised populations and secure the policy changes and sustainable social transformations necessary for enhancing the well-being of people and the planet today and in the future" (Dominelli, Nikku and Ku, 2018, p. 2). There are clear links to critical social work with an expectation of social workers understanding how political, economic and social structures influence active exploitation of the environment, implying it is a resource for humans to use at will as well as simply a lack of awareness of interdependence. Social justice here is centred "within a duty to care for and about all living things, animate or inanimate" (Dominelli, 2019 p. 233). Besthorn (2012, p. 37) points out this requires a significant shift from seeing environmental justice as preserving the natural environment for human welfare to a 'radical egalitarian ecological' justice where "non-sentient beings and natural systems are given equal moral standing … a justice of humanity in service of environment." Partly because of this, green social work takes a global view. Nadkami and Joseph (2014 p. 74) point out that in the globalised world, protecting the ecosystem is not just the responsibility of a single country but is an international political issue. Ecological social work or social work on environmental issues and environmental justice including climate change are emerging as critical areas for curriculum and practice in India and this is happening more broadly.

Green social work is also explicitly connected to the spiritual and the 'ecospiritual.' Dominelli, (2012, p. 194): says "green social work is underpinned by a moral and ethical approach. It is rooted in the spiritual notion that there are relationships between people, other living entities and the physical realm." This is congruent with eco-spirituality which "requires that humankind moves away from an anthropocentric or human-centred orientation towards reality, where wisdom, resources and traditions are used, to a life of cherished commonness, respect, gratitude and compassion for the natural world and all the inhabitants of Mother Earth (Ferreira, 2010, p. 16). This is made explicit in exploring how communities include spiritual ways of being in times of disaster: for example many people in the Caribbean use spiritualty to cope with adversity, build resilience and provide comfort (Rock, Joseph and Harper, 2018, p. 149) or in working to protect and replenish the environment: such as having Buddhist monks in Thailand designating trees as sacred and so preventing mass deforestation (Taylor, 2018, p. 337).

Green social work also resonates with and is influenced by First Nations relational worldviews, as a holistic approach which "emphasises interdependence between people, plants, animal and planet earth as the site in which life occurs, but which is affected by the activities of those deriving a living from its bounty" (Dominelli, 2019, p. 233). Green social work advocates for political change to reach a different place where local Indigenous knowledges are integrated with scientific expertise (Nipperess and Boddy, 2018) or with community practice where social workers conduct community assessments which draw on local and 'traditional knowledge' of the environment (Gray and Coates, 2015).

Working with communities is the main domain of practice for Green social work, cooperating with local people acknowledging their specific local knowledge to foster solutions for their own communities. There is a particular focus on the experience of disasters, both human and natural, from climate change to bush fires or floods in communities as well as the poverty and hardship related to these and to prevailing spiritual and/or religious beliefs. Communities are in specific places, so geography is also important, the specific nature of the physical environment, whether it is rural, remote, urban, an island, mountains or by the sea (Nipperess and Boddy, 2018). Ideally social workers and students would "include service users in the coproduction of locality-specific and culturally relevant solutions to the environmental issues that undermined their health and wellbeing" (Dominelli, 2018, p. 17) and for at least some communities this has a clearly spiritual connection. For example, after an oil spill

> Using their knowledge of currents and wind patterns, local Māori accurately predicted where the oil would wash ashore ... Participants told us it was important to follow their cultural and spiritual protocols in order to sustain the mauri (life-force) of the area and restore the balance disturbed by the oil spill (Hamerton et al, 2018, p. 424).

Seeing people from religious traditions as possible partners makes sense for green social work as for other social work in communities. In Sri Lanka, Perera (2018) worked with four social work students on action to separate garbage and plastic to reduce environmental waste and degradation. Part of her approach was to encourage

> a spiritual transformation ... promoting a love of nature and stewardship and evoking compassion and empathy for what is being destroyed ... mainly in conjunction with religious organisations [Muslim Buddhist and Christian) and incorporating religious teachings (insofar as they include these notions), reflections, rituals and prayer (Perera, 2018, p. 378).

Those writing from a spiritual and religious perspective also Taylor (2010 p. 8) says make similar connections: "a common feature of [contemporary spirituality is] a sense that nature is sacred and that ethical responsibilities naturally follow such a realization." Matthew Fox, an American priest (1983, p. 69) has been advocating for 'creation spirituality' for nearly forty years, as a way of recognising that we are "in the cosmos and the cosmos is in us" and that we need to seek healing, justice and creativity in caring for the earth. Just as Dominelli distinguishes between different kinds of environmentally oriented social work, Taylor (2010, p. 11) distinguishes "between green religion (which posits that environmentally friendly behaviour is a religious obligation) and dark green religion (in which nature is sacred, has intrinsic value, and is therefore due reverent care aside from its value to human beings." This also links to learning from First Nations peoples. From his research with opponents of mountain mining in Appalachia, Witt (2015, p. 390) found that dark green religion was a common thread in the mixture of people involved: some atheistic, some Christian, some across religious boundaries sharing views such as talking about love for land, retaining special connections to land, living with land not on it; for example "when asked about her thoughts on the impacts of mountaintop removal mining, one Catholic activist said, "we are so interdependent with the rest of creation, our Native American brothers and sisters got it right, we're all related."

Reflecting on practice is also an integral aspect of being 'green,' partly in enabling social workers to see how their assumptions can undermine or contribute to working in a 'green' way; but also how beliefs internalised from the prevailing culture can mean workers see the environment separately as a 'resource' or network to be used rather than of worth in itself. Such critical awareness can then encourage thinking about how greener practices can happen at all levels, individually and collectively.

Relational perspectives

You might ask here isn't all social work relational and of course, engaging in relationships is central to social work. The importance of relationships and interconnectedness between all beings animate and inanimate is emphasised particularly in First Nations worldviews and green social work. However, the relational approach takes a particular perspective on this, building on psychodynamic theory but combining it with ideas about being reflective, often critically. Jung (1959, p. 164) says the spiritual or psychological journey is a search for "the development of the Self" or the "wholeness that transcends consciousness." Part of this is bringing to awareness those parts of ourselves, including emotions that we are reluctant to acknowledge and integrate. In Ruch's (2012, p. 1317) article titled "Where have all the feelings gone?" she suggests that the pressures of managerialist approaches in organisations embeds an "understanding of human behaviour that privileges cognition, rationality and predictability and pays less attention to the emotional, irrational and unpredictable dimensions of human beings." A relational perspective is explicit that the nature of social work involves emotions and uncertainty which need to be recognised and engaged with; otherwise unconscious reactions will inadvertently affect and potentially damage relationships between workers and between workers and clients. Vince and Mazen (2014, p. 192) name 'violent innocence' as "not being able to tolerate what is negative in oneself [which] facilitates projecting the violent aspect of one's own unconscious onto the other." We need to look below the surface, using psychodynamic concepts such as defence mechanisms in the context of 'containment.' In a critical reflection supervision group, for example, "the containing process mediated through the group offers emotional understanding and tolerates the raw anxiety of an individual ... In such containing contexts presenters feel 'held' and able to confront difficult experiences that previously might not have been acknowledged" (Ruch, 2016, pp. 30–1). This also makes explicit the responsibility of organisations to contribute here and particularly the "responsibility of managers to help surface the hidden dimensions of practice and the anxieties they elicit. Equally, it is the responsibility of the organisation, and a core characteristic of reflective organisations, to support managers in undertaking this task" (Ruch, 2012, p. 1329).

Some writers from a relational perspective would suggest that critical social work needs to be reminded to pay enough attention to emotions, to ensure that the principles of seeking social justice are balanced by processes that ensure people work together effectively but also harmoniously. Critical reflection is most effective when you pay attention to the emotions that are arising from a particular experience, following up why you are having this particular reaction or reactions (Fook and Gardner, 2007). Kraus (2019, p. 101) for example, advocates for relational social work to guide the critical social work paradigm: if social work is about shaping society towards social justice and human rights social work can restrict its perspective neither to the individual nor to its environment…It is decisive that the focus is neither solely on the subjective perspective nor on the social perspective. In fact, it's about paying particular attention to the relations without losing sight of the individual and social requirements.

Similarly, Folgheraiter and Raineri (2012, pp. 474–5) say that rather than assuming science can solve people's problems, a relational view "suggests that it is the human energy that emanates from motivated people that 'resolves' the problem of the apparently growing inefficacy of welfare systems."

Recognising and engaging with emotions can be particularly important in exploring underlying meaning in the form of spirituality and religion. Often, the complexity of the reactions between individuals is illuminated by understanding the feelings of each. A relational approach reminds social workers to pay attention to the emotional reactions underpinning explorations of spiritual and religious differences. Establishing an authentic and respectful relationship remains central in the same way that it would in exploring any other social difference. Getting this right includes seeing how people relate to and are supported by religious communities but also how their perspective of their religious faith may differ from what is expected, listening for what matters to them, their emotions as well as their thoughts. Relational practice can be a way of recognising and working to challenge marginalisation, combining such qualities as empathic attunement and co-construction of meaning with "being familiar with historical and present social forces impinging on people as members of a vulnerable population (Rosenberger, 2014, p. 22).

So what are the implications for a critical spirituality framework?

I want to finish this chapter by suggesting an expansion of my ideas about critical spirituality, with a suggested framework which is expressed in Figures 3.1 and 3.2. The aim here is to integrate the learning from exploring the ideas about spirituality and religion from Chapter 1 with what emerged from exploring the theories in this chapter. The first figure shows the common themes that emerged in this chapter: which may be emphasised more in some theories than others. Remember that each of these has writers who would see connections to spirituality and/or religion. There are clear links between the interconnectedness of all things in First Nations and green approaches with the emphasis on relatedness in relational approaches and the connections between the inner and outer worlds in critical and postmodern thinking. This links to the importance of community, both as place and as people. All of these theories identify the importance of socially just action, understanding the place of history and social structure and of reflection, ideally critical reflection to understand the self and the influence of context on the self. Implicit in some and explicit in others is the need to move beyond dualities to a new

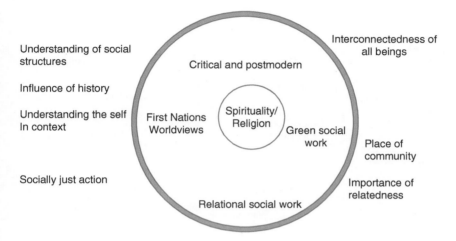

Figure 3.1 Theoretical framework themes.

understanding: including the value of both emotion and logic and how these can complement each other.

These are complemented in Figure 3.2 by five key themes from the first chapter on understanding spirituality and religion: the experiential nature of the spiritual which provides a way of connecting across spiritual and religious domains, the transcendent aspect of spirituality: that sense of something beyond the self, the transformational nature of spirituality: being restorative and healing and the celebration of diversity: acknowledging and valuing the many ways we experience the spiritual. Notice in the figure below, I have placed the experience of spirituality as central, with the four 'spiritual' themes in the middle or mediating circle. My suggestion is that these four themes can mediate our interactions with the 'theory' themes. If you are working with an individual who is feeling judged because of their spiritual or religious beliefs, for example, your belief in what is meaningful for them and in the value of diversity, would underpin your exploration of how this might be expressed in their environment.

Using circles emphasises that there is not a hierarchy of what is better or more useful here. Rather the aim is to think about how these might interact in any given situation. Depending on who you are working with, you and they may emphasise particular aspects of the circle. The aim would be that you maintain an awareness of other connections that could be made – either by you or them – that might be helpful.

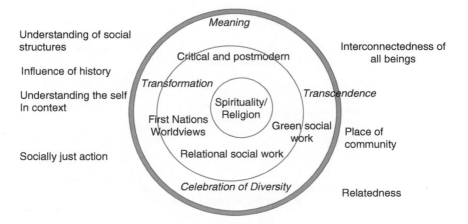

Figure 3.2 Theoretical framework for critical spirituality: key shared themes.

Tessa's experience

Imagine Tessa comes to see you feeling her mental health is fragile. She has previously been diagnosed with post-traumatic stress. What has tipped her over the edge now is that her children were teased in school about looking different. While Tessa doesn't usually wear a hijab, the family are Muslim. This has taken Tessa back to why they left Iran and the trauma of both that experience and life in the refugee camp. While she says her faith remains strong and is what sustains her, she feels flattened by feeling judged and fears persecution here for her family.

So how might the critical spirituality framework help you?
First from the spiritual perspective, you might want to ask Tessa:
So tell me about your spiritual experience?

What does it mean for you? Where do you get meaning in your life?

What helps you transcend what is happening now? What takes you to a more grounded, helpful space?

What would it mean for you if people valued what your spirituality had to offer?

From the theory perspective
What is community for you? What community do you have that supports you? What aspects of community would you like to be different?

What relationships matter to you? Where can you express how you are feeling and what you are thinking?

Who and what do you feel connected to? What aspects, if any, of the landscape comfort you? Foster a sense of belonging?

What is the influence of your history? What do I need to understand about your history and social context?

This might also encourage asking yourself?

How does this relate to my sense of meaning, transformation and transcendence?

What assumptions might I be making that could get in the way of understanding where Tessa is coming from?

What do I need to understand about our shared context and the structural issues that mayl be influencing what is happening for Tessa?

What do I need to take into account from a social justice perspective?

I will return to Tessa's experience in Chapters 7 and 8 in exploring how to explore this framework in practice.

Part II

Capacities and processes for embedding spirituality and religion in social work

This part of the book focuses on both the capacities or qualities you need to be able to include spirituality and religion in practice and on the processes that can help you to do that. There are several aspects of this:

First, it is important to identify your own values and beliefs related to spirituality in religion, your own sense of what is meaningful and how you express this. If for no other reason, this awareness will help you avoid imposing unconscious beliefs and assumptions on all those you work with including colleagues as well as individuals, families and communities. More positively, awareness of these will help you engage more constructively and openly with others. This may encourage you to pay attention to what matters for you in life enhancing ways leading to greater self-care. If you are flourishing, living in ways that reflect what matters to you, you are more likely to be able to care well for those you are working with.

Second, considering your own spiritual journey: the changes in how you have experienced the spiritual and/or religious over time, will sensitise you to how that might continue to change for you and others. This reinforces that these are not static aspects of people's lives, including your own, but rather ways of living and being that reflect responses to external and internal changes.

These processes foster the capacities or abilities that help with this. The ability to be open, humble and to listen deeply are reinforced by being aware of your own changing journey and the beliefs and values that are important to you.

On this basis, the chapters here are:

Chapter 4 focuses on the kinds of qualities, capacities and attitudes integral to spiritually inclusive and sensitive practice including openness, humility and vulnerability, the ability to sit with uncertainty and 'not knowing,' to listen deeply, and to understand the influence of history and social context and connection to place and space.

DOI: 10.4324/9781003132677-6

Chapter 5 focuses on how to use critically reflective processes to continually develop awareness of your own beliefs about meaning and about spirituality/religion. You might also choose to use the process of critical reflection with those you work with.

Chapter 6 encourages exploring the idea of spiritual journeys and how you can use this concept for you and others to see the different places people might be and so what kinds of changes might be possible over time.

4 Qualities of critical spirituality in practice

This chapter will focus on the kinds of qualities, capacities and attitudes integral to spiritually inclusive practice. You could think of these as qualities that are internal and those that are more externally focused. The inner qualities or capacities include openness, humility and vulnerability, the ability to sit patiently and lovingly particularly with uncertainty and 'not knowing,' to listen deeply and in the process of listening being compassionately attuned to the other person's experience of what is meaningful. More externally focused capacities include understanding the influence of history and social context and connection to place and space. These are complemented by spiritual and cultural responsiveness and the commitment to a socially just approach: to be actively inclusive in advocating for celebration of diverse spiritual and religious perspectives in communities and society generally. While I will explore each of these separately, in practice they interact with each other to form the complexity of engaging holistically with each person or community. Many of these connect with the ability to be critically reflective which is the focus of the next chapter.

Practitioners often discourage conversations about the spiritual or religious, feeling that they won't know the answers to questions that are asked or have sufficient knowledge to understand what people are talking about. My experience of providing training for palliative care workers was that they feared making people feel worse by somehow making an inappropriate response or not having the 'right' answer to give. In that particular field of practice, this feeling was intensified by concern about being asked questions like 'why is this happening to me?' or hearing comments like 'I feel as if my life has lost all meaning' and being unclear about what to say. This fear of 'not knowing' is one that permeates much of social work and related professions. It is an issue that workers often have to deal with such as not knowing about the complexities of particular cultures or religions or abilities/disabilities. This fear comes from often deeply held beliefs or assumptions that as a professional we should have answers and be able to be useful in some way. Usefulness is often linked unconsciously to having knowledge or practical skills that can be offered. Not knowing or being uncertain then becomes perceived as shameful or at least unhelpful and to be avoided. This also relates to an often unconscious

DOI: 10.4324/9781003132677-7

modernist perception of there being 'one right way'; the assumption that there is only one way of responding to such question and therefore there must be right answers.

The value of 'not knowing' and uncertainty, openness and humility

Ironically, from a spiritual as well as a general social work perspective, 'not knowing' can be a more helpful attitude or quality. It is also an inevitable part of life, to live with and manage being uncertain. Not knowing or being uncertain can encourage being open to many ways of being and a dialogue in a spirit of openness and humility (Michener, 2007) which is also part of a postmodern approach of recognising multiple truths (Morley, Macfarlane and Ablett, 2014). Vernon (2011, p. 159) suggests 'not knowing' is a state of mind that can balance the pressure to be rational and scientific: "the need to deliver certainty and the need to deliver relevance." You could argue that we never totally understand where the other is coming from. There can be more danger in thinking someone is similar to you and making assumptions about where they are coming from, than being clear that you really don't know. "While knowledge is indispensable, understanding is golden when it comes to effective cross-cultural practice. A stance of informed not knowing can provide a buffer against essentialism and stereotyping. Humility and respect are necessary to achieve cultural understanding and develop workable strategies (Danso, 2016, p. 416). This idea of informed not knowing is key here: we go through stages in learning of not realising what we don't know, to recognising that we don't know – a much safer place to be. From this place, we are able to seek knowledge as we need it.

This fits with what I mean here about humility in the sense of being open to the wisdom of others; assuming that those we work with have much to teach us. Implied in this is that we don't know everything, that, as workers, we too are human and have limitations. The interaction is more likely to be real if both see ourselves as learning and becoming more aware. This can be very freeing as a worker. Rather than assuming you need to know everything about all ways of being spiritual, you understand that those you work with will have the specific knowledge about what is important to them and that what you need to understand they will share with you. This also helps equalise the power in the relationship with each person seen as more wholly who they are with their own knowledge and wisdom. Leary and Banker (2019, p. 74) argue that "the core of humility is the understanding and acceptance that no matter the greatness of our personal accomplishments or positive characteristics, no one is fundamentally more special than anyone else because of them." This is a humility that reinforces deep respect for each person that you work with.

We can also experience humility in the sense of awe, of the natural world, including the power of nature, seeing ourselves in the context of a broader perspective. Narvaez (2019) suggests this needs to be a multi-layered and embodied attitude from the internalised and interpersonal to community and ecological levels. Her 'ecological humility' based on First Nations ways of knowing connects us to wider perspective of the natural world and our interconnectedness with and interdependence on it. This attitude fosters then not taking this world for granted as a resource, but rather living sensitively and in harmony with it, caring for the environment.

Humility is a quality that those who are religious have explored in some depth, seeing it from a variety of perspectives. Some Christian thinkers would see humility as relating to being or feeling unworthy, but others see it as a "central virtue" as seeing yourself accurately, including acknowledging weaknesses, being more oriented to others than self (Paine, 2017 p. 111). Similarly, from a Jewish perspective humility is partly about knowing who you are, assertively occupying your "rightful space within that context, appropriate to one's unique soul and responsibilities and eschewing" either arrogance or self-negation (Morinis, 2019 p. 39). Others have explored moving from a religious understanding to secular humility which can include a sense of awe particularly for nature, as well as recognising shared human limitations and fallibility and so being "disposed towards forgiveness, gratitude, open-mindedness, low self- focus, and feelings of awe" which can co-exist with a drive towards health and achievement (Wielenberg, 2019, p. 49).

This relates to the next interconnected qualities which are fundamental to all good practice of openness and vulnerability. What I mean by this is developing the ability to be aware of your own values and preferred ways of doing and being and at the same time to internally allow yourself to be open to what is different from these and what may feel fascinating, uncomfortable or even confronting. Being critically reflective (explored in Chapter 5) is a process that fosters understanding of where you are coming from and what needs to change. Underlying assumptions here may need to shift from *I know what I believe and am comfortable with how I express my spiritual self* to *there is something here for me to learn that I am feeling challenged by*. This degree of openness has a vulnerability and humility about it: it builds in the possibility of learning from the other instead of only being the helpful worker. This may simply be at the level of knowledge, realising how little you know about a religious tradition or spiritual practice. Equally it may be seeing how another lives their spiritual beliefs, asking why don't I have that kind of commitment?

Listening deeply

The ability to listen deeply is another related quality that emerges from a humble, open attitude. Social workers are trained to listen, but not always to the underlying spiritual nuances of what is meaningful. As Quaker author Douglas Steere (2000) puts it: "To 'listen' another's soul into a condition of disclosure and discovery may be almost the greatest service that any human being ever performs for another." Sometimes people need someone to listen so that they can hear themselves name what matters or hear at a more fundamental level who they are. First Nations people write about deep listening as 'Didirri,' a word from the Ngan'gikurunggurr language of the Daly River people, the sense of recognising "the deep spring that is inside us. We call on it and it calls to us. ... It is something like what you call 'contemplation'" (Ungunmerr-Baumann, 1988); this means waiting for clarity in 'quiet stillness.' McMahon (2017, p. 110) names how deep reflective listening or Gulpa Ngawawl in Yorta Yorta language is a key aspect of her research process:

> taking the time to process what I have heard and observed. Looking for signs from my Ancestors about the direction the research should take. This deep listening is informed by my dreams, learning from Aboriginal traditional stories and taking the time to wait for insights.

After deep listening comes "clear sightedness ... when a seed of thought or connecting thoughts have formed a picture." Deep listening in this sense encourages being internally slower, so that you are able to sit with the 'other' and wait for clarity to emerge. It also means listening for what is underneath the words to the essence of what the person is saying – or for what they are struggling to say. This can mean needing to wait, to take time. It is the antithesis of how social workers often feel in a busy organisational culture where the pressure is to move on and quickly make a decision. This quality means having the capacity to set aside that pressure and convey, usually nonverbally that you are willing to be present and listen deeply and reflectively, which in itself is enabling.

You could think of this as listening both deeply and in a 'spacious way' allowing space for what the other person sees as important to tell you. This means generating an atmosphere or climate in your work with them that feels spacious, that there is time for people to express what they want and need to. Organisational pressures can mean that social workers always feel time poor, and this can be unconsciously communicated to clients. Your body language gives away your desire to quickly find out what the issue is and how to respond, what to do. The danger of this is that people sense it and only feel able to tell you what seems the most urgent aspect of their situation or sometimes what they feel will be most acceptable to get their most urgent need satisfied. In the long run, this can mean that you miss what is actually important and only discover this when what you thought was agreed doesn't work. There is a skill in developing your capacity to sit with people, to be focused only on listening to them and conveying that they have as much time as they need even when you are time pressured. Ironically, this sometimes means that people become clear very quickly what the fundamental issues are, whether they want to do something about them and if so what. You may also find that allowing more time means the person comes to their own clarity and doesn't need you to do anything more. Listening thoroughly and deeply is enough in itself. Not all questions have answers: a person expressing frustration about why they have cancer and someone else doesn't, knows you don't have the answer to this.

Being attuned to the other

Finally, attunement or being attuned to the other is implied in this way of listening. You could think of this as being like being a tuning fork, seeking to get into harmony with a musical instrument. We sometimes talk about being sensitive to a particular atmosphere, picking up unconsciously changes in the environment or in a particular situation that mean something is about to change. In bush fire season, for example, I feel physically very attuned to any change in the atmosphere such as the smell of smoke or that might mean there is a danger of fire. I might also seek to be attuned to another person or group or community in the sense of aiming to have a 'sense' of what is happening for them, responding to the underlying variation you experience in how they are feeling and what they are thinking. Attunement comes from a relational perspective and from attachment theory, suggesting that parents need to be attuned to the needs of babies, sensitive to the nuances of their changing experience. Similarly, in listening to and working with others it is important to be tuning into what matters for them or how they are being affected by their interaction with you.

In some ways this is like being empathic, aiming to stand as much as possible in the shoes of the other to see how the world might be experienced from their perspective. The idea of attunement extends this further. Kossak (2015, p. 149) suggets that "[m]any people are out of tune with themselves and those around them, and out of tune with their environment and to a larger mystical or spiritual presence." He advocates for 'embodied empathy,' being able to tune into your own physcial and emotional being in order to understand how to be attuned to someone else and then also to the community you live and work in. Noticing your physcial reaction can help you notice what you are moved by, what is meaningul to you, whether that is in reactions like being tearful, feeling suddenly cold or hot or a sense of relief or relaxation. If you notice physcial reactions in those you work with, this can also prompt ex-ploring what this means and why it matters. How this is expressed will depend also on culture. In ancient Chinese culture, for example, because feeling and thinking are seen as inseparable, this leads to a more holistic view of the world, "not split into self/other, inner/outer, or even past/present...and calls for a different attunement, as being implicit—both known and unknown. Its in-tricacy takes shape when encountered, as embodied and unfinished" (Wang, 2020, p. 130).

Others would make links here between empathy and compassion, including self-compassion. Neff and Germer (2017, p. 371) name compassion as "opening one's awareness to the pain of others, without avoiding or dis-connecting from it, allowing feelings of kindness towards others and a desire to ameliorate their suffering." Self-compassion then is being open to your own pain whether it comes from something external or internal: being empathic towards yourself. Drawing on Buddhist teaching, Neff (2003, p. 87) identifies self-compassion with kindness, mindfulness and "in light of the common human experience, acknowledging that suffering, failure, and inadequacies are part of the human condition." Understanding this need for self compassion or self empathy reinforces the attitude of humility with those we work with, recognising that we all need compassion and empathy and to acknowledge our own needs as workers.

The capacity to wait, to be in the moment

Being attuned, combined with the other qualities of humility and openness can foster the ability simply to be with the other whether an individual or community, to wait until they are ready to speak or are prepared to be more open with you. When Alston, Hargreaves and Hazeleger (2018, p. 414) talked to those who had lost homes and community after the Black Saturday bush-fires in Australia, they found survivors "spoke of 'bushfire brain' and the need for time to make decisions, to absorb the nature not only of their tangible losses but also the intangible qualities of loss – their loss of community, of place, of the taken-for-granted certainties of life. Service providers on the other hand, spoke of a sense of urgency in addressing the enormity of the fire impacts – of needing to get in and fix things quickly." The learning from this experience was partly of the importance of working 'at the pace of survivors.' The idea of waiting is named very clearly in First Nations culture. In Yorta Yorta language, Mishel McMahon says the word: *Garraba* – means 'wait a little'; "a relational concept of sitting or waiting when trying to proceed in a particular direction or make a decision; you may need to be invited first, listen to Elders first, wait for a dream or revealed knowledge through a dream or a particular animal coming into your day" (McMahon and McMahon, 2019).

From a spiritual and religious perspective, learning to be in the moment is an important aspect of sitting with uncertainty while you seek meaning. This kind of listening also holds you and the person in a more transcendent space; where you might feel connected more broadly to other people, to the universal concerns of how to be in and relate to the world, listening to the spirit within a conversation. It might be as a worker listening to someone who is naming their loss and grief that you feel connected more broadly to the loss and grief in the world, both aware of the pain and suffering that exists but also how this is part of the overall pattern of life. The ability to be deeply connected in this way may sound exhausting, but is more often regenerating: there is a nurture that comes from the depth of relatedness and connectedness here. Cultivating this way of being still and listening can be fostered by practising what religious traditions would name as prayer or meditation. Mindfulness meditation is being increasingly advocated as a practice in social work and related disciplines and will be explored more in Chapter 7. While interest in mindfulness has been partly related to finding ways to manage mental health issues, this can also be a way for social workers to be present with clients and with their own reactions. From a worker perspective, "mindfulness is a way of paying attention with empathy, presence, and deep listening that can be cultivated, sustained, and integrated into our work as therapists through the ongoing discipline of meditation practice... a kind of shift from a 'doing mode' to a 'being mode'" (Hick and Bien, 2008, p. 4).

Understanding the influence of history and social context

Being attuned also relates to understanding the influence of history and social context individually and more broadly. How people express their spiritual selves frequently reflects their personal and family history. This might be in continuing family traditions and expectations or reacting against them, wanting to be different. For some, perhaps particularly those in a religious tradition there may be the solidity of generations of shared worship and community. Beliefs and practices that have been integral to how the family lives are so much part of who they are that they aren't questioned. For others, being part of a religious tradition may be something they have grown away from, related to family dynamics and frustrations and this may influence how they react to anything that is seen as spiritual. It helps to think about how this has emerged in your own life: what spiritual or religious traditions have been part of your family history? What was your parents' reaction to their experience? How did this influence them in your family? What have been your experiences of these as a child and adult? What assumptions and values does that mean you have about spirituality and religion?

Implicit in this understanding of the influence of history and social context is an expectation of being able to help others articulate that these are assumptions and beliefs and that these can change over time. Part of the dialogue is opening up the space of what is possible, that there are other ways of perceiving and engaging with spirituality and religion, not just one way. This can be a liberating and also a painful process for people to be. Most of us can acknowledge this kind of change for ourselves, the move from the certainty of *this is the way things are in my family/community and I am a part of this* to *I now see that things can be understood differently*. Part of our role as social workers in other aspects of working with people is to enable seeing that there are more possibilities, that change can be both possible and desirable. How to do this will be explored more in the next chapters.

The assumptions we have also relate to how the spiritual/religious beliefs experienced in our lives are similar to or different from the prevailing community norms and the history that informs them. As workers then, we need to be aware of how these have influenced and may continue to influence those we work with. If your religious tradition was the norm in your country of origin but is seen as less acceptable or actively unacceptable in your current community that might influence you to keep quiet about it or become more actively assertive. Lily Brett (2001) describes her parents' reluctance to be obviously Jewish when they migrate to Australia after the Second World War. Given their experience of the Holocaust, they understandably didn't want to stand out. For some religious groups, discrimination and active persecution continues to be an issue in both subtle and obvious ways. If this is the experience of someone you are working with, it's vital to see how you might be perceived by them. If it is your experience of being judged, this might affect your ability to work with people who seem similar to your persecutors. Part of this is not making assumptions about how a particular spirituality is expressed, but being aware of how this might be influenced by history and a particular cultural context. For example Firth (1999, pp. 165–166) points out that those who are Asian, and particularly elders in Britain come from very different geographic areas and speak different langauges, so that within each religious tradition – Hindu, Muslim and Sikh –

> there are also considerable differences depending on sectarian affiliation, caste or class, education, economic status and migration history … Attitudes to ageing will be influenced not only by the above factors but also by their own biography, education, family organisation, housing and health, and their place in the local social and religious communities.

Rena, for example, is a Muslim whose family were refugees from Afghanistan. Initially her family felt comfortable and accepted in Australia. In 2001 she was in her final year of secondary school, and after 9/11, suddenly felt it was no longer acceptable to be Muslim. She felt very angry at being judged when all the Muslims she knew advocated peace not violence. To her parents' discomfort, she decided she was going to start wearing a hijab to demonstrate her pride in being Muslim. This created more pressure for her including several incidents where she feared being physically attacked. This made her even more determined to continue and gradually, she also found that some of her friends became more interested in understanding why being Muslim was so important to her.

Working holistically

Next is working holistically: in a way that values all of who this person is and what matters to them. You could think about this as connecting to the spiritual aspect of who a person is in the same way that you would want to connect to or understand their health and well-being, the context and history of the person. Another way of thinking about this is adding the spiritual to the biological and psychosocial approach as Harms (2010) suggests. You could also think about this as connecting to the essence of the person, to the way of being that is fundamental to who they are. If you were building a relationship with a First Nations person for example, it would be essential to acknowledge that their First Nations way of being is the essence of who they are and that their spiritual self is an integral aspect of their being – although how that is expressed will depend on the individual, their history and community. Some people embracing a religious tradition would express this in a similar kind of way. Working mindfully and holistically also means using all of who you are so long as it is benefitting those you work with. This may mean for example, including your mutual use of humour. Bien (2008, p. 44) points out that it's important to enjoy being with those you work with "there can be jokes, stories and laughter in psychotherapy, even when talking about serious and sad things" provided we are doing this in a 'mindful' way that reflects our acceptance of and empathy with the perspective of the other person. Honesty is important here, being open about what you do or don't know: the expectation is not that you know everything about all spiritual and religious traditions, that would be impossible.

Place and space

Thinking about Kossak's (2009) idea of embodied empathy is a good reminder of the importance of tuning into the experience and meaning of place and space for individuals and communities. Zapf (2010, p. 38) says the idea of place "combines location and physical environment with character, meaning, and emotional significance for people; it is ... an interactive and holistic concept." He critiques social work's focus on person-in- environment which implies that people and environment are two separate entities where one dominates the other. Instead he advocates for what you could see as a more First Nations or green understanding of the interconnectedness of all things; people as place which "conveys unity and holism that brings us immediately to concerns of sustainability and stewardship." Those who live in rural communities often have much more experience of the influence of interacting with place. For me, living in a rural community means I am particularly conscious of the changes in my physical environment: the influence of the seasons on what I can do in the garden, how the days getting lighter or darker shifts what I do when during the day. Living next to a forest also fosters appreciation of natural spaces and how spiritually regenerating they can be. In my rural community there is also the need to be conscious of the possibility of bushfires, drought or flooding, all of which prompt paying attention to the environment and how it is changing.

Place and space influence how we are and can also be or reflect what matters to us. Our personal history is attached to places, our lived reality. Social workers are increasingly understanding the importance of 'place' particularly from a green social work perspective. This often highlights the importance of the physical nature of home and its surrounding landscape as the place that embodies feelings of meaning and of being 'at home.' Being linked to a specific environment can be part of a person's identity: how they understand who they are. People name themselves as feeling like a city person or a rural dweller, someone more comfortable with a particular kind of land. After bushfires "when 'place' is damaged, people suffer both from the physical manifestations of the disaster and also from the erosion of 'self' and the de-stabilised connection to 'place' that the disaster symbolises" (Alston, Hargreaves and Hazeleger, 2018, p. 406). The feeling of space is partly a physical one related to place, but also reflects an inner experience. People might talk about finding it nurturing to go to a particular geographical place, describing it as a 'space' that evokes certain memories for them, or having a feeling of spaciousness that allows them to expand internally. As explored in Chapter 3, First Nations people remind us how critical it is to understand how we are interrelated to all things, animate and inanimate. Mishel McMahon (2020), a Yorta Yorta woman, suggests we all need to ask ourselves what kind of environment resonates with us, regenerates us spiritually. If we were to know ourselves from this broad understanding: is it river country with red gums or desert country or hills rolling down to sea? If we can't live where we feel nurtured by our environment, how can we compensate for that? She makes it clear that for First Nations people specific places have individual as well as community meaning, and that all land has significance historically. It is a completely different way of looking at the landscape to see it all as imbued with sacred meaning in the way that was explored in Chapter 3.

As well as the physical nature of place, it is critical to include how place and space are perceived and experienced, what they mean for individuals and communities. Often places have a feeling of space that is often important. A particular landscape may feel constrained or spacious. I moved to live in a very flat environment after years of living among hills. For several years, I felt somewhat distanced from the environment, it didn't nurture me spiritually. Then I went to visit a friend who lived in densely wooded hills where little light could penetrate. I found that I missed the feeling of spaciousness from the flat country, the openness to the sky, the awareness of clouds, changing weather and light. Without realising it, I had begun to find a different kind of being 'at home' there which was spiritually nurturing and equally connecting to the landscape.

The closest most of us can come to what place and space mean for First Nations people is to think about our own memories of particular places and what they have meant for us. For all of us the subjective experience we have of being in a particular place can mean we remember it differently from another person. An obvious example is that if you go on holiday to somewhere where you have perfect weather, great company and the kind of activities you most enjoy, you are more likely to have a warmth of memory about the place. If you have been to the same place and spent the time arguing with your friends or family and the weather means you can't do anything you planned, your experience and feelings about the place will be very different. Similarly, certain places evoke important memories, nostalgia or meaning. People who are grieving might want to revisit places that were important in their relationship with the person who has died, or be reluctant to leave the house or area they lived in. More often now people are putting markers by the side of roads where someone they loved has died; for others being able to visit a cemetery is an important way of still feeling a connection.

When I asked people in a regional city hospital what nurtured them spiritually as part of a research project (Gardner, Tan and Rumbold, 2018), many responses included memories of place, usually of the natural world or for some what they could see from their hospital windows: sky, trees and gardens. One was nostalgic about fishing in the Murray river; another for being on their farmland where they could see far into the distance. Many missed gardens and seeing the sky; some longed for fresh air, the feeling of sun. The hospital had recognised the need for garden space, at least flowers if not trees and had started to build a courtyard that would allow patients to sit in a somewhat more natural environment. Particular built places can also evoke for many people a spiritual or religious feeling – churches, mosques or synagogues would be obvious examples. Those who do not see themselves as religious may still feel moved by these. Brunn (2015, p. 5) points out that place has long been studied as a theme by those looking at pilgrimages, sacred places and landscapes as well as the built environment, and that "the origins of all major world religions are associated with specific place and regional attributes, that old and new diasporas mix in different place settings and that new age, animistic, agnostic and secular movements have specific place features." Increasingly, people are going on pilgrimage that once would have been for religious traditions, but have become a way of seeking meaning for others. Others go on nature retreats or pilgrimage walks as a form of finding time and space for a sense of renewal (Maddrell, 2013). Béres (2012) writes about experiencing the island of Iona as significant spiritually: partly the combination of seeing it as both a specific place and part of a vast space.

It is useful to ask yourself and those you are working with how does your physical environment influence you? This might include asking is where you live spiritually nurturing and if not, how can you foster this? How can you create a room or part of a room or garden that nurtures your spirit? Are there ways that you can make changes in your local neighbourhood that change how it feels to be there? Is there a park nearby that you can visit? We often make assumptions about what kind of housing can be life-affirming, but it may be more about how we engage with it. It can also be too easy to assume the same things will be life-affirming for everyone. Some people actively dislike gardening or actively engaging with nature, so the question always needs to be what place and space is life-affirming for you? For some people, the physical space of their religious or spiritual community is what is life-affirming: the church, mosque or synagogue or the yoga centre or neighbourhood house. For others it is about where they connect with people that matter: having somewhere to meet or to do something with others, access to places to work, learn, socialise, volunteer. Some of this may well be finding a place or space online for spiritual connection, for meaningful interaction about death and dying or establishing relationships (Carroll and Landry, 2010).

Dominelli (2012) points out that money can be a factor in place and space and that we need to be attuned to the structural influences of this. Lack of money is a significant factor in what kind of housing you can have, the choices you can make about where you live, the access you can have to the kind of environment that you find nurturing. People often have to move to cities for work and for those from rural environments that can be undermining spiritually. Governments make choices about funding to make environments more appealing: wealthier suburbs may well be those with more parks and space for children to play. Social workers need to be advocates for spaces that everyone can access in ways that feed their spiritual selves. This connects to accessibility to transport as well.

Place and space is an issue in the workplace as well that can contribute significantly to spiritual wellbeing or undermine it. Some workplaces are conscious of this and seek to create an environment that makes inclusion of the spiritual explicit, including specific places for prayer or meditation such as a chapel or meditation room, garden spaces for people to sit and gather energy. In some, it is possible to create a feeling of spaciousness for yourself and those you work working with, making your office a welcoming and inviting space. I once visited a government department where workers were in 'pods' in a large and basically uninviting room. When I was walking round the pods to see people, I could see that nearly everyone had found ways to make their pod more homelike with what mattered to them: photos, ornaments and so on. Being able to work at home has the advantage of people being able to use mediation or prayer as they need to and as fits with their religious tradition.

Courage

A quality that also fits here is that of courage. Given the current taboos about naming and exploring spirituality and religion in social work, it takes courage to be willing to do this. It also takes courage to look at your own assumptions and values, the perhaps sometimes unjust expectations you have had about those for whom religion is important. This links to the underlying value for all of these qualities of working from a socially just perspective. One of the criticisms made of religious traditions, often fairly, is that they are not suffi-ciently conscious of advocating for the rights of all people to live full and rich lives. There are significant examples of those who are not heterosexual being excluded, victimized or simply not having their sexuality accepted as a valid way of being. Some would point to excessive wealth for those in power or to ways in which women are excluded from ministry or other positions in the hierarchy of their faith tradition. Cultural insensitivity is expressed in all sorts of ways, the use of religious beliefs to justify terrorism and the abuse of minority groups in many countries are other examples. On the other hand, it is important to remember that there are some faith traditions and members of others for whom social justice is integral to their religious practice. Judd (2013, p. 178) points out that "Advocacy for social justice can be seen throughout organized religions in their support of causes such as civil and welfare rights, the labor movement and various peace movements." This can mean another kind of courage: naming what is not acceptable behaviour justified in a spiritual or religious way.

Putting this altogether affirms how to be as worker as well as how to do social work (Figure 4.1). The hope is that you can find in yourself the capacity

Inner focused

Externally focused

Openness, humility and
vulnerability

Understanding influence
of history and social context

Sitting with uncertainty and not knowing

Working holistically

Listening deeply

Place and Space

Attuned to understanding, emotion, meaning

Empathy and compassion

Courage

Being in the moment

Figure 4.1 Qualities of critically spiritual practice.

to be open, humble, vulnerable, compassionate and from that place to listen deeply, attuned to the other. This way of being will enable you to better sit with the person, allowing uncertainty and not knowing until it becomes clear whether this in itself what is needed or to allow clarity for moving forward. Awareness of external issues such as history and social context, the importance of space and place as well as remembering the knowledge from previous chapters will encourage these processes.

5 Using critical reflection to engage with spirituality and religion in practice

When I asked workers in palliative care whether they thought spirituality should be included in training for them, workers were both convinced that spirituality needed to be part of their practice and unnerved by what that would mean. Some feared not knowing what to say or having nothing useful to offer. What they reported several months after the training was the value of becoming more aware, recognising the need to start with their own 'stuff'; their values and beliefs about spirituality and religion and how that might influence others, the importance of 'not making assumptions.' One participant commented: "I have learnt about accepting people where they are at and I'm learning not to judge or become frustrated. I've noticed quite a profound change" (Gardner, 2012, p. 455). What I am suggesting in this chapter is that using the processes of critical reflection is a way of developing this kind of awareness and ability to recognise your own assumptions and not impose them on others, particularly here in relation to spirituality and religion.

For most of us, our personal history is significantly, but often unconsciously, influenced by and interconnected to our social context and related history. The resulting assumptions we make have considerable potential for inadvertently undermining the beliefs and values of those that we are working with. When I interviewed a Jewish woman about her religious experience, she talked about how much she appreciated that the rural community where she lived recognised how quickly she wanted to bury her mother after she died. In the Jewish tradition, the person should be buried within 24 hours, initially perhaps partly related to hot climates, but now inextricably linked to socially and culturally significant rituals for burial and mourning. I noticed my own, fortunately inner, surprised reaction to this and my assumption that it would be 'better' to have a longer time between the death and the burial. When I thought more about this, I realised I had made assumptions based on my own historical and social context. In Scotland, a colder climate, the expectation was that there would be at least several days, often a week, after death when people could come and sit with the dead person and also with the family. My underlying assumption was that it was good for people to have this kind of time to be able to make their farewells. Notice that I held this assumption even though I had left Scotland many years before and no longer lived in the kind of climate where that would always be

DOI: 10.4324/9781003132677-8

possible. It's also an assumption that is simply my belief, not based on any kind of checking in with what others might prefer or see as desirable.

My reaction in this particular example highlights the need to be constantly critically reflective in engaging with what matters spiritually to you and to those you work with, as you would with any other aspect of your practice. We are conscious of the need to be sensitive to assumptions underlying social and cultural differences related to age, ability, gender, sexuality and race. Because of this, it is likely that as a social worker you are already familiar with how to use critically reflective processes in exploring your reactions to particular experiences. Similarly, as a student, you are likely to be learning how to embed a critically reflective approach for your future practice. Critical reflection or it may be called reflective practice is a significant aspect of social work and other professional training. In the particular critical reflection approach I am using here, critical reflection is defined as a theory and process which "involves a deeper look at the premises on which thinking, actions and emotions are based. It is critical when connections are made between these assumptions and the social world as a basis for a changed action" (Fook and Gardner, 2007, p. 14). It is a way of asking the "big, ultimate questions of life" (Fook, 2017, p. 28) going deeply into the meaning of an experience.

This approach to critical reflection is underpinned by a set of theories that inform being critically reflective. Two of these: critical theory and post-modernism were explored in Chapter 3, so I will only briefly explore here how to connect them to the processes of critical reflection, then add reflexivity and reflective practice in the context of a spiritual approach to critical reflection. As Hunt (2016, p. 34) points out reflective learning or practice "cannot be separated from the process of personal meaning making or, therefore, from the asking of "ultimate questions," such as "who am I?" If we don't use processes like critical reflection to understand our own meaning-making, the danger is that we don't hear what the other is saying and unconsciously impose our values and beliefs on them. What we need to recognise is how often "we require others to conform to our ideological structures and ways of expression before we will receive truth as they see it, how unprepared we are to trust in the capacity of others to work out their own solutions with divine assistance" (Loring, 1997, p. 161). If you live in an essentially secular family and develop an interest in Catholicism, for example, it helps to understand the personal and social history and context that may make it hard for your family to accept this. A critical understanding can provide a sense of the history and structural influences that mean they perceive Catholicism in a particular way which may or may not reflect your experience.

Critical aspect of critical reflection: seeking socially just change

A critical perspective also fosters seeking socially just change within a human rights framework. From a religious perspective, liberation theology makes explicit the value of this connection. Bennett (2007, p. 41) compares reflective practice and critical reflection as similar to the difference between practical theology and liberation theology where "in some contexts, professional reflective practice becomes an instrument of conservative political and religious ends" such as the current neoliberal emphasis on efficiency and conformity, whereas liberation theology brings" liberation and humanisation through radical, transformative social and political change." The kinds of questions fostered by a critically reflective approach could include:

> how is this experience influenced by the assumptions and values of the community and society you live in?
> how have you and the others in your experience been influenced by these?
> what are the power issues here?
> how is the prevailing power dynamic supported by these assumptions?
> what kinds of socially just change does this suggest you need to advocate for?

Postmodern thinking: celebrating many ways of being

Postmodernism also encourages understanding the dominant discourses in society: what are the main ways of thinking about this in this culture and how does this influence your experience? In many Western societies, there is a confusing combination of dominant views. There are often unconscious assumptions that the society is essentially Christian built into the fabric: a strongly Protestant work ethic, decisions about women's reproductive rights based on religious values and a privileging of Christian religious traditions. On the other hand, such societies see themselves as secular, making decisions on a purely rational basis, rather than acknowledging that all decisions are value-based. Postmodernism helpfully fosters seeing that there are many ways of being, many valid approaches and strategies, and celebration of diverse religious and spiritual ways of being. This moves exploration of a particular experience beyond a one right way: all Muslims believe this or all Hindus do this. It also fosters moving beyond a dualist or either/or way of seeing things. Rather than seeing people as religious or not, spiritual or not, ask such questions as:

> how else can this be seen?
> what are the many ways that this experience can be understood?
> If we move beyond seeing how these are apparent opposites, what new learning or ways of seeing this are possible?

Postmodernism also encourages asking how language is used, and how what language is available to use influences communication. For example, it may be that there isn't a word in English for an aspect of their spiritual or religious beliefs that a person from a non-English speaking background is trying to share.

Use of reflexivity

Next reflexivity: ideas about reflexivity have partly come from research "a stance of being able to locate oneself in the picture" (Fook, 2016, p. 56). What I find particularly helpful about reflexivity is that it encourages asking yourself both how do I see other people, but also how do they see me? It reminds us that how we see ourselves is not necessarily how others see us. For example, someone might ask are you Christian because you are wearing a cross. You might hesitate to answer, conscious that while you share some beliefs with other Christians, you don't share all beliefs. You may fear that if your client is an unmarried parent, they will have felt rejected by some forms of Christianity and so that will colour their view of you. From a critical reflexivity perspective, included in this is an awareness of how each of these sets of perceptions – yours and the other person's is influenced by the social and historical context in which you both live. To work effectively you need to be able to hold both your own perception of yourself (that being a Christian is a positive experience for you), but also recognition of the perception of the other person and their validity in the context we are in. This will be influenced by how each of you is able to 'position' yourselves, depending on who has power and why, which "relates to issues of recognition which themselves are informed by issues of race, class, gender and sexuality" (May and Perry, 2017, p. 184). Similarly, from a relational perspective, Goodman (2014, p. 48) suggests workers need to "be transparent to both their own cultural beliefs and open to those of their clients … to remain simultaneously aware of their own cultural proclivities and existing ideas about those of others in order to potentiate the relational aspect of the therapeutic encounter."

Reflexivity is particularly valuable in enabling you as a worker to see the complexity of how you might be seen from a spiritual perspective by a client, the assumptions and fears they might have developed from someone they perceive as spiritually different from them – as well as how you might also have such assumptions and fears. If you are a white man wearing a cross, meeting as a client a woman of colour wearing a hijab, you may be perceived at least initially by the client as having a significantly different experience of life in general and specifically of spirituality/religion. You may be concerned that your lack of understanding of Islam may get in the way; you may assume that the woman will not want to talk to you as a Christian. On the other hand, it may be that the client assumes if you are wearing a cross, you must take religion seriously and that's a good start. Understanding reflexivity helps you stand in the shoes of the other to see how you might look from their perspective: how their past experience of dealing with professionals might feel oppressive or overpowering. Rather than making assumptions, this encourages asking:

> how might this client be perceiving me?
> how might they think I am perceiving them and how might that influence their reaction to me?

It may be that you can ask the client about their perceptions directly once you have established a relationship with them, particularly if it seems as if these are getting in the way.

Reflective practice: unearthing assumptions

Finally, reflective practice encourages unearthing the assumptions and values that influence how you act and react, often unconsciously. As I illustrated in the example beginning the chapter of the Jewish funeral, it is alarmingly easy for us to think that our ways of being and doing are the norm that everyone else will share. In critical reflection practice, the word assumption is used to suggest that this is a value, attitude or belief that is assumed or taken for granted; it is usually unconscious. The aim is to make these conscious so that you make an active choice about whether you want to continue to work from this position. It isn't that all assumptions are unacceptable. In my initial example, this was the case: I had assumed that it was better to have longer after a person's death to farewell them before burial or cremation, my new assumption was that this depends on the person's religious and cultural background and I need to check what this means. If my unconscious belief had been people have very different ways of engaging with death, that would have been a useful assumption to make conscious and operate from. This exploration of assumptions also helps us be more aware of when we think we are operating from a conscious or espoused value of belief, but are being influenced by an unconscious one. *Jamie for example believed that she was operating from a value base of accepting and celebrating diversity, but noticed that as a practising Buddhist, she was frustrated by people who dismissed religion and spirituality as 'nonsense.' She realised that her assumption for herself had turned into a 'should' for others: everyone should be curious about or value spiritual and religious diversity and that she needed to understand that others' past experiences meant they didn't share her views.*

Reflective practice also has an intuitive and creative aspect: a valuing of engaging with others in ways that suit their particular ways of being. Schon (1983, p. 19) suggests that it is important for professionals to move beyond 'technical rationality' to value "making sense of uncertainty, performing artistically, setting problems and choosing among competing professional paradigms." Like relational practice, this affirms using the process flexibly and creatively in ways that fit with you and those you are working with, perhaps using art, rituals or symbols to encourage people to name what matters. Reflective practice also names the difference between espoused theory: the assumptions you believe you are operating from and the theory in practice: what your reactions are actually based on. The kinds of questions encouraged from reflective practice could include:

what assumptions and values am I operating from?
which of these are influencing me unconsciously?

am I acting inconsistently with my assumptions? (i.e. are my espoused values different from my values in action)

what do I intuitively know about myself and about what is happening here that I need to put into words?

Dan, for example, was vaguely aware that something wasn't working in his relationship with a colleague, Seren, a Sikh, who had recently joined the staff. He didn't pay attention to this until Seren became angry with him in a meeting when Dan made a comment about men no longer having sensible short hair cuts pointing out that for some men like him, it was a religious practice not to cut their hair. At the time, Dan denied making this connection, but when he thought about it afterwards, he was conscious that he did feel challenged by the visibility of Seren's religious connection. His espoused theory of celebrating diversity had been undermined by his theory in action, an underlying assumption that people should 'fit in.' Once he recognised this he was able to consciously change his underlying assumption to fit with his preferred theory and to apologise to Seren.

Critical reflection process identifying meaning

Overall then, what I am suggesting here is that we can use a critically reflective process underpinned by these theories – and the other theories from Chapter 3 to articulate meaning, our fundamental values and beliefs and our understanding of the spiritual or religious world: our own and those we are working with. This includes how people connect to the key underlying questions of how we live, what really matters to us. These are not easy questions and it is important this process be carried out in a supportive and enabling environment, where each person feels able to be vulnerable in unearthing and naming aspects of their more fundamental values and beliefs. The theories above can help with this reinforcing there is not one right way, that diversity is to be valued, that the aim is to inspire and embolden each other to become clearer.

Essentially the critical reflection process in this model (Fook and Gardner, 2007) involves taking a particular experience, usually an experience that has concerned or puzzled you in some way, an experience you want to explore more deeply or feel there is more to be learned from. This process means identifying the emotions, thoughts and reactions that relate to that experience as well as the underlying meaning connected to the experience. There are two stages to the process (see also Box One):

Stage one

The first stage focuses on exploration, including your reactions, how you felt and what you thought, exploring what matters to you about the experience at a more fundamental level the kinds of values and beliefs you have, the assumptions that you might make that would influence how you have reacted.

This exploration needs to include understanding the influence of your own personal social context and history as well as that of the culture and society that you live in.

As part of the first stage, you could explore how the experience might look from the perspective of another person involved – most experiences do involve at least one other person. You would speculate from a position of positive curiosity about what the experience might mean for them, how they too might be influenced by their social context and history and past experience. Having done this, you revisit your own experience to see whether trying to see from their perspective has shifted your own.

Stage two

The second stage focuses on the implications for change. The expectation is that this greater understanding of where you and the other person/people are coming from will lead to some kind of change in your understanding and so in your practice. This might also mean you seek change in your organisational or social context. Both of these stages are important: the expectation in the process is that the exploration and deeper clarity about meaning in the first stage will lead to either changed perceptions and/or assumptions and/or linked changed behaviour or a decision to seek other change.

The examples below will explore this process. The questions in the box outline in more depth what these questions might be using the general critical reflection framework but adapted to focus more on spirituality and religion (adapted from Gardner, 2014). The critical reflection process can evoke strong feelings, often the experience you are exploring is one that you are not comfortable with, at least partly because of your own reaction. Because of this, it is important to think about who you might want to work with and how. You can use the questions in Box One to work through your experience yourself, though it can be harder to elicit your own underlying assumptions and values. If you do decide to do this, journaling can help or writing your responses to the questions, then sitting with them to see what your responses bring up for you.

The critical reflection process can be used in individual supervision and having one dedicated listener can be very helpful in the process. You might consciously make a choice about whether you feel this will work: is your supervisor familiar with this process? Do you feel comfortable to speak openly about your spiritual self? Alternatively, you might choose to use the process in a critical reflection peer supervision group, formally or informally in your organisation. The group process means you are sharing with others in a more mutual way, and at the same peer level, so more similar in terms of power which can feel safer. Similarly, Drummond (2020) a Meriam and Daureb traditional owner, advocates the use of 'yarning circles' for nursing students creating safe spaces for students and staff to more deeply and critically understand their reactions to Indigenous knowledge in relating to Indigenous health issues. You could use the process with a trusted friend also interested in using this process (Gardner, 2014).

However, you choose to do this, it is important to set clear expectations about the culture first: confidentiality, mutuality, how the process will be used, deeply non-judgemental acceptance and respect for each other's experience and perceptions. The kinds of qualities or capacities outlined in Chapter 4 are relevant here: listening deeply, being open, humble and vulnerable, allowing silence and sitting with the other person/people, while also being prepared to ask respectfully what other perspectives there could be. While critical reflection can be used in many ways, here I am focusing on using it to explore experiences that include spirituality and religion and the questions in the box below reflect this. The box is followed by three case studies illustrating the use of the critical reflection process.

Box One: *The Stages of Critical Reflection: Possible questions related to including spirituality and religion.* Note these are examples of questions to give you ideas, but need to be adjusted to suit you and those you are working with.

Stage One: Exploration

1a From your perspective:
What was the experience? What were you feeling? What were you thinking?
What fundamental values and beliefs connect with this experience? What assumptions were you making related to a sense of meaning, to who you are fundamentally? Were there connections there to spirituality/religion? What feelings and thoughts are there about these?
How did this experience connect with other past experience: your own personal experience and/or family history? What about connections to other aspects of your life? Relationships, education, work, taking part in spiritual or religious activities?
How do your assumptions fit with your own family history and social context? Are these assumptions about meaning ones that encourage you to flourish and grow? Or are they assumptions about meaning that are undermining? What are your reactions to these: how are you now feeling?
How did this experience and your related assumptions connect with the broader social context and history? What were the prevailing views about spirituality/religion in your community? The society you live in? How was difference between those who saw themselves as religious/spiritual perceived? Is that relevant here?

1b From the perspective of another person in the experience:

What was their reaction? What might they have been thinking and feeling?

How was their reaction influenced by their values and beliefs, to their sense of meaning? And is there a connection for them with spiritualty/religion?

How did this experience connect with their family history and how meaning (which might include how spirituality/religion is expressed?

How did this experience and their related assumptions connect with the broader social context and history, to the community they live in, particularly related to questions of meaning, to religion and spirituality?

1c From your perspective: having explored your own and the other person's perspective, where are you now, what are you now feeling and thinking about your experience and your reaction to it?

Stage Two: What needs to change?

What meaning is now clearer to you?

What do you now want to change about your reaction/assumptions and values/your way of acting in this experience?

Are there values and beliefs that you want to more consciously affirm or change?

What difference would this make to your practice?

How does thinking about this mean you feel about your experience, about meaning and possible change?

How could you translate this into practice?

How will you remember this new learning?

Examples of using critical reflection to reflect on practice:

The following examples illustrate how you can use critical reflection to explore what is happening in a particular experience, using the theories above and the structure of the process to explore your own and another person's reactions. Remember exactly how the process unfolds will vary, you need to be attuned to this person and their preferences, using deep listening and the other qualities explored earlier rather than to stick rigidly to the questions.

Case Study One: Fran's experience

Fran was in her early 40s when she moved to work in a community health services agency offering counselling to individuals and couples. The experience she brought to her critical reflection group was of gradually getting to know a couple, Mark and Donna. Over time, when Mark became more trusting of Fran, he disclosed that he had been abused by a priest in his local parish church when he was eight. He believed that some of his continuing issues with trust in relationships stemmed from that experience. With more publicity about abuse in the Catholic Church, he had become more confident about speaking about his experience, which previously he had felt very ashamed of and assumed must be his fault in some way.

Stage 1a

Fran had been a staunch member of her local Catholic church all her life and sees the value system as underpinning all of how she lives. Of course, she was aware of the building criticism and concerns related to abuse in the Catholic and other churches which at a conscious level she was also considerably concerned about. However, she noticed that as Mark continued to haltingly talk about his experience, a part of her wanted to diminish it and deny it. She had to stop herself from making comments like are you sure that this happened and that you didn't misunderstand something that was going on? As a social worker, she also was very conscious of the need to affirm Mike's experience, to believe and respect the pain of his story and to support him if he wanted to take action against the priest.

Initially, her critical reflection group members found it difficult not to react from their own beliefs about sexual abuse. However, they remained true to the process and encouraged Fran to explore where her reactions were coming from. She identified her feelings of both shame at doubting Mark, and surprise at the strength of her desire to defend the Catholic Church. She described her local church community as a place of deep spiritual warmth and wisdom. She was in tears as she outlined what it meant to her. Her very deeply embedded assumption was that *the church and her faith was a place of meaning, life-giving for her and for others.*

Stage 1b

As she explored the question of meaning, she dentified how as a Catholic, she felt she was constantly now defending her involvement in the church. Because of this, rather than exploring Mark's assumptions she thought it would be more helpful to take her social work colleagues as the 'other' in this experience. In brainstorming assumptions for her colleagues she identified:

> the church is wholly corrupt;

> all priests are likely to be damaging others in some way;

> people don't appreciate any of the good things the church does.

Her colleagues added assumptions from their different perspectives:

> some priests are great!

people always talk more about the negative than the positive

any organisation has good and not so good people.

Stage 1c

Fran realised as she considered these that she also assumed that people, including her social work colleagues were <u>all</u> making negative judgements about <u>all</u> the Catholic Church and that she sounded as if she assumed it was <u>all</u> positive. When she sat more with her reaction to Mark, she also realised that her family assumptions were that *it's more important to notice the good, and to ignore the bad.* Partly, this came from their church community as children where the emphasis was on a loving God, but also came from her mother's family where discussion of anything negative was seen as unhelpful and strongly discouraged. The family assumption that Fran had internalised was: *peace is more important than anything else.*

Stage 2

When she could put all these together Fran could see that she needed more helpful new assumptions. These binaries weren't realistic from either perspective: the church was both uplifting and flawed as were those who worked and worshipped in it. She created new assumptions: *the church and the people in it are both good and not so good and I need to engage with all of that.* She also separated out her faith from the church: my faith is separate from the church and I can foster my beliefs and values. When asked what difference this would make Fran could see firstly with Mark that she would more fully engage with his need to criticise the priest and the church for the lack of action to support him and others. She also acknowledged there were times in her faith community and in her workplace where she would ignore what was destructive and that she needed a new assumption: *peace needs to be balanced with justice.* Ironically, she could see how this fitted with the church's teachings that she had ignored or assumed meant only seeking justice for the oppressed in other parts of the world. This she could see significantly changing her attitude to her practice in general.

Case Study Two: Jane's experience

Jane works in the children's ward of a large regional hospital which has a significant First Nations population. The example she brought to her critical reflection group was of a First Nations family, the mother Kerry, father Dave and daughter Tanya who was six. Tanya was seriously ill with leukaemia and having regular treatment that meant she had to be hospitalised sometimes for a week. When Tanya came for treatment, other family members, her grandparents, aunts and cousins would often come to offer support, which was against the hospital rules that only immediate family members could visit. Jane had become increasingly irritated that Kerry and Dave seemed unable to tell family members they shouldn't come. They also wanted to bring plants into the hospital for Tanya's room rather than flowers that could be in a vase, that also didn't sit right with Jane. This finally erupted one day when she saw Kerry arriving with her mother and one of her aunts, she could hear herself being close to shouting at them that they were ignorant.

Stage 1a

As Jane told her story, she sounded very angry and frustrated, and she agreed that was how she felt. As group members asked her to say more, she articulated that she felt she had to enforce the rules and that they were making it hard for her. One of the group asked what she thought about the rules and she was able to say she didn't agree with the rules necessarily, sometimes it would help to have more family around, Tanya really responded well to them. As the group asked more about Jane's reaction what surfaced was: it isn't fair for them to get different treatment. This translated into: First Nations people get special treatment and that's not fair. Jane was as surprised as others in the group that this assumption had emerged. When asked where that came from she remembered that in her family and community, there had been a perception that First Nations people got more benefits, more services. She remembered that, as a young child, she had seen a teacher give a First Nations child a bag from a local shop. She had assumed that these were presents that only this child was ever given and resented that the teacher like this child best. This had become entwined with the family and community assumptions. With an adult understanding, she could now see that this might well have been something the child needed or that the family had arranged for this to happen. As an adult and social worker she was well aware of all the unfairness and discrimination First Nations people experienced.

Stage 1b

When she was asked where she thought Kerry and Dave might be coming from, Jane was able to name their assumptions:

> we should do everything that might benefit Tanya even if it causes conflict.
> family helps provide healing,
> nature is healing
> all these need to be present in the alien environment of the hospital.

Jane could also see that her attitude meant they might see her as yet another example of a white person who didn't understand and for whom rules were more important that what really mattered for a patient and family.

Stage 1c

When the group moved to exploring where Jane was now, she said she had suddenly had an'aha' moment, identifying that part of her reaction was that she felt cut off now from her family and community. She had rejected their conservative atheist beliefs that she found stifling, but had no idea about the spiritual. When asked what kept her going when things were hard, she said where she felt most spiritually nurtured and healed was when she spent time in her garden or walking at the beach, but she had seen these as hobbies, just something she did, rather than a valid part of her spiritual life. As she talked, she could see that she envied the closeness of Tanya's family and their belief that they could collectively care for her and each other in a stressful time. She could also see that their way of relating to nature was also something she wanted, that feeling of being interconnected to the natural world. Her resentment and envy had translated into an assumption of *if I can't have it, why should they*? She was horrified to identify this underlying feeling which so strongly contradicted her preferred and explicit assumption that *people should be able to express what's important to them and to have those needs met unless they are harming others*.

Stage two

With humility, she acknowledged that she yearned for what Tanya's family had and that her new assumption needed to be *I can learn from this family*. She also acknowledged that she had somehow lost with this family her usual assumption: *if the rules aren't working, I need to challenge them*. In this case, she could also see that the rules were often restrictive and undermining for other families too. She decided she would start by apologising to Kerry and Dave and asking what would help them and Tanya and to be assertive about seeking the flexibility they needed. More broadly, she would raise the issue of being more responsive to what families needed and greater flexibility in what was possible for them. She also articulated that she needed to focus on her own spiritual well-being and so actively include nurturing herself by being in and caring for the natural world, validating time being in the garden or walking as vital not just optional extras. She also wanted to express this in her work, perhaps to bring plants to work and in raising issues about how to care for the earth more broadly.

Case Study Three: Dave's experience

Dave works in a family counselling agency, primarily with couples addressing issues in their relationship. The experience he brought to his critical reflection peer group supervision was his frustration with a couple, Matt and Liz, who wanted to use Tarot cards in their counselling session with him in making decisions about their future. This was their fourth session with Dave and they had worked hard through a series of issues, mainly related to their very different personalities and the conflict this caused in caring for their two young children. One of the main areas of conflict had been competing to prove who was working hardest in paid employment and why that person should be expected to do less housework/care for the children. They had reached agreement that part of the problem was their work/life balance and assumptions about being valued for the income they could bring rather than their worth as individuals. In this session, they wanted to explore how their life together could be different and suggested using Tarot cards to help.

Stage 1a

Dave was surprised at the strength of his negative reaction to this. He felt as if they were undermining the counselling process by bringing something that seemed a simplistic way of fixing fundamental meaning of life and relationship issues. In the session, while he made a superficial reference to the Tarot cards, he effectively ignored their request. While they continued to explore what seemed to be relevant issues, he felt the life or spark had gone out of their interactions. He couldn't, in the moment, work out how to manage this differently and the session ended without their usual affirmation of how useful it had been.

In response to being asked more about where he was coming from, what the strength of his feelings related to, Dave said that this resonated with his feelings about leaving the church his family belonged to when he was a child and adolescent. He sometimes felt that the way the church operated was too 'magical' for him, that he was expected just to believe in what didn't seem real or logical to him. When he was baptised with full immersion as part of a group of adolescents, the others all talked about how they felt 'made new', but he just felt wet and cold. In Matt and Liz wanting to use Tarot cards, he felt he was again being invited to join in a ritual with a kind of meaning he couldn't grasp. In his late teens he left the church and said he would now describe himself as an atheist, someone who had rejected unscientific and unproven beliefs, preferring to work from a logical and rational way of being. Working to understand his underlying assumptions, what emerged most fundamentally was *I am not this kind of person: I can't connect in this kind of intuitive, symbolic way.* When challenged about how this related to his ability to work intuitively with clients, he said this still felt based on logic to him, picking up on physical reactions, gestures, tone of voice that suggested what might be happening for them.

Stage 1b

The critical reflection group then asked where Matt and Liz might have been coming from. Dave struggled with this and so asked the group to brainstorm possibilities. This is a technique often used in critical reflection to generate other possible ways of seeing or understanding. It doesn't matter if these are accurate, the process helps generate an attitude of other ways of seeing being possible. The possibilities included:

> They have previously found the Tarot cards encourage discussion between them
>
> The Tarot cards are a metaphor for different journeys
>
> They read into the cards what might be hard to say openly
>
> Tarot cards bring up ideas they might not have thought of
>
> The cards are a neutral way to work out a direction.

Stage 1c

What this meant for Dave was being able to translate Matt and Liz's experience of the Tarot cards into something he could also make sense of. He had often used cards with images to help clients name something they found it hard to put into words. He could see this as a 'reasonable' way forward. The group then asked why it was so hard to accept that people might want to make decisions that might not be seen as rational for someone else, but had their own logic to them. What would it mean if Matt or Liz had belonged to a faith tradition and wanted to make decisions based on where they felt 'called' by their faith to be?

This took Dave back to his own family experience where people did frequently make decisions on that basis which he often felt irritated by. When asked about this irritation, Dave initially went back to affirming logic, but after some time – and a question about whether there were other feelings involved, he acknowledged that he also felt significant sadness that this was not an experience he had. When he thought back to the baptism experience, he remembered also feeling excluded and lacking, questioning what was missing in him that meant he didn't also feel 'made new.' In retrospect he could see that his move to affirming being logical and rational was a defence against exclusion. The assumption was *there is only one right way to be religious* – and if he couldn't fit with that he would assume *it is better to reject the unexplainable and irrational*.

Stage two

One Dave had reached this clarity, it was easy to move to Stage Two, to see that a more helpful assumption is that *there are many ways to be spiritual – and religious*. Dave was also somewhat embarrassed that he felt he had assumed this was nonsense, rather than what he thought his default position would be of respecting the other person's perspective. The group also brainstormed ways of being non-rational that included feeling inspired by music or the landscape, making a choice that is value based – this is important for me – rather than logic based. Dave could acknowledge that he too had times when he felt moved by something in ways that he couldn't logically explain. Noticing the spark had gone out of the session with Matt and Liz was an example of that. He could also see that he needed to affirm with Matt and Liz that the Tarot cards were useful to them. He could ask them about what they meant for them and work with that meaning. While he didn't want to explore this further in the group, Dave also named this unhelpful binary of logic versus intuition as something that often caused conflict in his personal life and that he needed to sit with the implications of the session there too.

Conclusion

The three case studies here illustrate how critical reflection can be used to tease out the underlying meaning in interactions including where there is a connection to spirituality and religion. Notice what is important in the process is workers being willing to explore challenging reactions, including their feelings and what they know may be seen as less acceptable assumptions and values. The listener/s need to be open too, to hearing experiences and reactions that are not part of their 'norm' to hear the underlying depth of meaning. This often means using the qualities explored in Chapter 4, particularly listening deeply and openly. The examples used also illustrate the connections between the personal and the professional that can emerge when workers explore their reactions to troubling experiences. It is important that workers feel able to name these to the degree they feel comfortable – and establishing trust and mutuality in the group is a key aspect of this.

6   Understanding the spiritual journey

I find the metaphor of a journey a useful way to encourage standing back and reflecting on what has been significant in your life, the times of joy as well as the times of struggle. A journey is also a metaphor that can include the complexities of how life unfolds: we have all experienced actual journeys where we have lost our way, the journey takes longer than we thought, or, to our surprise, things go more smoothly than we expected, or where something totally unexpected but life-changing has happened. Taking time to contemplate more specifically the spiritual aspect of a person's life journey can also be a very helpful way of understanding how their sense of meaning has changed and developed over time. This can illuminate what has changed perhaps with periods of greater or lesser clarity or interest and sharpen what has emerged as meaningful now. Using this idea to reflect on where you sit as a person and a worker can also foster understanding what this might mean for how you engage with others. It can also help you see what kinds of ways of being or doing – what I will call spiritual practices – might help you to live life from what makes life more meaningful, satisfying or value-based for you. Spiritual practices will be explored in more detail in the next chapter.

Religious traditions often use the language of a spiritual journey or stages in the spiritual journey to help people identify how their beliefs and experiences have changed over time. This chapter gives an overview of ways of thinking about this so that you can see how these might apply to your journey and those you work with. How this is experienced also varies culturally: a more mystical understanding of spirituality common across many religious traditions is often lost in the Western need to live in a more apparently rational and certain world. On the other hand, many First Nations people, while they vary in how this is expressed, have a similar fundamental understanding of the existence of the spiritual all through their lives that deepens over time. "Children are born with innate connectedness to their spirit world, to their Ancestors and to animals, landscapes, seasons and human community in/of their world. This is their lifeworld, their family. As awareness grows, their ability to name their lifeworld deepens and they are gradually enabled to understand and attune to the greater complexities of what this understanding means and the related expectations of increased responsibilities to everyone or

DOI: 10.4324/9781003132677-9

everything that is a member of their family" (McMahon, 2017, p. 140). I also make explicit here that change over time is to be expected, the inevitability of both challenging and joyful experiences and the subjectivity of this journey. This might include, for example, understanding the relative simplicity of a new convert's religious beliefs compared to the more nuanced experience of someone who has wrestled with the complexities of connecting across religious traditions. It might be seeing how a person's spiritual practices change after a life crisis from something seen as incidental to life to something essential to their wellbeing or how there is a sudden awakening or desire to see life differently. Just as in critical reflection groups, what is important is having a positive curiosity, a desire to understand the journey of the other person.

Changing aspects of the spiritual journey

For most of us in retrospect, we can see that there are many different periods of our spiritual journey i.e. the journey of changed understanding of what is meaningful in our lives, what nurtures and sustains us. I'm going to talk about this in terms of times when we feel that we are "in the light" compared to times when we feel that we are "in the dark." What I mean by being in the light is those times in our spiritual journey when we feel that we are most attuned to our spiritual selves, our inner lives. You might think of this as when you feel most wholly yourself, your best self, most able to express all that you see as your gifts and qualities. In these periods you would feel as Sneed (2010, p. 180) expresses that you are "flourishing," growing, developing and able to express this in the world in some life-enhancing way perhaps being more loving even to those you do not like. Some people might talk about this as feeling resilient or that their well-being is at its best. Others might say they feel they feel deeply connected to their experience of God and doing God's work in the world. It can help to pay attention to what is happening in those times of light and doing or being this more consciously. There can also be times of struggle in the light as well as the dark: you might recognise that you need to change from something that you continue to enjoy but that it is time to move on, to focus on something new or that you can't keep on doing all the things that are life-enhancing and survive, something has to go.

What I mean by being in the 'dark' is when you feel that you have lost this sense of inner connection to your spiritual self, to your sense of what is meaningful. Many writers in the religious traditions name times of being in the dark as a dark night of the soul. What they mean by this is a time of feeling disconnected from God or spirit, a sense of alienation from themselves, their inner being and often a related sense of disconnection from others as well. It might be focussing on ultimately destructive aspects of life or struggling with the wrong question. How exactly this is expressed, will depend very much on the person. For some it can be a significant time of depression or feelings of alienation from much in their world, a loss of sense of purpose and connection or anger against themselves or others or the world in general. For others it can feel more like a sense of ongoing uncertainty, loss of clarity of direction and meaning, irritation, mild unhappiness, simply a sense of things not feeling right. It is important to recognise that whatever the expression is this will feel like a time of struggle. Sometimes a person who simply experiences this as irritation can feel this is not significant compared to those who are deeply distressed, but what's key is seeing what this means for the person at the time. One of my own experiences of being in the dark was feeling I was in the wrong job, in an agency I thought I should enjoy working in. I wasn't deeply unhappy, simply a bit irritable, feeling annoyed by things that weren't really important. When I acknowledged these feelings, I was able to recognise that I needed to move on to other work where I felt much more in the light, able to express myself more fully.

Part of what is useful about naming these as aspects of a spiritual journey, is that it normalises that these times of light and dark are expected parts of life. This can help put into perspective both the times of light, understanding that we are not likely to live at this level all the time, as well as the times of dark, awareness that these times will also pass. It also helps us to see that we can learn from all of the aspects of our journey, perhaps particularly the times of struggle. Parker Palmer (2000, pp. 56–7), writes very powerfully about what this experience was like for him: "Midway in my life's journey, 'way closed' again, this time with a ferocity that felt fatal: I found myself in the dark woods called clinical depression, a total eclipse of light and hope. But after I emerged from my sojourn in the dark and had given myself several years to absorb its meaning, I saw how pivotal that passage had been on my pilgrimage towards selfhood and vocation." While he is explicit about not wanting others to have to have this experience, he can see in retrospect that his depression was grounding, encouraging him to stop trying to be something he wasn't, but rather "the ground of my own truth, my own nature, with its complex mix of limits and gifts, liabilities and assets, darkness and light" (Palmer, 2000, p. 67).

Ideas about stages in the spiritual journey

We are familiar in social work with ideas about life course development: how individuals grow and develop over time, making their way through various life stages. What is often not covered in these is how people also develop and grow spiritually and Harms (2010, p. 10) seeks to include spirituality across the lifespan though still "particularly in the aftermath of experiences of adversity." There is a significant literature about this from a religious perspective which can be useful in exploring both religious development and how spirituality may change over time. For those who have not had contact with religious traditions, it is particularly useful to have a sense of how you might see stages in the spiritual or religious journey, because it illustrates how differently people can experience these. This reinforces the need to understand how individuals see themselves at this stage of their journey rather than assuming for example, that an older person will be at a particular stage. The danger of all life stage approaches is also the implication that they are linear, whereas what we know in practice is that people will vary considerably in how they engage with these. Some people would argue that we are all born 'enlightened' or in tune with the universe, but lose this as we are influenced by the prevailing norms of our culture, religious or otherwise. Canda, Furman and Canda (2020) suggest that children can express significant aspects of their spiritual experience, and that adults need to listen to how these are expressed rather than imposing their expectations. What can also happen is that people re-engage with what have been earlier stages for them possibly at a deeper level because of new circumstances in their lives or a new understanding of what their spirituality means for them. A person who is facing a major life event, such as having someone very close dying a painful death, or experiencing a disaster such as fire or flood or an assault may find that the assumptions underpinning their life and their spiritual selves are severely challenged. Such a person might shift from a position of unquestioning faith to questioning their source of meaning or might move to a more fundamentalist position. They might change assumptions from *I am always hopeful and optimistic about life* to *life's challenges are overwhelming, more than I can manage; I am not safe and have to rely on myself for protection.* It is more helpful than not to make assumptions but to ask what does this mean for them, how does each person locate themselves at this stage of their life journey, where are they spiritually?

From a religious perspective, a number of writers have explored the idea of stages. These vary depending on the writer and the faith traditions they are influenced by, but often have 6–7 stages (Fowler, 1981, Wilber, 2007). Some Hindus would say there are three stages: moving from blind faith (simply participating without knowledge or lived experience) to informed conviction (based on knowledge of Hindu philosophy) and then personal realisation where "personal experience transforms informed conviction into certainty" (Veylanswami, 2009). What I have done here is to use a combination of these ideas combined with writers such as Trelfa (2005) and Canda and Furman (2010) who have applied these to working in social work settings. Fowler identifies particular ages for each of his stages, linking cognitive growth with spiritual growth. Wilber makes more explicit than Fowler the connections between individuals and their social context, seeing parallels between stages of development for individuals and societies, but both have been criticised for being too Eurocentric and too focused on individual development, rather than making explicit interconnections with culture and community.

Ways of being or aspects of the spiritual journey

However, I think rather than naming these as linear stages, there is value in naming these as different places or ways of being that people can inhabit at different times in their spiritual journey, while also seeing how these are influenced by culture and context and how they change over time in complex and often unpredictable ways. Trelfa (2005) found that many students in her youth and community work course began with seeing this kind of work as a 'calling' from their usually Christian backgrounds, but often became disillusioned during the course, finding it challenged their faith. She uses the idea of Fowler's stages to explore how this disillusionment fits with their spiritual development, but also advocates for reflective practice to be seen as "as a way of being in the world" through which students can understand and develop their 'faith' in practice, the underlying beliefs and values that influence them. Similarly, Lindsay (2002) suggests students need to be supported to grapple with moving often from a more conventional understanding of their beliefs and values to a more reflective and questioning point, as they would in other areas, such as understanding the complexities of gender or culture. She also suggests this will continue throughout life as a worker: "Finding a sense of meaning and purpose in life is an ongoing process throughout the adult years, new situations and experiences challenging cherished beliefs and values which appeared adequate at an earlier age. The spiritual quest is driven by the human need to find meaning in life" (Lindsay, 2002, p. 116). The image below affirms these ways of being as aspects of the spiritual landscape rather than a neat linear development. Moving from one to another is challenging: there is often a sense of loss, perhaps of the certainty of beliefs or the safety of belonging to a community as well as the flourishing that comes with deeper complexity and the strengthening of fundamental beliefs and values. It may be an external event or experience that encourages change – doing a course as Trelfa suggests or a personal or community crisis or it may be an internal desire to be different that grows over time.

One of the vexed issues in social work about including spirituality is how do you recognise the difference between people who have a mental illness being 'delusional' and genuine spiritual experiences. This can lead to reluctance to include spirituality in mental health. Starnino and Canda's (2014) study of mental illness and spiritual growth shows the complexity of how these can be linked. They combine understanding of Fowler and Weber's stages of spiritual development with how those with serious mental illness can develop spiritually in ways that fit with recovery from their illness i.e. the two can have synergy. They reinforce that this kind of growth is not a linear process, identifying four kinds of journeys. First, those for whom their spirituality has only a slight impact on their mental illness; second those who considered spirituality to be important for them, but where their mental illness and spirituality created a barrier to recovery: for example, those hearing voices with negative spiritual themes. The third group was those starting to use spirituality in their recovery process, to foster a sense of meaning and the fourth was those who had a high synergy between the two: for example, letting go of such ideas as sexual abuse as a punishment from God and able to take positive action to achieve what they identified as meaningful. While they affirm seeing spirituality as a potential benefit rather than deficit, Starnino and Canda (2014, pp. 292–3) do point out that integrating spirituaity positively in recovery from mental illness "can be a complex and lengthy process ... partly because neither the spiritual development nor recovery processes are linear" but if "providers view spiritual struggles as a natural part of one's growth process, they may be more likely to support clients as they work through their struggles, draw on spiritual strengths, and reap spiritual benefits."

Starnino and Canda's experience makes explicit the need to actively ask about spiritual and religious relevance. Hodge (2001) suggests that it helps to think of taking a spiritual history as similar to taking a family history, using narrative and strengths focused questions that encourage the person to tell their story. Alternatively, you could integrate the spiritually focused questions into hearing the person's story overall – there is more on how to do this in Chapter 7.

You might ask questions like:

> What has been meaningful for you at different points in your spiritual journey?

> When would you say your life was flourishing or most of what you were doing and being was life-enhancing?

> What times in your life have felt life-denying?

> When would you say your life felt like a time of struggle or most of what you were doing and being was life-denying?

> What have you missed, forgotten or not wanted to remember?

> What did you know as a child?

> How have you related to the natural world?

> Looking back, what shifts and changes have you seen?

> Are there patterns it is useful to notice? What is their underlying meaning?

> What have been the challenges of shifts in understanding and experience?

> Where are you now in your spiritual journey?

> How would you describe what nurtures you now?

> What do you need to do to build this now into your life?

First, it helps to have clarify what these different aspects of the spiritual journey or different ways of being might look like (Figure 6.1).

Ways of being or aspects of the spiritual journey

1   Unquestioning beliefs: in this aspect of the spiritual life people have internalised their own family's beliefs (which will include their beliefs about religion/spirituality) without questioning them and these may be reinforced by the beliefs of their community. A strong sense of belonging and/or

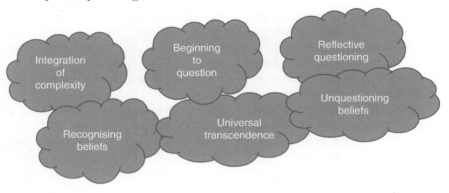

Figure 6.1 Aspects of the spiritual journey.

concerns for safety means that the beliefs and values here are not questioned and may not even be particularly articulated, they are so firmly ingrained in the person and their context. Some individuals may not have been exposed to other beliefs or spiritual attitudes; for others the strength of their family/ community beliefs is so strong that they are unable to take seriously other beliefs or feel that questioning these would mean betraying their community. They may simply not be aware that there are other beliefs, that others see the world differently. This can mean they unconsciously or consciously reinforce oppressive social values. Experientially, individuals may experience deep connections and a sense of transcendence, fostered by their spiritual community through shared worship, music and ritual as well as social activities. For those who have not been questioned about their beliefs before, being asked about these may be experienced as negative judgement or unhelpful criticism. Students in social work classes that focus on sharing values often comment that they are surprised at the differences in beliefs and values. A typical comment might be: *I never thought people would see that as important.* Or *I haven't ever though about spirituality that way.* Sometimes people who convert to a religious tradition or those who join a religious tradition for the first time can also be in this way of being for at least a period of time. The strength of their experience can mean that they simply need to embrace the experience of being part of the tradition rather than to question it. *Freda, for example, who chose to leave her Christian tradition to become a Muslim took very seriously praying at the expected times, decided to wear a hijab and altered other ways of being to express her commitment to her new beliefs. One of the other students in the class, also a Muslim, suggested she be a bit more relaxed about it, so she didn't alienate other students. Freda saw this as totally unacceptable. After more discussion, they agreed they just saw how to express their religious beliefs differently.*

2   Recognising beliefs: in this aspect of the spiritual journey, people start to ask about their family beliefs, to make them conscious and want to

understand for themselves what their spiritual life means. This may partly come from being asked by others about what they believe and why. They are able to name the spiritual as important, but usually name this in a literal and descriptive way: for example, they can name what is considered important in their faith tradition and describe it to others, and to name what is important for them in how this influences their lives. Usually, the focus is on recognising and articulating beliefs rather than questioning them. The danger of this aspect can be an emphasis on what can be described, rather than acknowledging the experiential and mystical. Also, if these beliefs are questioned explicitly or implicitly it challenges a person's internal sense of coherence. They may want to reject the person who is questioning them rather than simply seeing that there may be other perspectives. While questioning may be helpful for growth in the sense of seeing other alternatives, it can also be experienced as unnerving and the person is likely to need support and understanding to move through this. What maintains people in this aspect is often the sense of community and belonging, the safety of a group that believes the same things and sees the world in at least similar ways. *For example, Sally, a Christian student social worker, felt she needed to defend her faith in a class about gender and affirmed more traditional roles of men and women, based on Bible interpretations, such as believing that the man should be the head of the household. When other students challenged her, she was unable to explore this further, simply saying, this is the way I see things and it works fairly in my relationship.*

3   Beginning to question: at this point, people are starting to question their spirituality or faith tradition; understanding that more complexity may be beneficial or that they are starting to be interested in how others may see things differently. It may be that deepening relationships outside the family and community, study, work experiences bring the need to be able to explain to others more about the way spirituality or religious is expressed. Perhaps because family and/or the spiritual and religious community is very important for them, they still generally accept the prevailing expectations without questioning too much. Trelfa (2005, p. 209) suggests people in this place/stage "have not a clear grasp of their own identity and lack autonomous judgement to build/maintain an independent perspective." The ideas from their faith tradition may be so strongly internalised, it is hard to separate them out from who the person is. However, there might be something that means the person begins to question aspects of what they believe such as a tension between the teaching of the religious tradition and the person's other experiences. For example, a person at this point, might still affirm her religious tradition's teaching on sexuality: that only heterosexuality is acceptable, but struggle with integrating that teaching with becoming friendly with those outside the religious tradition who are not heterosexual. Knowing and liking someone who is not heterosexual and seeing the pain of their exclusion from a religious tradition might encourage questioning of why this person's experience is not seen as valid.

Alternatively, it might be that something happens in the church or spiritual community that contradicts the espoused values and the individual starts to question the certainty of their thinking. Here the experiential nature of spirituality may be present in a sense of community or transcendence in worship or the person might find this elsewhere.

4   Reflective questioning of the self: here people are more able to identify their individual experience of the spiritual and what that means for them, to separate out beliefs and values from their spiritual community or religious tradition. Fowler (1981) calls this 'individuative-reflective': individuals start to own their own reactions and assumptions, they can reflect critically on their experience and the ideas and ideology underlying a faith tradition or their own spiritual expression. They may also have more emotional literacy and be more able to articulate what they believe. The danger here is focusing too much on the conscious i.e. being overly analytical and judgmental and not also validating the experiential. In this way of being people often describe feeling disillusioned about the gap between their faith tradition's teachings and how these are expressed in their church or spiritual community, including by the leaders of the tradition. Sacred texts that had been understood in a more literal way are now judged as simplistic and may be rejected. People might become angry with the attitudes in their church on discovering children's experience of child abuse and so decide to leave their church, rejecting the teachings of the faith tradition as well as its structures. Becoming aware of the inadequacies of how a faith tradition is expressed and may lead to rejecting the faith altogether and/or moving to a new faith tradition. From a more broadly spiritual perspective, someone might begin by questioning their faith in a political party or a social movement they have been involved in. *Rose, for example, had been part of a yoga community for many years, but began to question some of what she now felt wasn't complex enough in the teaching there. She said: I feel something is missing in my life, nothing bad has happened but a sense of meaning is missing, nothing I do really seems to matter, my belief in just working hard for ever in that way doesn't feel important any more.*

5   Integration of complexity: at this stage, people are more able to live with the contradictions and complexities of their own beliefs and those experienced in their faith traditions. They are aware of the deeply held beliefs that underpin but also transcend the structure of their individual faith tradition. At the same time, they can be critical of their social context and able to live within it. This would include, for example, people who continue to worship in a faith tradition and feel nurtured by it overall, while being critical of some or even many of its practices and actively seeking to change them. For some, this can be a time when people feel caught between how they would like things to be and the challenges of achieving this in practice, the risks Trelfa (2005, p. 210) suggests are people becoming "complacent, 'paralyzing passivity' and/or cynical withdrawal as their changed worldview, vision and commitments encounter an unchanging

world." However, others feel freed by the possibilities of adhering to the essence of their beliefs and what they value from their religious tradition, but also feeling able to challenge it. They may also engage with people and practices from other spiritual or religious traditions. *Jo, a social worker, felt affirmed by his Jewish community, its rituals and the breadth of ways of being within it, the cultural and social connections. While remaining deeply sceptical about some of the structures and leaders, he quietly worked to foster what he felt was meaningful which he felt paralleled his social work practice.*

6   Universal transcendence: here, people are focused on what is shared across spiritual and religious traditions, even if they continue to participate in a particular spiritual or faith community. This is more likely to be expressed as a mystical sense of the spiritual, the interconnectedness of all things: the embedded spiritual experience for First Nations people in all of their lives. Individuals may choose to continue to participate in one faith tradition partly because of their connection to community there and at the same time take part in aspects of other faith traditions. Alternatively, they may no longer want to identify with one religious tradition or spiritual expression, but live from their underlying connected spiritual experience.

   Liz had moved around various faith traditions and spiritual healing practices including Wiccan and First Nations experiences for much of her life. Looking back, she described herself as a restless seeker after truth. In her 70s, she came to feeling that there was a connection between all of these, that if she paid attention to the essence of each of them, that more was the same than different. She decided that she would simply meditate each day and attend whatever she felt like at the time.

Drew Lawson (2021) writes:

   my pen moves across the paper
   in a spirit of thanksgiving
   for all my teachers who enticed
   me deeper, deeper until i find
   myself somewhere else now
   beyond the need for all labels
   whether Catholic, Quaker, Sufi or Buddhist.
   i recognise myself sailing through the infusion
   of the one-ness of all-that-is

How might this work in practice:

I have included two case studies next to illustrate how using the idea of aspects or places in a spiritual journey can be helpful both for you as a worker and those you work with. This is followed by exploring the value of your exploring your spiritual journey as a worker with a final case study from a worker perspective.

Case Study One: Mark and Abbey

Mark came to see a social worker, Abbey, a year after his partner of 30 years died unexpectedly in a car accident along with his 20-year-old son. He and his partner would have described themselves as atheists, seeing family and friends and work as what gave their lives meaning. Both had been very sceptical of religious traditions, describing them as peddling unproved beliefs. Some of his friends and family had expressed concern about him not 'dealing well with grief' because he continued to talk about his partner and son as if they were alive. They were also concerned that Mark had joined a Pentacostal Christian church community, attending services several times weekly and actively promoting their beliefs which included prayers with those who had died. As Abbey and Mark talked about what was normal in grieving, he explained that the certainty of these Christian beliefs gave him something to hang onto while he felt his world was falling apart. He didn't want to question what they said, simply to believe that his wife and son were in heaven and that he might see them again. This felt supportive and comforting and the community simply accepted his outpourings of grief as natural in a way many of his friends felt challenged by.

For Abbey, Mark's way of dealing with his grief was not something she had experienced before. She wasn't familiar with prayer and dubious about images of heaven. She had a friend whose increasingly feminist beliefs were challenged by her local Pentecostal church, all of which made her feel uncomfortable in simply supporting Mark. However, she could see that what he needed in this time of significant grief was not to be challenged about gender or other aspects of the church community. His experience meant he questioned the fundamental aspects of his life. It made sense that he wanted people who had certainty, not questioning when he felt everything had been turned upside down. Clearly, the church community was providing him with the kind of support that she as a worker couldn't and his friends couldn't either. What she could do was to normalise the extent of his grief and to reassure him that it was understandable still to feel so grief-stricken and to want to converse with the dead. She also encouraged Mark not to give up on his friends, so asked where he thought his friends were coming from. After expressing some frustration, he was able to say they were concerned for him and even to say I can see why – I would never have thought I would end up in this church. She asked him to say more about what the church offered and asked tentatively if there were areas that he felt challenged himself. He said of course there are, but that's not where I am now, I just need to fit in.

For Abbey these were clear messages to accept that Mark had found what he needed for this point in his life at least – and possibly ongoing. It was important that she along with his friends accept this, while acknowledging that this way of being. like all others. might change over time as might his feelings of grief. Abbey recognised that the temptation was for her to challenge Mark because she found his acceptance of this church difficult, rather than respecting that this community was providing what he needed at this time.

Case Study Two: John and Diane

John is a social worker in a community-based palliative care service covering a large regional area. People are usually referred to the service when they are expected to have eight weeks or less to live. He has been seeing Diane, a woman in her early 70s, who has late-stage cancer. Initially, Diane wanted to focus on her relationship with her children. She remains close to her son who visits regularly, but has been estranged from her daughter, Kylie, for over 20 years. They had what seems in retrospect to Diane, a ridiculous argument about how Kylie should bring up her only child. At the time, Diane expressed concern about what she saw as her daughter's inability to set limits. She can see now this related more to her anxiety about whether Kylie had managed to break her drug habit. Now she is dying, Diane wants to be reconciled with Kylie and John has been helping her think about how to do this. They had finished writing a letter to Kylie and John was about to go when he hesitated feeling that there was something else that Diane wanted to say.

What Diane did say was that she wanted to talk about where she was spiritually. John knew that Diane practised Buddhism because she had Buddhist symbols around her room. He felt comfortable with this because he had attended Buddhist meditation himself for some time and felt that Buddhist philosophy was congruent with his own values. He assumed this was what Diane wanted to talk about. However, what Diane expressed was, for both of them, a surprising desire to be reconciled to the Catholic Church. She thought she could now see the connections that transcended the differences between these traditions and wanted to acknowledge the coming together of these different aspects of her life. When she was in her early 30s she left the church after an argument about the place of women. She missed her involvement with a faith tradition and a friend had introduced her to Buddhism. For the last nearly 40 years she had been actively involved with her local Buddhist community, meditating daily and attending retreats almost annually. She felt disconcerted by her desire to be reconciled to the church and fearful that her Buddhist community would see this as a rejection. She was wondering whether there was any way that John could ask a priest to give her the last rites in a way that nobody else would know about.

John was very disconcerted by this. He struggled to understand how someone so committed to Buddhism could also want to be reconciled to the Catholic Church. He also found it challenging to think that this could be meaningful. A previous patient had been Catholic and had asked John to be present when the last rites were given and John had found this quite confronting as a ritual. He was aware that he really had no knowledge of what this meant and why it was symbolically so important. From a social work perspective, he also felt that he needed to be hearing this as what clearly meaningful to Diane even if he found it incomprehensible himself. He was able to respond positively to Diane and said that he would find out what was possible.

When John explored this in his critical reflection supervision, he realised that his assumption was that *people should be consistent and loyal about their religious affiliations* and perhaps another assumption was that *it is only possible to have one religious affiliation at a time.* The group at his request generated other possible assumptions including:

- People can resonate with the essence of more than one religious tradition
- Religious traditions have more in common than can seem apparent from the outside especially if you're looking at fundamental beliefs
- People now are more likely to form their own spiritual understanding from a combination of religious and spiritual beliefs and experiences.

One group member reminded the others of the different places people could be in their spiritual journey and that for some what is shared across spiritual and religious traditions becomes important, especially mystically: developing a sense of universal transcendence. John found this useful; it reminded him of experiences with friends that had puzzled him who had in his view seemed overly flexible about their involvement with different religious traditions. He realised that he tended to have this kind of assumption in general i.e. that people should be consistent and stick to their values (and faith tradition) even if they thought there were contradictions between the ideal and the practice. Looking back, he saw himself as having moved from being reflectively questioning to integrating complexity in his own spiritual journey. His new assumption was *people continue to develop and grow and to adapt their underlying beliefs and values according to what is meaningful to them at the time.*

From this perspective he could see that Diane was in a place of seeking universal transcendence and was able to actively encourage her to follow up reconciliation to the Catholic faith, while maintaining her commitment to and nourishment from the Buddhist community and related practices and beliefs. He also felt more open to what this might mean for his own spiritual practices and understanding and decided to speak to the representative from the Buddhist community for himself about what it would mean to seek a sense of universal spirituality.

Exploring your own spiritual journey

Given the potential to be working with people in ways that include exploring their spiritual journey, it's useful to do this for yourself. This can be helpful in fostering self-care: paying attention to and embedding life-enhancing spiritual practices. What we explored in Chapter 5 using an experience in a critically reflective way is one way to do this. Another way is to draw your own journey, i.e. to visually represent on paper how your sense of meaning has changed over time. Sometimes drawing or using symbols can help free you up to see your life differently from when you use words. There is no set or right way to do this, you might be someone who draws a line and then marks particular events or changes at times along the way. Alternatively, you might have symbols of different events dotted over the paper or might use colours to represent different experiences of meaning. You might choose to do a line of your life and first list the obvious external events, then put in the internal changes that might or might not relate to these. Be sure to include times that are more about being as well as events that influenced your life. For example, you might identify a period where you felt very fulfilled in your family life or in your religious tradition as opposed to a specific event like finishing study or taking on a new role. If this doesn't appeal to you, you could write a time line for yourself or use poetry or stories from your life to identify important changes.

It is useful than to sit back and look at the journey and to ask yourself the questions we identified above to use with others:

> What has been meaningful for me at different points in my spiritual journey?
>
> When would I say my life was flourishing or most of what I was doing and being was life-enhancing?
>
> What times in my life felt life-denying?
>
> When would I say my life felt like a time of struggle or most of what I was doing and being was life-denying?
>
> What have I missed, forgotten or not wanted to remember?
>
> What did I know as a child?
>
> How have I related to the natural world?
>
> Looking back, what shifts and changes have I seen?
>
> Are there patterns it is useful to notice? What is their underlying meaning?
>
> What have been the challenges of shifts in understanding and experience?
>
> Where am I now in my spiritual journey?
>
> How would I describe what nurtures me now?
>
> What do I need to do to build this now into my life?

Case Study Three: Alice

Alice, a social worker in her early fifties, who had worked in juvenile justice for ten years, started to explore in supervision her need for change in her working life. As she did this, she realised that she was influenced by her children growing up and leaving home – her youngest child had just moved away to go to university and so she was living on her own. She was feeling that the drive and commitment had gone out of her life, she said she just felt 'flat' a lot of the time. On her supervisor's recommendation, she went to see a social worker who suggested doing a 'life map' outlining the changes in her life. While she initially struggled with how to 'draw' this, gradually Alice could see how it helped to 'stand back' and see her life from a different perspective.

Alice chose to start with a long line looping in a semi-circle round the page, beginning with the obvious main events in her life: her family had moved several times when she was a child because of her father's work, her father had died when she was seventeen and she had left school to work in a bakery, marriage, children and divorce, the decision to go to university and do social work. Gradually, she added in times when she felt life was flourishing, that she was happy and fulfilled – being a parent, being a student, times that were life-denying, when her father died, times in her marriage that were undermining and the feeling of failure at her divorce. She also could identify some smaller significant events, an unexpected conversation with a friend that led to doing social work, a week's holiday with her husband and children that felt infused with wellbeing, giving up smoking, going to drawing classes and a community choir that gave her a lot of pleasure.

What she started to see was the changes in how she experienced her life happened when she had paid attention to what really mattered to her. Her parents were not religious, but had clearly expressed values about what they thought was important simply put: *you should have commitment to family, working hard and working to make the world a better place.* Alice had internalised these values, but her experience was also that when her parents worked hard for community and the world, she and her sister often felt neglected. Because of this, she had tried to work from an assumption of *what matters to me is family and friends first, then saving the world.* She could see looking at her life map that her life looked like a struggle between these, trying to get the balance right. In practice, it felt as if her internalised family values constantly fought with each other. Why then, she asked now that my children have left home and I can fully concentrate on work do I feel my life is lacking? As she asked the question she answered it: because they helped me keep the balance of meaning. *I now need to consciously do more to be with family and friends.* What was newer was recognising that the times she spent drawing had also fed her sense of flourishing, of wellbeing. It also became clear that while this could seem to be a way of doing, for Alice it was also a way of being still, take time to be present and relish the moment. She added a newer assumption: *I also want to give myself permission to draw as a way of being, a choice that gives me a deeper connectedness to the universe.*

Having reached this point, Alice asked herself, 'is the problem my job or the way I have been thinking about my life?' She remembered that her manager had been talking about the value of engaging young people in juvenile justice in drawing or other forms of art after reading the benefits of this and wondered if she could be involved in making this happen. She decided to wait and rather than seeking a new workplace to explore whether if she was more focused on getting her own inner and external balance right, she would find that work became more rewarding as well. She decided to join another drawing class as a way of affirming this new understanding and to commit to making time to draw each week.

Part III

Application to practice: how to include spirituality and religion in ethical social work practice

This third part of the book focuses more specifically on how to embed spirituality and religion across domains of practice and how to engage with the ethical dilemmas this will raise. The underlying questions include how do you put all these ideas into practice? How can social workers be actively inclusive of spirituality and religion in ways that reflect social work values and ethics? How can you embed spirituality in your life, to ensure your own flourishing and well-being?

More specifically:

Chapter 7 explores working with individuals and families, complementing the theoretical framework from Chapter 3 with narrative and strengths approaches and the capacities of Chapter 4. The kinds of question that can help you engage where appropriate as you engage with others, work together on assessment and seeking change are outlined. Finally, the chapter suggests a number of spiritual practices that can help with embedding the spiritual, paying attending to what is meaningful for both workers and the individuals and families they work with.

Next, Chapter 8 explores how you might embed spirituality in working in and with organisations, communities and policy development. Some social workers work in secular organisations, others in 'faith-based' organisations and each can generate dilemmas for workers about how to practice including the spiritual. Policies influence all domains of practice and reflect social structures and expectations which social workers might affirm or seek to change from a socially just perspective. Social work also has a part to play in fostering celebration of religious and spiritual diversity in communities.

Finally, Chapter 9 considers some of the ethical dilemmas this work can raise and how to engage with them. How do you respond to situations where there seems to be no 'right' answer but a decision has to be made? How do you help people wrestle respectfully with their deeply held but opposing value positions? These questions are even more challenging when you have your own beliefs that may contrast with those you are working with or where they touch aspects of your own experience. Possible frameworks for thinking about and engaging with ethical dilemmas are outlined and applied to practice examples.

DOI: 10.4324/9781003132677-10

7 Embedding spirituality and religion in practice: working with individuals and families

This chapter focuses on how to include spirituality and religion in working with individuals and families, something social workers – and those from other disciplines often find difficult to do. My own experience of this was that I had to first overcome my own reluctance to include the spiritual before I could work effectively with others. I was surprised by how strongly I had internalised the messages that social work is a secular profession and the spiritual was strictly personal. Once I more consciously made explicit for myself that spirituality and religion were important aspects of life and that needed to be taken into account I could more readily have discussions that included them. This meant discerning what this meant: for some people it meant understanding and engaging with a religious tradition; for others, it was more about understanding what gave meaning in their lives in a fundamental way.

A significant example for me was engaging with a student who over the four years of the social work degree wrestled with her changing relationship with her church community. Her family was a member of a community church that she described itself as having a strong Christian evangelical base. The church leadership was all male and the ways of operating essentially reflected what Connie later described as a conservative, patriarchal community. When she began social work, Connie's husband was pleased that she was undertaking a course that would prepare her to serve the community, particularly the poor and disadvantaged. However, neither he nor Connie was expecting that Connie's own view of the world would change as she studied. Towards the end of her second year, she came to see me to express her concerns about her changing attitudes to assumptions about gender and to the LGBTIQ+ community. These were starting to create conflict with her husband and to some extent in the church. However, Connie felt she had a lot to lose if she was seen as too different in the church community; she felt very close to many of the women there and her two children's lives were so much part of the community.

Part of me wanted to say to Connie: maybe it's time to move on from your church community; maybe their attitudes and values are going to be incompatible with your developing social work values. I had to accept though that this was not where Connie was at: she feared losing both her marriage and

DOI: 10.4324/9781003132677-11

a strongly interwoven community that had seen her through many personal and family struggles. I had to actively practice both critically reflecting on my own experience, my different spiritual journey and using the qualities identified in Chapter 4. I needed to be open to listening deeply and openly, with humility to what really mattered to Connie and to be very carefully respectful in opening up the space of how her family history and social context, as well as the broader social context influenced her reactions and decision making.

What I came to realise is that what Connie wanted from me was the provision of a safe space where she could talk freely without being judged. She needed somewhere to verbalise the tensions and contradictions she was feeling, to clarify them for herself. Her church community or her husband could not be that space because they were too invested in her staying the same. The social work students often had too much invested in her changing to share their experience and values. Allowing a space where she could feel heard, deeply listened to and encouraged simply to explore for herself was what she needed and valued. Over time – and we only met very intermittently, this enabled her to work out for herself what to challenge in both worlds. This included identifying some of the assumptions that she had internalised generally as a woman, from the church community but also from society about 'knowing her place' and changing these to asserting her right to be heard for her own views.

My experience I think has parallels for others: to work effectively with individuals and families in including spirituality and religion means recognising first who you are and how your own assumptions, values and beliefs may get in the way of engaging with others. It is key to take seriously understanding your own journey with the 'spiritual and the assumptions and values you have internalised from your own past experience, your family, community and the society you live in. Next, it means understanding and accepting that spirituality and for some religious beliefs are an integral aspect of life and need to be included in practice as desired by those you work with. It also means recognising that you do have a theoretical background, skills and values that provide the ability to engage with this, and the confidence that you can find the knowledge and develop the skills you don't have.

Before we get to the more specific, practical ideas about how to include the spiritual, I want to briefly reiterate the critical spirituality framework from the first part of the book which form the background for these more specific practices. This integrated theories to provide a way of thinking about how to include spirituality being mindful of the relationships between individuals and their families and communities and the historical and social structures in which they live. A critical, postmodern, green, First Nations and relational understanding emphasises awareness of the historical and social context and celebration of the different ways in which the spiritual may be expressed including paying attention to the natural world and the interconnectedness of all beings. These approaches are congruent with and many underpin the processes of being critically reflective which encourages people to make explicit connections to the broader social context and how it is influencing people's stories to foster their capacity to use their understanding of underlying meaning to bring about change.

Including narrative and strengths approaches

Two practice theories that can complement and reinforce using these in practice are narrative and strengths approaches. "Narrative care can be simply defined as the art of *storylistening*. It is the art of attending closely to – and for – the stories by which we understand our identities and experience who we are" (Randall, 2020, p. 448). A narrative perspective draws on postmodernism and reminds you to expect people's 'multiple' stories as well as including the influence of underlying social structures. This makes explicit that we all have many ways that we are seen and that we see ourselves and we might describe ourselves differently depending on who is asking and why and how they ask. Béres (2014, p. 129) points out "the importance of *inviting* people to tell us about themselves, rather than asking them very direct questions, and of being *curious* about the details of their stories so that they can embroider the series of events with the taste and feel of the experiences they are recounting." This frames the worker as interested in understanding where the person is coming from and allowing for the complexity of what may be or appear to be contradictory stories. Facilitating conversations that allow for different perspectives allows moving to 'alternative stories': it might be that someone who has experienced abuse can move between stories of seeing themselves as a victim or survivor, and make an active choice about which to live from or whether to live from both – or move beyond this dualism to a new, more flourishing place. Implicit in this development of alternative stories can be increasing awareness of and questioning of the social context, whether this needs to change as well or instead of the person.

Similarly, a strengths perspective encourages people to identify or remember their strengths and resources, the times they resolved an issue or crisis well, not only those times they struggled. Asking about such times can elicit what the underlying meaning was and the capacities that were enabling. Spiritual or religious beliefs, the communities that people are connected to can all be named as strengths and resources. "A practitioner who is committed to these ideas assumes there are no boundaries to potential, and that growth and change are not only possible, but also part of an innate restorative capacity that humans possess" (Harms and Connolly, 2019, p. 122). Saleeby (2009, p. 1) sees this as a collaborative process honouring "the innate wisdom of the human spirit, the inherent capacity for transformation of even the most humbled and abused" through focusing on "interests, capacities, motivations, resources and emotions in the work of reaching their hopes and dreams." Arousing hope in seeing that other ways are possible is an integral part of this.

How to embed spirituality and religion in practice with individuals and families?

How then might these theories combine with your existing and expanding skills and values in working with individuals and families?

Social workers are well trained in listening to others about many issues and in hearing underlying messages that may not be explicit in what the person is saying. Typically, social work training includes awareness of the non-verbal as well as verbal communication, the importance of actively listening, including reflecting and summarising, asking questions to encourage deeper exploration of feelings and thoughts and how these connect to underlying values and beliefs and the influence of social context. In working with any individual or community, social workers also use skills of engaging with the other, assessing collaboratively what is happening and what issues there might be and generating ways of working together that are satisfying and effective. All of these are integral to actively including the spiritual dimension of life.

A key aspect of beginning to work holistically with any individual is demonstrating that you want to build a relationship with them that is respectful of who they are and what it is that they want to work on with you ie making clear you are interested in all of who they are. Openness, humility and vulnerability are important attitudes to demonstrate such respect. These attitudes fit with what a narrative approach would describe as inviting the person to tell stories, being positively curious. These are also connected to deep and spacious listening: demonstrating your ability to be fully present or mindful remembering that you don't need to focus on coming up with answers. Sometimes, it becomes clear that the person simply wants to feel heard. If you don't have time for this or are feeling too internally pressured, it may be more helpful to say you are running out of time and make another one. People can sense when you really want to be somewhere else and mostly prefer you to be honest. What can be surprising is that if you truly listen deeply truly being with the other person, you may arrive at the essence of the issue very quickly.

Being truly respectful implies an attitude of equal worth; that while there may be perceived and actual power differences in terms of role and status, that you see yourselves as working together, each bringing what is needed. Part of this is conveying your enjoyment of working with others, an attitude that this work is mutually rewarding. Hurley, Marin and Hallberg's (2013, p. 270) in a study of child protection social workers, found resilience was a two-way process "in which both participants can benefit from the strength and resourcefulness of the other" with workers feeling "inspired and strengthened" by their clients. There is the potential then for this to also happen in terms of the spiritual, workers learning from the experience of those they work with. Béres (2014) suggests we need to affirm there is vicarious resilience, not only vicarious trauma.

Paying attention to language will also be important: people who would describe themselves as spiritual but not religious might well use different language, but still want you to understand what they see as fundamental to who they are and what really matters to them and how they live. What this means then is that you need to be able to be flexible about the language that you use, while ensuring that you provide openings for people to be able to describe this. With some people, there will be non-verbal cues – ways of dressing or symbols that people wear that demonstrate their commitment to a particular religion. With other people, it will be a matter of asking about a person's spiritual and religious beliefs. For some people, it will be a relief to be asked about an aspect of their lives that is significant to them, particularly those who are active members of a religious tradition. They will also want you to understand how their particular understanding of their religious tradition influences them and to ensure that you don't make assumptions about their religious or spiritual expression based on inaccurate knowledge.

We tend to depend on spoken language which can be challenging for some. It can help to explore other ways of naming what matters through the use of images and symbols, drawing or other forms of art. You can now buy a sets of cards with images which may also have a word from organisations such as Innovative Resources. One set of cards is called Signposts – exploring everyday spirituality in photograph-based cards "designed to invite anyone to talk about meaning and significance in their lives whether or not they couch this in religious terms." Asking people to select one or several cards that say something about where they are now, can be a way in for people to name this and can elicit surprising information about their strengths and resources. You might choose to be creative in using art or small toys/figures to use as symbols of experiences as ways to enable people to name and explore them (Wood and Schuck, 2011).

All of these ideas contribute to how you set the scene for being ready to engage with individuals and families in ways that foster embedding spirituality and religion. So how to get started? It is useful to work out ways of asking that are respectful and open up conversations, open rather than closed questions that allow the person to respond in the way that fits for them.

Tessa's experience

To make this more concrete I am returning to Tessa's experience from Chapter 3:

> *Imagine Tessa comes to see you feeling her mental health is fragile. She has previously been diagnosed with post traumatic stress. What has tipped her over the edge now is that her children were teased in school about looking different. While Tessa doesn't wear a hijab, the family are Sunni Muslims. This has taken Tessa back to why they left Iran and the trauma of both that experience and life in the refugee camp. While she says her faith remains strong and is what sustains her, she feels judged and fears persecution here for her family.*

So how to start? Engaging

You would start as you normally would: being welcoming with beginning conversation, then moving to asking why the person has come to see you, what they are hoping will happen. Depending on where their answers lead, at some point, you might ask questions that focus on what is meaningful, in ways that open up exploration of how they use their spiritual resources. Examples of questions that do this and incorporate an expectation of strengths and resources are:

> What helps you keep going when things are hard like this?
>
> What qualities do you have that help you with this?
>
> What is it that really matters to you here?
>
> What's really meaningful to you?
>
> What kinds of things make a difference to you, restore your spirit?
>
> What gives you hope that things can change?

More specifically, for example, from a narrative perspective you might ask something like:

> "We'll get to what has brought you in soon, but could we begin with you perhaps describing what has been keeping you going during the last little while as you have been dealing with all the effects of the end of your relationship?" (Gardner and Béres, 2018, p. 106)

Tessa responds to these questions by talking initially about her fears: what her children's experience might mean, her struggles with her mental health, her concern about not being able to cope and care for her children and husband. She is surprised by the question of what keeps her going, but readily names her faith as an important part of her life, and that the hope of a better life for her and her family is what sustains her. Being with others in her faith community helps and seeing her children be able to play and walk to school without fear.

If the person is explicit about a specific spiritual practice or religious tradition that has been significant for them, you might then ask:

> So tell me more about what this has meant for you?
>
> How have things changed over time in your spiritual (or religious) experience
>
> How has this ......influenced how you were able to be and what you were able to do?
>
> How else could this make a difference for you?

What really matters about this for you now?

(see also the questions in Chapter 6).

If it's clear the spiritual or religious has been part of the issue, you might say:

So it sounds as if your belief in ... (or experience of) was an important part of what happened? If yes, then could you say more about where you were coming from?

Where were other people in your life or in your community coming from about this?

Tessa's responses to the first questions lead very easily into asking these kinds of questions. She is able to explain more about how important her religious faith is and how this sustained her in Iran and in the refugee camp. This has also been an important aspect of settling into the community, finding other Muslims who welcomed the family. As you listen more, sitting with her feelings of distress, she explains that she doesn't at this point want to talk about what happened in Iran, it brings back too many memories, but she does want you to understand and value her faith, which she finds many Australians don't do. She also wants you to understand the depth of her fear for her children and not to simply dismiss it as her husband and friends do. It is important for Tessa that you are able to sit with her feelings, respectfully, with embodied empathy: demonstrating that you are seeking a deep understanding of where she is coming from. Building this relationship needs time and space, for her to trust that you will not also dismiss her fears or her faith.

Assessment: clarifying what is happening, what matters

As you move more into a stage of 'assessment' again working out together what it is that the person wants to work on, it may feel helpful to ask more specifically about connections to religious or spiritual traditions or practices, particularly if the person has already started to make this explicit. Given the critical spirituality framework, you would expect to explore what connections and relationships the person has that are significant to them: family, friends, involvement with people and organisations related to work, health, being social, part of a church, the physical as well as the cultural and social environment. As you would generally, it would be important to take the lead from them in identifying what it is that they want to work on initially and what that means about how much you explore with them their spiritual experience. If someone is seeing you because they are worried about an imminent crisis with their housing, it may be that you do not see it as relevant to explore other aspects of their lives including what is fundamentally meaningful. However, it is important to have enough general background to make sure this is the case and allow the family to tell you if and why this matters. For example, a family might be particularly worried about losing their rented property because of rent arrears, and therefore be also very worried about where they might end up living next. Part of their concern might be having to move away from a community that has both a church, mosque or synagogue and so on that fits with their religious tradition and also a school where their children can learn within this tradition. So although housing is the primary concern, this still does have a link to their religious beliefs and this influences where they would prefer to live.

I do need to mention that there are a number of assessment tools related to religion and spirituality that have been developed particularly for health settings and you may be in an organisation that likes to use these. Some organisations use these systematically to ensure that the spiritual is included. These have the advantage of making sure that spirituality – or often more particularly religion are included. The danger of these is that they can become too prescriptive or use language that doesn't fit the individual's experience. They do often focus on religion rather than spirituality more generally. Because of this, some professionals prefer to use them as prompts to encourage asking about what is meaningful. Others have developed more inclusive tools. Rumbold (2007), for example, developed an assessment tool called the 'web of relationships' that prompts being attuned to the different areas in a person's life that might be meaningful: their relationship to the transcendent, to self, to other people, to social networks and to 'space' which includes activities meaningful to the person. His research with staff in three palliative care units using this tool found it became a dynamic and shared assessment process: they gradually collected information from their patients to identify their spirituality and so what would help their process of dying. Puchalksi and McSkimming (2006, pp. 30–2) developed the FICA tool with two hospitals:

F = Faith, Belief, Meaning: do you consider yourself spiritual or religious?

I = Importance and influence such as what importance does your faith or belief have in your life?

C= Community – are you part of a spiritual or religious community?

A Address/Action – how would you like me to address these issues in your healthcare?"

They found using the tool led to culture change – staff felt it gave them permission to name and discuss spiritual issues.

Canda, Furman and Canda (2020, p. 351) designed a spiritual interest screening tool with three basic general questions "What things or activities give you a sense of peace, hope, joy, meaning or purpose, especially at difficult times of life?" and "Are there certain spiritual, religious, faith-based, or holistic approaches to health and well-being that are important and helpful for you (such as prayer, meditation, yoga, participation in a religious or spiritual group, or spending time in nature?" The third question asks if they would like to discuss any of these during their health care. However, they suggest that the least intrusive form of spiritual assessment is implicit: "by cultivating a spiritually sensitive relationship with the client, without talking explicitly or directly about religion or spirituality; we cue the client to our openness, receptivity, interest, and respect for whatever is important to the person." This can be "facilitated by open- ended questions that tap themes related to religion and spirituality through use of everyday nonreligious language (Canda, Furman and Canda, 2020, p. 353).

There are some tools that organisations have developed for themselves that use a combination of words and images as ways to start a conversation about spirituality. North and West Metropolitan Regions Palliative Care Consortium in Australia, for example, created a page image of brightly coloured balloons with the kinds of words they felt meant spirituality for them: transformation, sense of being, grounding, sacred, love, values, transcendent, relationships, fundamental hunger. Some balloons were left blank and a separate worksheet created with no words in the balloons so people could make their own image of what spirituality meant for them. A one-page worksheet 'captured the conversation' summarising the person's response and significant issues raised.

From the theoretical perspectives in the critical spirituality framework outlined in Chapter 3, you would expect to ask about relevant history and the influence of the person's own social context and the broader context:

> What relationships have been significant to you?

> Are there particular connections to groups or organisations that are or have been influential in your life?

> What spiritual or religious influences are there or for you or your family? What's important to you? How do you go about making sure that's part of your life?

> How has your experience been influenced by the broader community's attitudes to your values and/or your religious or spiritual beliefs?

> What connections do you have to the natural world?

You might at this time feel you can ask about creating new understandings, for example:

> How did the other person/people involved see this? Where were they coming from?

For Tessa, what emerged at this point and was new, was firstly naming the natural world as important to her. Her family in Iran had been farmers and she really missed not having land to grow anything in the refugee camp. Having a garden and being able to grow vegetables is really nurturing for her. Having seen the degradation of land in Iran and the bleakness of the refugee camps, she is also fearful of what is happening in the world about climate and the environment. Second, she identifies not only her concerns about her children's experience, but also how the community in general sees Muslims. She mentions, almost in passing, that she is concerned about the opposition to building a mosque in the community and how this might mean her family are targeted in some way. This also has resonance with her past experience, the violence to her family that meant they had to leave Iran.

This encourages you to ask a bit more about how she thinks others might see this, including those who teased her children. As you explore this more, Tessa can see that it is possible the children in the school were simply speaking from ignorance. She can remember being teased in Iran as a child just because she was taller than most girls of her age. This is helpful in lessening her fears about her children at school, but clearly other broader fears remain.

Working together

Perhaps I need to reiterate here that what you are working will be what the person wants and needs you to work on: if that is the urgency of housing or income relief or the need for advocacy to access services, it may be that attending to spiritual or religious issues is not what the person wants or needs. What to work on together and whether and if so how spirituality fits will gradually become clear. Useful questions might be:

> Where do you think we should go from here?
>
> What do you think it would be useful to focus on?
>
> What seems to be the way forward for you?

It may be that the exploration means the person has become clearer for themselves about their reaction and whether their new understanding is enough for needed change. Alternatively, they may want to work with you on particular aspects of what they have brought to you. It may be that using some of the critically reflective processes help: encouraging the person to name their assumptions, what they have taken for granted about how things are, then brainstorming with them what other assumptions might be possible. Sometimes this frees up perception: what was seen as impossible to change can be understood differently. You could also think of this from a narrative perspective as finding exceptions, times when the person has felt or thought differently from what seems to be the current 'dominant' story. Freeing up thinking in this way can then lead to different actions feeling possible too.

Including spiritual and religious practices

What I am also suggesting you might add here, depending on the person and the situation, is asking about spiritual or religious practices that are important to them. This can foster new understandings or ways of being or reinforce what has been useful in the past. If you have asked about what has helped keep people going in times of crisis or struggle, they may already have talked about this. Notice I am stressing here asking about what works for them. If you do make a suggestion about a spiritual practice, it is important to do this tentatively and only if people are finding it hard to think about what this would mean – and want ideas. This would be similar to how you might ask with caution and respect if someone is open to a therapeutic practice. For people who are religious, this idea will be familiar: they may already use prayer or meditation regularly, affirm the place of music or rituals that are part of their religious tradition. Attending religious gatherings at for example, a church, mosque or synagogue or community setting may be important reminders of spiritual values. However, even for those who are religious it is easy to forget the value of spiritual practices in time of crisis. Some of those involved with religious traditions would say that they still don't have practices that fit with what gives them meaning or that are truly restoring for them.

Tessa acknowledged that while she formally participated in Muslim worship that sometimes her fears were so great that she felt hardly present. She was aware that some Muslim women in the community met for shared prayers weekly, but had not felt able to go. As she talked more about where she was coming from, she could see that she had made assumptions about not being welcome because of cultural differences in her way of being Muslim. She was able to say I need to leave behind how things were in Iran and see how things are different here. As you explore this and her love of gardening, you ask if she might be interested in volunteering in an organisation for people with disabilities who produce vegetables for the café they work in. Tessa is initially taken aback at this idea, but says she can see it would be helpful to meet others who are outside her usual community.

What I mean by spiritual practices is ways of being or doing that remind the person of their fundamental values and makes those more real, more actively part of how they are living. These are likely to change over time, so it's important to explore what works for them right now. It helps if you are clear about what is important for your own spiritual practice, so that you understand why some kind of spiritual practice can also be helpful for others.

Having your own spiritual practices also means you are likely to be in a more grounded space from which to listen as a social worker. The ideal is to move from doing spiritual practices to seeing how the spiritual, acting from what is meaningful is an attitude to all of life: your ability to be spiritual can then underpin all that you do. This is a life's journey, but something we can start to feel the more we practice. The attitude of spaciousness explored earlier comes from being with people rather than thinking about what it is that needs to be done. The doing can then emerge in a way that is more attuned to the being self of you and the other. It also makes sense that if we are to be integrating spirituality into working with others, we also need to ask what it would mean to do this for ourselves. Links between spirituality and self-care have emerged in research with human service workers including social workers: what Ho, Sing and Wong (2016) name as spiritual resilience and tranquility. In McGarrigle and Walsh's (2011) research for social workers, sessions included meditation, body scan, relaxing, mindful walking and listening as well as mindfulness-based activities. Participants felt they became better at both self-care (and so less stressed) and that this had meant they were more actively attentive to their clients.

When I have asked what makes it hard to carry out spiritual practices, responses often include: *this seems selfish or indulgent when other people have a more difficult life than me, I don't have time, it feels uncomfortable to do something just for me; I don't think I will be able to do this well.* It is important to move beyond the kinds of assumptions that these imply: *I am not as important as other people, my needs don't matter, it is only valid to do this if I can do it perfectly.* More helpful assumptions might be: *we all benefit from practices that nurture us spiritually, they benefit us and all those we have contact with; spiritual practices have to be learnt like any other and will be more fluent the more we do them, I don't have to stick with the same spiritual practices for ever, I can choose what works for me now.* What works will depend on your personality, your history, what is happening for you currently. Some people find what they need is more physical, bodily, active, such as yoga, running, walking fast or dancing, others need quiet and withdrawal, others connection with people or with words and ideas. You may need to consciously give yourself or encourage the other person to give themselves permission to undertake the spiritual practices that feel right for them.

A practice that can underpin and reinforce all other spiritual practices is journaling, writing and/or drawing about these experiences and what they mean for you. Keeping a journal should be a private and safe space which you can use as a way of noticing and articulating an experience, in a way that means you have recorded it and can revisit it later if you want to. Looking back to how you felt and reacted to an earlier experience can reinforce how you have changed or illuminate old patterns that you still want to change. It is important that you don't judge what you have written in any way, the aim is to write without worrying about language or perfect expression or saying the 'right' thing, but simply allowing words, ideas, images to spill onto the paper.

Some examples of what spiritual practices might be:

- Paying attention to moments of connection, of joy, of gratitude, of feeling in tune with yourself and what matters in your world. There may be simple, small aspects of what happens in your daily life that foster your feeling of wellbeing provided you notice them. Calman (2019) suggests this might be as basic as enjoying a cup of coffee that is just right or noticing acts of kindness to you or between others. It might be the pleasure of a newly cleaned room or the satisfaction of completing any task. This might be as simple as asking yourself at the end of each day what did I value about today? What do I feel grateful for today? Once you are doing this regularly, it encourages you to notice this as it happens, something you or others have done or simply being happy or joyful. You could note these in a journal and perhaps monthly or annually notice what changes are emerging.

Daniel felt overwhelmed by the sadness in his social work role with refugees. He decided to avoid being burnt out, something needed to change. After a conversation about this with his supervisor, he started noticing what made him feel happy or connected during the day. He realised firstly that the refugees were often a source of joy as well as sadness; their zest for life continued in spite of or sometimes because of what they endured. His deep sense of connection with them was also renewing and satisfying. Secondly, he began to more consciously also value small moments of gratitude, for his own family, for the changing seasons in gardens on his way to work, the mutuality of time with colleagues. He decided to keep a journal of these and looking back after six months, was able to see how much more easily he was able to notice and name what nurtured his spirit. This fitted with his sense of being more internally grounded and able to nurture others as well.

- Regular meditation or prayer. Mindfulness meditation has become increasingly recognised as a way of slowing yourself down, being focused or "keeping one's consciousness alive to the present reality (Hanh, 1976). For those who are spiritual or who are becoming conscious of their spiritual selves, this is a way of practising being, changing from being distracted by thoughts to allowing them to pass by. Those of you who are religious are more likely to be familiar with the many forms of prayer and meditation that are part of religious traditions. Prayer may in some traditions be more likely to be spoken or sung, might be specifically related to prayers of gratitude, of asking for help, sharing experiences of suffering. However, across religious traditions there is also a form of what you could call more mystical prayer that is more likely to be silent, meditative prayer, that aims to still the mind and ideally to also foster the experience of transcendence and/or the interconnectedness of all. Mindfulness meditation, which is generally based on Buddhist meditation has become increasingly popular as a tool stilling the mind for workers and clients. Rogers and Maytan (2012, p. 7) for example, see mindfulness as a way of learning to live more fully in the present" which includes developing qualities of 'wisdom, patience, and compassion.' Ways to slow the mind down and help with focus are often simple, such as:

- Concentrating on your breathing, counting it in and out
- Focusing on a symbol – a flower, tree, image that you like
- Being aware of different parts of your body in turn and relaxing them
- Walking focusing only on the experience.

Sometimes it helps to start with a guided meditation in a class or listening to one online; someone speaking the meditation can help you be less distracted. With practice, you can use any activity in being mindful. Families may also be interested in using mediation with children (Garth, 1994).

Sue Wilson (1996, p. 10) *writes: One morning I had a powerful sense of love and tenderness in the air, streaming through the gully and around the suburbs and throughout the world. I pictured how it would be if everyone was touched by this spirit and if we all sat silently on our back steps, as a community of neighbours, worshipping this tender goodness together.....*

As I came out of this meditative moment, my mind put words to it. With great wonder, I thought, "It's a spirit of holiness"

- Naming and practising what nurtures you spiritually. Ask what is important to you spiritually and what can help you remember to include these. Again these will vary for each person and it may be that the key is for people to give themselves permission to do what seems to be indulgent but is fundamental to nurturing their lives. For a person for whom relationships are important, Saturday morning tea with family or friends might be a key spiritually regenerating ritual. If being with nature is key, it may be building into your life regular walks on the beach or in a park. It could be regular yoga or joining an advocacy group seeking social change.

- Having times of silence in your life. Western culture discourages silence and many people feel uncomfortable with silence, they are so unused to it. For some, there is a fear that being in silence will allow uncomfortable thoughts and feelings to emerge, perhaps painful memories or nagging doubts. For others, silence is something to be relished that is deeply renewing. Silence, or solitude or stillness, all are ways of allowing spaciousness in our lives. For me the quiet of being in the forest allows me to be aware of where I am internally, to connect to what really matters to me. As we moved out of Covid lockdowns and children returned to school, many people affirmed their need for silence that had been lost. As workers, we need to be able to allow silence in our conversations with others to give space to people internally wrestling with what they think and feel. For some people having a spiritual practice that gives permission for being quiet and still is what will most nurture them. This might be in the form of building some silent time into the day, while walking, driving to work, pausing between work and home. Some religious traditions offer essentially silent retreats often with a trained spiritual nurturer who can be a sounding board or give support as needed. These are often open to anyone, not only those who are religious or from that religious tradition. For those who find silence anxiety-provoking or are not familiar with their own silence, being on a retreat that is supported like this can be a good place to start. More people are now going on pilgrimages either to what are seen as sacred sites or in nature and these may also be silent – or not, so you may able to choose how much silence you have.

- Consciously connecting to the environment. A spiritual practice that specifically pays attention to land or country can be spiritually grounding. This might be taking time each morning to be aware of the landscape around you, to give thanks for the beauty and nurture of the earth that sustains you, to acknowledge that "life is an interdependent web of which all are a part" (Dylan and Coates, 2012, p. 141). It could be taking this further to care of the land around you or being more conscious about how you use the earth's resources. This might include seeking to live more simply, to actively choose to consume less or to volunteer with a landcare group.
- Creativity of many kinds might be part of spiritual expression: the more obviously creative arts: painting, drawing, sculpture, writing, poetry, dancing, knitting, pottery and so on but also the creativity that is part of activities like gardening and cooking. Kossak (2009, p. 16) writes about drumming but this might apply to other shared activities too: "When rhythmic synchronisation is a shared experience... the phenomenon of attunement extends from an inner sensitivity to self to an outer sensitivity with another person's reality, which may include a transpersonal or transcendent experience."

  Tracy, for example, said that as a social worker and parent, she spent her life running from one thing to the other. She was constantly exhausted and sometimes felt unable to keep going, but that nothing could change her life. After a car accident caused by falling asleep at the wheel, she spent three weeks in rehabilitation and began to question her way of living and her need for perfection at home and work. Part of the rehabilitation was doing craft work to build strength in her damaged arm and shoulder. While she was initially irritated by this, she came to relish how absorbed she became, so that she felt restored and increasingly creative. When a passing pastoral care worker said that looks like a meditative practice, she suddenly realised that was right and that she would really miss not doing it, it brought joy to her life. She decided to give herself permission to build this into her life believing that her different attitude would benefit her and everyone else she connected with.

- Music is a source of spiritual nurture for many people, singing alone or with others, listening to people playing, writing music can all be restoring and lead to a sense of transcendence, awareness of what is greater than the self. Where I live there has been a significant increase in choirs of all sorts, built on the assumption that everyone can sing enough to take part. For many, these are places of companionship and fun as well as for renewal at a spiritual level.

  Jake noticed that if he played music on his way home from work instead of listening to the news of the day he arrived home in a better space. It was easier to leave work behind and to arrive grounded and refreshed.

- Paying attention to your dreams. Writers from First Nations people to psychoanalysts like Jung suggest that dreams are an important source of information for us if we pay attention to them. Jung suggests understanding dreams metaphorically, seeing each aspect of a dream as a part of our selves and asking what that aspect might be expressing (Johnson, 1986).
- Acknowledging vocation. For some people naming work as vocation can mean seeing paid or voluntary work that you do as part of your spiritual practice, part of what gives your life meaning. If you take this seriously rather than work being only something you do to be paid, it can become more fundamentally part of who you are. Not everyone has the choice of work as vocation, but you can also think about your vocation as a way of being in the world that is your attitude to life more broadly. You might be someone whose life vocation is to be receptive and listen to others – family, friends, neighbours and also, if it fits, at work. Alternatively, your vocation is to be an initiator, an encourager or someone who brings harmony to conflict.
- Critical reflection can also be seen as a spiritual practice, that helps you both clarify who you are, what motivates, sustains and nurtures you, what gives you meaning. Hunt (2021, p. 271) has advocated for "critical reflection in, and on, professional practice and indicated the potential for personal and social transformation that lies in exploring what and how we know and, especially, in asking 'Who is the "I" that knows and practices?"
- Community connectedness: which might be anything from participating in a religious tradition, being an active community group member or being neighbourly.

Spiritual practices and rituals

The idea of seeing spiritual practices as rituals can help here. Religious and spiritual groups all have their own rituals: patterns or expectations about carrying out particular activities that reinforce spiritual practices. These would include worshipping together, prayer, social activities after services, celebrations at particular times of the year.

Rituals are often culturally determined or at least influenced. It is useful then to help people work out what this will mean for them. More people now decide their own form of wedding or funeral, for example.

Rituals can be practices that you do specifically or occasionally: ways of celebrating and marking change such as the rituals of school graduations, weddings, funerals. More people are devising their own ways of carrying out these and devising other celebrations: for 'significant' birthdays, birth, progression to work or divorce. Rituals can also be an activity that you do regularly and routinely as a way of building in a spiritual practice. It could be anything from regular meditation or walking in nature, to a weekly family meal. Committing to a ritual can mean that you carry out a new spiritual practice enough to experience the benefits and want it to become part of your life. A spiritual practice as ritual doesn't necessarily take a long time, but it requires commitment. It might be as simple as a minute's meditation entering and leaving work or an activity where you want to bring all of your resources, spiritual and other.

Acknowledging your limitations: referring on

While I have suggested that it is not vital – or possible – to know everything about another person's spiritual or religious preferences and that it is more important to learn from them, there will be times when you recognise you need to know more. You can gain knowledge partly from asking those you work with and so recognising and validating their greater knowledge, but you might also at times need to gain more knowledge, using your research skills and/or consulting with people who are the experts or specialists in this field.

From a religious perspective, that is likely to be those employed in the religious community and most would now have websites where you can find who to talk to.

However, it is important to recognise, in this aspect of practice as in any other, when your knowledge and skills are not enough and you or those you are working with need more specialised knowledge and skills. Carrington (2017, p. 297) points out that "Although as a social worker my practice may be guided by a spiritual paradigm, and I may utilise spiritual theories and practices, or even discuss spiritual or religious concepts with people, it is not within my role to give spiritual instruction. For that, I would suggest there is a need for appropriate referral to a suitable spiritual practitioner." Spiritual practitioners would include those employed as pastoral care or faith-based workers or chaplains in an organisation primarily for that purpose. If you are based in a health agency such as a hospital or rehabilitation centre, it is also likely that representatives of religious traditions will also have a connection there and be available for those who want that. People who are firmly connected to a religious traditions are likely to be visited or supported by someone employed there either as a minister/priest, rabbi, etc or as a pastoral care type worker. It is important to make connections with them whenever you start to feel out of your depth. If those you are working with do not want someone from their immediate community contacted, you may need to ask them about the value of contacting someone else. Trained spiritual directors or companions or counsellors who work as private practitioners are increasingly available in most countries and often work across religious and spiritual traditions. Spiritual Directors International or simply looking for a website for spiritual directors in your own country will help you find people.

Case studies

Case Study One: Clarifying underlying meaning

Grace was referred to Jake, a hospital social worker, because one of the nursing staff overheard her having an argument with her mother Margaret who is dying and was significantly upset afterwards. Jake began by asking Grace what she was hoping for from seeing him. She replied that she wanted someone to make sure her mother didn't do anything stupid that would undermine her care. She explained that Margaret wanted to leave palliative care and die in a small holiday shack in a forest environment that she sees as her spiritual home. Jake had previously talked with Margaret as part of her admission to the palliative care unit and was already aware that she wasn't happy to stay there, but that she also wanted to have Grace's blessing, if possible, on where to die.

Partly because of this, Jake asked Grace to tell him more about her and Margaret, what kinds of things were important for each of them? Initially, Grace just really needed to express her frustration at Margaret being stubborn and *'wanting to make life difficult for everyone else'*. She was also concerned about what other people would think of people letting Margaret die in what is a very basic shack. Jake acknowledged her frustrations, then asked *what keeps you each going when times are difficult like this?*

Grace was tearful at this point, saying that relationships were important to her and particularly still her relationship with her mother. She wanted her mother to live as long as possible and this idea of going to the shack seemed to be her mother giving up, wanting to leave her. Jake responded with *'that's really hard, to be facing not having your mother with you'*. Grace agreed and added, *I know other people will support me too, but I will miss her so much.* Jake asked, so *who and what will support you?* Grace was able to name friends and family members and also to acknowledge that part of what would support her would be something she had inherited from Margaret, loving being in nature, feeling connected to the universe. She and Margaret had talked about Margaret's ashes being buried or spread near the shack and she felt it would help to be able to visit her there.

Jake felt this led well to asking: so where do you think Margaret might be coming from? What is it that keeps her going? Grace was able to say *relationships do a bit, but it's being in nature really, being at the shack and the forest has always meant a lot to her, especially in hard times, it's renewed her, I can see why she wants to die there. I just didn't want to face what this meant.* She could also say she found some of the practical aspects daunting and Jake was able to say there were services that could help with those. This took Grace back to worrying about what others might think of this decision, so Jake asked *where do you think those pressures come from, the expectations that things would be done in a certain way?*

Grace struggled with this initially, but eventually talked about an image that had stayed with her, an advertisement showing people dying in a beautifully decorated room surrounded by caring nursing staff. She had taken on board that this is how death 'should' be done and would demonstrate her love for Margaret, but could see this was never what Margaret would have wanted and that no one who knew her would expect that. She expressed a sense of relief at letting that go and said she would talk to Margaret herself to explain how she felt and that she would help her go to the shack. Jake agreed he would set up a meeting with the coordinator of the home based services that would help support them both.

Notice this conversation was not time-consuming and was constructed in the here and now. It required some micro-skills and deep listening to reach a negotiated outcome that left everyone satisfied.

Case Study Two: Family relationships counselling

Paul met with Clare and Jenny in a family and relationships counselling centre. When Paul asked why they had come they said the main issue was conflict about where their child should go to school, but this question had generated other issues for them, so that they were now concerned about whether this was going to undermine their relationship. Paul explained that he liked to work by hearing each person's story and asking the other to listen, affirming that he would make sure each person would be heard.

Clare explained her background meant she had very mixed experiences of religion. Her mother was from a Catholic Irish family and a firm believer and supporter of the church all her life. As a child Carol felt enfolded in the warmth of the church community, she loved the ritual of the Mass and because she also went to a Catholic school, the values and beliefs expressed in her life were very consistent. Her father's background was Jewish, but he was not practicing and because of the Holocaust was strongly opposed to religious beliefs. He accepted her mother's practices and that their children would be baptised and brought up Catholic but was not prepared to talk about religion except occasionally to say he thought too much religion caused wars. As she got older, Clare felt caught between her parents' conflict. When she was fourteen she rebelled firstly about going to church then against many other aspects of her childhood, left home at 16 and started living with her partner Jenny in her late twenties. For several years before that, she experimented with drugs as a way of achieving altered states of consciousness and went to several Buddhist and Hindu retreats to practice meditation. She still meditates regularly.

Jenny's family was not religious and she had very little experience or knowledge of religious traditions until she met Clare. What she did know was from media information about the various kinds of conflict caused by religious differences. She was initially fascinated by Clare's history which cemented her assumptions that it was better to avoid religion altogether, although she could see the value of meditation as it often restored Clare in ways she couldn't explain.

When she and Jenny's oldest child was to start school, Clare realised that she felt she really wanted her to go to a Catholic school. This was so far from her and Jenny's agreed attitudes and beliefs that it caused a lot of tension between them. They started having arguments about all sorts of things that they had previously thought they agreed about. Fearing the ending of their relationship they decided to see Paul, a relationship counsellor.

After hearing why they were coming to see him, Paul asked each to say something about what really mattered to them and for the other to listen deeply in the sense of hearing the underlying messages and feelings. He suggested that rather than only using words, they also choose an image that spoke to them about these issues from a pack of card images he had.

Jenny began by outlining why she didn't want their children to go to a Catholic school given the abuse in the Catholic church, outmoded attitudes to women and particularly to lesbian women ending with *I just cannot understand how you could even think of this*. Josie asked her to say more about what she was feeling. Jenny said considerable anger and frustration how she felt that Clare had undermined what she felt was their shared values and beliefs, but as she talked more also identified her sadness at losing their easy companionship. Paul asked her to say more about what really matters, to take a different way in, what helps when things are difficult. Jenny took more time to answer this, responding that what really mattered to her was Clare and their children, and what helped when things were difficult was to take time to walk by herself to sort out what she was feeling and thinking and why, what she called a meditative walk. Jenny's image was of a circle of candles: she described this as what she felt after a walk, that she was restored and the circle with light represented harmony and inspiration.

Turning to Clare, Paul asked the same question about what really matters. Clare started by also saying her relationship with Jenny and their children, then she said there was also something for her about the church that she was finding it hard to identify. She said she found what Jenny said about undermining their shared values very painful, because she saw these are church values she wanted their children to have too: caring for others, social justice, the importance of love more than money. The question about what helped when things were difficult took her to meditation and somehow that was connected to those values, remembering really fundamental values, but feeling these transcended whatever she was struggling with.

Paul reflected back what he was hearing: that what really mattered most to each of them was their relationship and their children and shared values, and to some degree shared spiritual practices, both meditating though in different ways. He then asked what do you each see as spiritual about how you live?

Clare's response was she felt that the spiritual was part of her life, that she was always looking for meaning. While she no longer believed in God in the way she had as a child, she did believe in something greater and valued the glimpses of that she got when she felt deeply connected to Jenny, to some others and sometimes in nature. Jenny said while she didn't use that language those things were important for her too, but she didn't see them as only connecting to a church. She added that what she feared for their children in a

Catholic school was how they might be ostracised. Paul asked is there a way you can make this spiritual stuff part of your lives in a way that works for you both? This was an aha moment for Clare: she suddenly saw that she was repeating her parents' pattern of it's my way or yours, one of us has to sacrifice our preferred way for the other. She wanted to move beyond that to valuing the spiritual in ways they could both be comfortable. They agreed they would send their daughter to a Steiner school and to work together on how to make the spiritual more explicit together including for their daughter.

8 Spirituality, religion and the broader context: organisational, community and policy practice

Here, I move from focusing on engaging with individuals about their experience of the spiritual and religious to the influence of the organisation, community and policy contexts you work in. All of these can significantly affect how people are able to express their spiritual selves and it may be that the focus of social work action needs to be on the context rather than individual experience. Each of these contextual levels will have an implicit or explicit set of assumptions that may be related to spirituality and religion. A community, for example, may see as acceptable one form of religious expression but negatively judge another. A Sikh who is verbally abused for wearing a turban needs community change rather than only individual support. Policies enshrined in the legal system may encourage or discourage forms of religious expression in ways that may or may not fit with social work values. First Nations people, for example, would name their experience of the spiritual with their environment, the land from which they are born as well as the community they are part of. It follows that government policy decisions about land use that doesn't take this into account will feel actively harmful for them. This is increasingly also a concern for others who feel spiritually connected to the earth and aware of how it is being undermined by government policies. Given varying degrees of acceptance of religious and spiritual diversity, social workers need to work actively with their organisations, communities and at a policy level to foster celebration of spiritual as well as other forms of diversity, creating communities that generate flourishing for all aspects of community, animate and inanimate.

While the focus of action may be different, my experience is that we still need to use the same qualities and processes as working with individuals and families. When I am able to engage respectfully and openly with colleagues and managers, being prepared to listen deeply, to sit with uncertainty and wait as needed, I can more readily encourage naming of values and beliefs, assumptions about how things are done. If I am in this space, I am more often able to reach agreement about how to act. This can include courage in challenging what seem to be untested or limited assumptions, naming value differences and seeking more socially just change. In one voluntary organisation I worked in, for example, some members of the management

DOI: 10.4324/9781003132677-12

committee expressed frustration about other members 'sabotaging' decisions that had been agreed on by a majority decision. As the social work co-ordinator, I asked whether we couldn't more often work to consensus, waiting to make decisions until everyone's voice had been heard. After considerable discussion, it was agreed that very few decisions had to be made urgently and that we would try this way of working. What was made explicit in the discussion was that this meant respecting that each person's opinion reflected what mattered to them and that we should all be open to hearing all views. In practice, once someone's opinion was heard, they were usually more prepared to compromise so a consensus position could be reached and decisions were made more harmoniously from an agreed value base.

These broader ways of taking action could be thought of as a key aspect of the critical or structural aspect of critical spirituality: asking what needs to change in the organisation, community or policy to generate more socially just and inclusive practices. This encourages seeing the integration of how assumptions in the broader social context are embedded in interactions between individuals and in organisational and community practices. As agents of social change, social workers at any level can be seen as being at least small 'l' leaders. Some would name this as 'unleading' asking how power and influence can be shared so that everyone is able to influence how they would like things to be. This means needing to unlearn leadership practices that "promote hierarchy, individualism, compliance, power over, silence, and a culture of fear" partly to include the experience, knowledge and leadership of the "global majority, including Indigenous people, Black and African diasporic people, and people of color as well as people with multiple and intersecting marginalized identities" (Shah, 2021). Essentially this means being able to name and act from the values that you see as fundamental to the kind of society, organisation and community you want to live and work in.

The broad policy context

I am starting with the policy context here because this will influence how you are likely to be able to work at both organisational and community levels. This level includes the expectations that nations make explicit about human rights and how these are enshrined in policy. A policy at a national or international level is generally thought of as a way of governments responding to an issue and enshrining this in legislation or particular strategies or programs carried out by funded agencies – sometimes government departments, sometimes other agencies. Bacchi (2009, p. 1) points out that how a particular issue or problem is represented in the policy context matters because it "carries all sorts of implications for how the issue is thought about and/or how the people involved are treated, and are evoked to think about themselves." In the same way you would use critical reflection to understand personal and professional assumptions, you can question policy assumptions: what is taken for granted in how an issue is represented, how do the beliefs and values embedded in policy represent a way of thinking? does this policy assumption reflect social work values? This kind of search includes "deep-seated cultural values – a kind of social unconscious …basic or fundamental worldviews" (Bacchi, 2009, p. 5). However, policies can also be generated from the ground up. Individuals and groups expressing their values and beliefs about what matters and taking action, can over time – and sometimes it takes a long time, achieve policy change.

In countries that have historically had mainly one religious tradition or where one religious tradition still dominates, for example, it is likely that the collective social unconscious will continue to be influenced by the beliefs of that tradition. This means that even in nations that consider themselves secular, long-standing assumptions from religious tradition continue to influence how decisions are made. The question is how these become part of policy and legislation and what impact that has. The Ontario Human Rights Commission (2013, p. 34) in Canada makes this explicit in recognising that "neutral" or "secular" views often privilege agnostic or atheist traditions and worldviews" and are "residually and normatively Christian." This leads to systemic faithism, which the Commission defines as: "the ways that cultural and societal norms, systems, structures and institutions directly or indirectly, consciously or unwittingly, promote, sustain or entrench differential (dis)advantage for individuals and groups based on their faith (understood broadly to include religious and non-religious belief systems)." This can affect anyone, meaning that non-Christian religious traditions or those who are 'spiritual but not religious' are disadvantaged, their practices seen as not compatible with Canadian identity. Mistry (2021) for example, left Canada in his early twenties to live in India for a year with his extended Hindu family. When he returned to Canada, he was sharply confronted with the difference between living in a country where your own religion is integral to how things are done and a country where it isn't. He could see in a way he hadn't before he left how Christian assumptions were built into how the country operated: Christian public holidays, Sundays as a day of rest, Christian values influencing policies and assumptions about how to live.

This kind of policy analysis also benefits from the interrogating of language seeking to understand the meaning that particular words have for different people and how meaning becomes part of policy. France, for example, as a secular society, has banned the wearing of all religious symbols for public sector workers on the basis of seeking *impartiality* and *neutrality* for over sixty years, but new policy focuses on extending this to parts of the private sector for Muslim hijabs and burquas only. This has become a debate about religious freedom versus the need for secularism/neutrality, but perhaps the implicit assumptions are: *religion is divisive and we should avoid it* or *we want people to have the same beliefs not assert different ones*. This language reinforces unhelpful binaries: the opposite of neutrality and impartiality perhaps seen as bias or conflictual with negative implications. You could instead see neutrality as being a point on a continuum of a variety of interesting perspectives – and so value diversity as enlivening not dangerous. In Australia, for example, usually also described now as secular, initially First Nations, then colonised by Christians, there is an expectation that funding be provided to support faith-based schools of all kinds. This policy was initially developed because those from the United Kingdom and Ireland wanted to send their children to schools representing different aspects of Christian traditions: Catholics and Protestants. The policy was written to be inclusive of all expressions of Christianity, but broadly enough so that it now includes also subsidising, for example, Jewish and Muslim schools. Implicit in this policy is that Australians expect to have the choice of sending their children to a religious-based school, even if they are not themselves religious.

Religious traditions are part of this policy context and do actively seek to influence them. However, they naturally do not always agree about policy developments and it is important to remember that not all within a religious tradition will agree either. A Guardian newspaper editorial points out that the Catholic vote was equally divided in electing Joe Biden with some US Bishops talking about the challenges of having a liberal Catholic in the White House. However, it is important to recognise that religious traditions and their leaders can positively contribute to changed attitudes and so policy change. In 2021, the Pope met with the Grand Imam Ahmad Al-Tayyeb in Abu Dhabi where they both signed a document calling for shared dialogue and common commitment to recognise that "God has created all human beings equal in rights, duties and dignity, and has called them to live together as brothers and sisters" with an expectation of rejecting violence and extremism and living in tolerance and peace (Document on Human Fraternity for World Peace and Living Together). Similarly, Justin Welby, the senior bishop in the church of England at Easter 2021, advocated for people in Britain to seek a society benefiting all not just the rich and for the government to continue to provide international aid at pre-Covid levels (Waterson, 2021).

One of the human rights most nations agree with is to treat people equally, but what exactly this means is not always the same and the underlying expectations can be contradictory. The use of 'religious freedom' can be a way of affirming the rights of each person to be able to express their religious beliefs as they choose, but as part of a more neoliberal, individually focused agenda this can also be used to deny people other forms of expressing themselves. A recent example of policy change in Victoria, Australia related to conversion therapy: the use of prayer to convert those who identify as homosexual to being heterosexual. Those who were part of a Christian faith tradition and who were also LGBTIQ+ felt they were being unduly pressured to change their sexuality – or at least to deny their preferences. This concern was reinforced by social workers and other professionals seeing the undermining impact of this, including mental illness and suicidality. Because of this, the Australian Association of Social Workers campaigned for policy change on the issue releasing a number of media statements (Yin, 2019). Groups like Catholics for Renewal also questioned Christian and other teachings that allowed people to be pressured in this way. In the ensuing debates about the need to make such conversion practices illegal, some members of a number of religious traditions argued for their right to pray for such change as part of their religious freedom. However, the government decided to move to policy and related legislative change that made conversion or suppression practices illegal. The assumption in this policy was that individuals will express their sexuality in a variety of ways and that this should not be undermined by religious beliefs. Implicit here is an expectation that religious traditions should become more inclusive to allow for those who are not heterosexual to be able to participate. Peter Wilkinson, the president of Catholics for Renewal is quoted as saying that "conversion practices are based on the assumption that heterosexuality is the only 'orthodox' form of sexuality" and hoping "that the passage of this bill will stir the official Catholic Church to recognise such moves as reflections of the signs of the times, calling upon it to rethink its now-outdated teaching on diverse sexuality" (Ilanbey, 2021).

More generally, people who see themselves as spiritual might feel their concerns about what really matters to them are not recognised by decision or policy makers. Their opportunities for expressing this in policy may be limited by not being seen as an established group or tradition. Post COVID-19, for example, more workers wanted greater flexibility about how to manage a work-life balance. Many people found being forced to stay at home and severely limiting social and other activities meant they had time to reflect on what really mattered in their lives. For some this translated into embedding spiritual practices in their lives: walking, meditating, yoga or simply spending more time with a partner or family and/or having time to themselves. These experiences generated questions about the need for policy and organisational change: should people be allowed more flexibility in the workplace to allow this better balance? How might this be enshrined in policy when there was also pressure to have people return to work and so keep businesses going, buying lunch/coffee and using public transport, shopping at lunch time. For many, the desire for policy change comes from feeling interconnected to the earth, spiritually connected to the environment and seeing the impact of climate change.

Workers often feel that being able to bring about policy change is beyond what is possible for them. However, much policy change begins small and comes about as the issue is gradually recognised as one that is important to many. Hodge (2012, p. 20) argues that social workers need to argue for human rights at all levels; micro, mezzo and macro, recognising that the 'insider knowledge' of those who have experienced persecution and discrimination for their religious beliefs is what is needed to address these issues. Hicks (2008) for example, writes about attitudes in foster care practice to those who are lesbians and gay men, a policy likely to be based at least partly on what were seen as Christian values (and would still be by some). As more applicants and workers came to question the underlying assumptions that children could only be adequately fostered by heterosexuals, gradually policies were questioned and changed. Similarly, after the marriage equality vote was successful in Australia, some people expressed surprise how quickly this had happened. Others pointed out they had been campaigning for twenty years. From a broader context, policies can seem to change quickly, but with years of lobbying and awareness-raising in the background.

Useful questions might be:

What policy issues related to spirituality and religion affect your practice?

What policies affect those you work with?

What kinds of changes would be desirable?

How could you start to seek change?

Organisational practice

How you are able to practice will be influenced by the organisation you are employed by, its vision and mission and how it is funded. Much has been written about the current neoliberal influence on and in organisations: the pressures of managerialism, standardisation, focus on measurable outcomes as indicators of quality (Gardner, 2016). These can work against a person or community-centered approach and the inclusion of what might be seen as the more elusive qualities of spirituality, compassion and care. A more business-oriented model of service provision is challenging for those wanting to work holistically and inclusively and requires the capacity to stand back from what is expected to work creatively to manage these competing expectations.

How these issues are experienced and expressed will vary depending on how organisations are funded and auspiced. Many organisations that employ social workers would consider themselves to be secular and are funded by secular governments. However, given governments may reflect implicit re-ligious values as identified above, these will continue to influence organisa-tional policies and funding. Particularly in the West, the emphasis on nuclear family values in religious traditions may mean that welfare agencies also focus on nuclear families, compared to the more community orientation of First Nations or the global South. The broader cultural values implicit in policy generally are frequently part of the culture of the organisation, but may also reflect the local community or communities the organisation is based in and the personal and professional backgrounds of those who work there. An or-ganisation based in a highly multi-cultural and multi-religious community may well respond or need to respond differently from one in a more mono-cultural and religious one.

Alternatively, your employing organisation may be a faith-based organisa-tion that is explicit about the value of its particular faith or religious tradition. Crisp (2014, p. 11) defines a faith-based organisation as "a social service agency which explicitly identifies with a religious tradition and/or is auspiced by any religious organization or religious community or organization." This faith tradition might provide some funding and will certainly have representatives on the organisation's managing body. This will affect the policies and practices of the organisation and in some organisations means only working with those from that faith tradition. However, for many faith-based organisations this is complicated by also receiving government funding which means working with anyone needing these services. Similarly, those employed in the organisation may or not be religious themselves which can make more complex their interactions with the organisation and how it operates. Those who share the faith tradition may have high expectations of being able to live out the ideas of their faith community. Secular workers wonder whether it is their responsibility to seek to understand the implications of being in a faith-based organisation or whether the secular funding means they just work 'as normal.'

Danny, an experienced counsellor moved to work in a Catholic auspiced agency because of their innovative family relationship counselling service. Initially, he felt welcomed and the service, funded by the national government operated in very inclusive and flexible ways. However, he frequently felt increasingly uncomfortable about the weekly staff meeting starting with prayer. As a gay man he also felt that his sexuality was tolerated rather than celebrated and that this attitude might permeate to those the agency worked with. This came to a head when he put up a poster on his door advertising a LGBTIQ+ festival in the local community. The Director, Jenny, asked him to take it down as it might offend some staff and clients; he responded that he felt offended by attitudes towards his sexuality. This led to a more general discussion about how he felt excluded by not being Catholic including the prayers at meetings. Jenny asked about how he would describe his spirituality, which he struggled to do. He and Jenny agreed to each think about what the other had raised and to meet again. In the meantime, Danny articulated what he saw as his spirituality: the values that influenced his work which were similar to the agency's main values of building a more inclusive society, where everyone could live life to the full. He wondered if he was excluding spirituality in his work with families, and how to include more kinds of spirituality, including his less religious based version. In their next meeting, he was surprised to find Jenny open to this and she suggested his team take the 'prayers' at some staff meetings, in the form of reflecting on values and meaning. For Danny, this was an 'aha' moment, seeing that the prayer time could be a way of orienting positively to the day rather than seeing it as forcing religious beliefs onto others. Jenny added that from her perspective being inclusive meant respecting that views varied, seeking understanding while promoting wider acceptance. They agreed to compromise on the poster: he would have it up inside his office and would tell staff in his team about the festival.

The explicit values of a faith-based organisation may or may not be similar to those of a secular organisation. For example, Jewish Care, Victoria, Australia, is explicit about providing services within the Jewish community. Its purpose is "Delivering excellent care and support, underpinned by Jewish values for the community we serve" meaning values of respect, community, inclusion and social responsibility (Jewish Care, 2021). Catholic Welfare Services in Singapore says it is the "Action Arm of the Catholic Church of Singapore" but that its mission is to "journey with people-in-need to live life to the fullest" particularly those experiencing poverty or distress, regardless of race or religion (Catholic Welfare, 2021). These are both similar values to those expressed in a secular organisation: the Victorian State Department of Families, Fairness and Housing which says it "works hard to create equal opportunities for all Victorians to live a safe, respected and valued life."

As well as considering how your organisation is inclusive of religious traditions, it is also important to ask how spirituality, in the sense of what is meaningful is included. Rego and Pina e Cunha (2008, p. 55) interviewed 361 people from 154 organisations finding that spirituality at work meant "employees who view themselves as spiritual beings whose souls need nourishment at work, who experience a sense of purpose and meaning in their work, and a sense of connectedness to one another and to their workplace community." They conclude that if organisations foster these spiritual needs, individual workers are more likely to bring all of themselves to work in ways that benefit them and the organisation. Most people have had mixed experiences of organisational life from this perspective. However, many social workers would have what I called a sense of vocation in Chapter 7; a belief in the value of what they do, so that meaning and purpose might come from the work itself. My experience in critical reflection supervision groups is that what people find challenging is more often the frustrations of organisational systems rather than the work itself. Part of being a leader in the unleading sense might be promoting connections between workers, generating a sense of mutuality about your work practice. Critical reflection supervision in can foster this kind of deeper connectedness: participants come to see that what they assumed were individual issues are often shared and to understand the fundamental values that influence each other's practice. As discussed in Chapter 7, some organisations now include questions about spirituality and religion as part of their assessment process.

Gradually in some organisations, questions are being asked about wellbeing for staff and how this can be influenced, what policy and practice changes need to be made to promote purpose and nourishment at work. For this to happen, we all need to affirm its importance for us as workers and those we work with. McGarrigle and Walsh (2012, p. 228) suggest that "The challenges of changing one's habits and day-to-day methods of dealing with one's stress may require the integration of meditative skills at all levels of the workplace—between managers and staff, coworkers, and clients." A simple, practical issue is how people are able to experience their own religious holidays. If you live in a country like Australia as I do, several public holidays are based on an assumption that Christian holidays will be celebrated. A secondary school student (Rahman, 2021) wrote an article for the Age newspaper pointing out that as a Muslim her religious celebrations are not only not recognised as holidays, but organisations such as her school disregarded them in organising school camps and ironically an inclusivity conference during Eid, when families would celebrate the annual ending of Ramadan. She points out "My Christmas matters too. I hope that schools all around Australia can acknowledge the negative impacts of ignoring these special days, and the importance of amending the school calendar so that students no longer have to choose between their education and their celebration."

Related to this some organisations have programs in organisations with a specifically spiritual orientation. For example, camps for young people to connect to nature, mindfulness meditation used in mental health services and schools. Use of art can help people express the essence of what's important in different way. You might teach mindfulness meditation as a way of managing anxiety to children and young people at school, for all students rather than only those who express this as an issue. Some organisations have rooms set aside for worship, either inter-faith rooms for any form of spirituality or some specifically for religious groups. Taking the interconnectedness of all things seriously also means asking how organisations and those employed in them care for the environment. How are broader policies about climate change translated into organisatonal practice? The experience of COVID-19 significantly changed expectations about travel for work and conferences, for example, encouraging organisations to think about other options and making them work. Many organisations now have policies about recycling made explicit in how they gather and dispose of waste.

Organisations may also employ staff specifically to engage with spiritual and religious issues, who might be called pastoral care workers, chaplains, faith and wellbeing workers or similar (Carey, Swinton and Grossoehme, 2018). Generally, the expectation would be that they would be able to work with anyone from any spiritual or religious preference. They would also have connections with people from specific religious traditions for those who prefer to talk to them. When I interviewed people about what kept them going in a hospital in Bendigo, many named the pastoral care staff as people whose visits reinforced a "sense of connection or validation in the hospital for their religious beliefs" as well as the symbolic affirmation of having a chapel (Gardner, Tan and Rumbold, 2018). Some also wanted to be visited by someone from their faith tradition, who could use the symbols and/or prayers specifically meaningful to them. You could think of all of these as the specialists in the spiritual care field and then it makes sense you need to be aware of when to refer on to them. Ideally, these conversations with such specialists are available for all those in the organisation; to staff as well as those they are working with. Such workers may also provide activities in the organisation that create a culture of naming and acting from a spiritual place, from a sense of connections to nature, to each other and/or to the transcendent. In a faith-based organisation such as a Catholic hospital, there might be a shared prayer time to acknowledge suffering and death and the place of hope; in a secular organisation a time for shared meditation on a similar topic. However, it can be unpredictable when people will want a conversation about spirituality; it may be the cleaner in a hospital or the hairdresser in an aged care setting who creates the time and space for someone to explore what really matters to them.

The hope is that most social workers will be able to have spiritual conversations at least at a beginning level and to refer to others as needed.

Useful questions to ask about your organisation:

How does this organisation include spirituality/religion for those staff and those who use its services?

How are staff educated/trained to understand and actively include spirituality/religion in their practice?

What flexibility is there for me/others to be able to express what we need spiritually?

How does the organisation demonstrate its willingness to be inclusive to all expressions of religion and culture?

Is there for example, a prayer/meditation room that can be used?

Is there something explicit about religion/spirituality in the organisation's vision or mission statement?

How are those who are not of the dominant religion in the country catered for in terms of significant holidays and religious practices?

How does the organisation engage with nurturing the environment?

Sandra worked as a social worker in a large regional hospital. When the hospital was allocated funding for a new building, staff were asked about what they thought was important. Sandra met with the social work and First Nations staff also based at the hospital and together they developed suggestions for increased wellbeing for staff, patients and families based on feedback from the previous five years as well as addressing concerns about climate change. These included having:

- *Gardens with locally appropriate plants and trees around the new building with many seats for sitting and contemplating and/or having breaks*
- *Small pockets of planting on building walls which could be seen by those inside and outside the hospital*
- *Culturally diverse images on the walls particularly in the entrance to convey welcoming attitudes to many cultures and religions*
- *First Nations staff located on the ground floor with the outside of their office space with images by local First Nations artists*
- *A Spirituality Room which could be used by anyone for quiet prayer or contemplation or be booked for a religious service*
- *Using renewable energy and orienting the building for passive solar*
- *Recycling practices that made explicit care for the environment including reduced use of non-recyclable products*
- *No single use plastics in cafes and encouragement to use own coffee cups and water bottles*

- *Policies that encouraged use of public transport wherever possible or ways to avoid the need for travel.*

Working in communities

Seeing the value of an organisation as a meaningful community links well to identifying the community context explored in Chapter 3. First Nations people are particularly explicit about how community is an integral part of being spiritually attuned. Most of us have some idea of a community or communities that are important to us whether they are geographical or communities of interest, places and/or connections that give a sense of meaning, often of belonging, feeling valued and affirmed, which may also include times of challenge or conflict. Those you work with are likely to have or seek community that is a place of belonging and mutual support, where people feel valued for who they are as well as what they have to offer. Those involved in religious traditions often find this sense of community there, but may also want to feel included and valued in the wider community. Similarly, those describing themselves as spiritual but not religious may have a community connection: a yoga class or meditation group may be where they feel more deeply connected. Emerging online communities continue to reflect spiritual and religious expression connecting people and providing a sense of meaning in their lives (Gardner, 2012, p. 379).

Your role as a worker then might be to work with individuals to nurture community connections, but at least equally to work with communities to encourage them to be more inclusive of all spiritual/religious ways of being. Sadly, there are many examples around the world where people from very different religious and spiritual backgrounds have been living in harmony until a particular incident creates conflict that generates its own momentum. 9/11 was an example of this, where Muslims suddenly felt judged even though they were generally equally critically of those who destroyed the twin towers in the US. Community tensions partly related to religious differences in Northern Ireland flared after the Brexit vote when some community members feared separation from the UK. Media representation of these often simplifies conflicts and exacerbates these tensions which are often expressed in people abusing others: negative comments in the supermarket or shouting at people walking along the street; some are physically attacked. You may find that in your social work role these kinds of differences are expressed in the community you are based in, either in the sense of the geographic community broadly, or the school community or a particular community of interest.

If you are in a city with a mix of religious traditions, it may be that you actively include these communities in working on general community issues. Some religious traditions or some people from religious traditions will be interested in participating in and/or being advocates for community change. Not including them as part of your network of organisations to work with can mean you exclude potentially valuable partners. Interfaith Councils or

Networks have become an important place of mutual support in communities as well as sources of working to bring about community change. Religious leaders can play a role here. As part of his latest writings across the globe, the Pope (Wooden, 2020) suggested that "a community can be rebuilt by men and women who identify with the vulnerability of others, who reject the creation of a society of exclusion, and act instead as neighbours, lifting up and re-habilitating the fallen for the sake of the common good." The overall aim is to discern what gives life and helping everyone to develop their full potential and flourish. In my own city, Bendigo, it helped to bring together representatives from groups across the community, including religious traditions, to form an overall planning group recognising that other groups also experienced dis-crimination and that what was needed overall was broader community change. Sporting clubs held special come and try days targeting those who didn't usually feel able to participate, cultural festivals celebrating music, dance, food fostered greater appreciation of what different cultures and religions had to offer, businesses undertook training in, for example, unconscious bias related to employment and in house attitudes.

First Nations communities are also explicit about why they need to be involved as a community in any decisions that are made about services that will impact them individually or collectively. They affirm that it is critical to start with valuing the knowledge they have and their capacity to support each other building on the integration of spiritual practices. First Nations communities critique Western social work as using a deficit model that can undermine the holistic nature of their way of being. Grieves (2006, p. 66) reports research findings on the persisting cultural values of the Pintupi people "It became clear that these people as a group are driven by some core values that are very different, even antithetical to the values of the modern western society in which they are located, even submerged or embedded, as a minority group. And their identity is at least in part shaped in opposition to what they see as the lesser western values of not being able to share, for example." This is as helpful reminder to check with communities generally: what are the values that they really want to embody, how do they sit with what is seen as the norm and how might a community advocate for other values.

How then does using the critical spirituality framework, the qualities and processes influence your practice here?

Back to Tessa's experience

As you continue to meet with Tessa, it becomes clear that her fears about reactions to the proposed new mosque are justified. A social work colleague, Diane, who works for the City Council tells you that the Council has received a number of public protests against the planning permit. The protestors have lodged an appeal against the application citing the building of a mosque could lead to it becoming a focal point for terrorists. Diane has been asked to facilitate mediation between the two parties and asks you to support her.

Diane's private response was one of disbelief at the level of anger and fear in the community. She also experienced a polarised response from colleagues, some in quiet agreement with the Islamic Community; some vehemently opposed and some not wanting to be involved stating they felt intimated by the community anger. She acknowledges she knows little about Islam and Tessa agrees to meet with her to introduce her to her faith.

From a social work perspective Diane wanted to support the Muslim community. However, she also feels she needs to professionally acknowledge the protestors' fears, not simply ignore or ridicule their beliefs. Rather it was important to take the time to understand and facilitate a process where the protagonists and representatives from the Muslim community came together to better understand each other and hopefully identify common ground.

Diane supported by you negotiated a process using principles of critical reflection to guide the discussion. This took a commitment from both parties and Council staff over a period of three months. The Muslim representatives provided an overview of their faith and examples of traditions and rituals. The community representatives of the protestors described their fear and desire to protect their community. Each identified their desire for a sense of belonging and relevance in their community and each walked away with a feeling of greater understanding and acceptance. Diane acknowledged the bridge of goodwill was built on the principles of curiosity, reflexivity and respectful challenge of each other's assumptions; not necessarily in fierce agreement or to gain or impose a forensic knowledge of Islam rather a greater awareness. The Council also accepted that they needed to do more work on generating social inclusion and started to work on a Cultural Diversity Inclusion Plan which involved a cross section of community members representing business, sport, recreation, relevant agencies related to multiculturalism and health as well as from a newly formed Interfaith Council.

For Tessa, this was a hugely reassuring and empowering experience. While she still experienced some discrimination in the community, she now felt the Muslim community overall was generally better understood and actively supported by those at the Council and a range of community leaders. This coincided with one of her children wanting to go to a Climate Change School Strike activity. While she was initially reluctant, her husband encouraged her to go. A number of community groups were represented and she was approached by the local sustainability group and she decided she would join some of their activities.

Case Study One: George and a school community

George worked as a social worker in a primary school in a large city with many different spiritual and religious traditions. Over time, the school changed from having children who were mainly Christian or of no particular religious or spiritual background to a combination of First Nationals, Muslim, Sikh, Jewish, Christian with a small number of others such as Bahai and Buddhism. He noticed that children who were obviously religious were more likely to be teased and raised with the principal how this might be dealt with. They decided to start including information about different religious and spiritual traditions and the need to accept them from early on in classes. He suggested this meant starting with teachers who often made judgemental comments in the staff room. George and the principal decided they would ask someone from each spiritual or religious tradition to send a representative to a staff meeting each week until all they had all been covered to speak for about twenty minutes on the key aspects of their tradition, how children might be introduced to these and why these were important to families and to answer questions.

While some staff initially doubted the value of this, over time most were able to see how their own assumptions had influenced their judgement and to start to explore ways to value this diversity in the school community. They were able to work with the children in their classes to name and value difference, rather than unconsciously conveying negative messages.

Case Study Two: Saria and Kate

Saria, a Sikh from Afghanistan was referred by a hospital nurse to see Kate, a social worker. The nurse was concerned about Saria being depressed after a diagnosis of bowel cancer. Kate was initially concerned about her lack of knowledge of the Sikh religion and of Afghani culture. Saria was reluctant to talk initially which combined with Kate's fear of saying something inappropriate meant it was hard to establish a relationship. Eventually, Kate decided that it might help to put into words what she was feeling and said: *Saria, I really want to be helpful to you, but I am worried about saying something that isn't respectful to your culture or your religion, I feel so ignorant about both. I'm not even sure if I should be working with you as a woman. Could we start with you helping me understand where you are coming from, what's important to you about these?* This shifted the dynamic between them and Saria was able also to be more direct in saying *I was worried that you didn't want to work with a Sikh.* They explored first where this came from and Saria gave examples of how he felt negatively judged in the community and by his GP, feeling that people made a lot of assumptions that weren't accurate. Kate again expressed her desire not to do that and her hope that Saria would help her understand what his faith and culture meant for him. She asked Saria to say more about where you are coming from, what's important to you about your faith and culture?

Saria named faith as foundational to his life, but explained that he practiced being a Sikh in a way that fitted with his culture. When Kate asked about the nurse's concern about depression, Saria's response was *I don't think I am depressed, I think I am sad about something else going wrong now and I have good reason to be sad, I miss my country, my relatives, family members have died and I am grieving for them. What I need is to be heard and to be welcomed here instead of people being suspicious of me. I also need to be able to practice my faith at work and in all of my life.* He also expressed his fear that doctors would not treat him well given the prejudice he has experienced in the community.

This was a challenging experience for Kate, she had heard similar comments from other patients and was aware of racist attitudes in the community towards people who were obviously religious – such as Saria wearing a turban. She and Saria talked more about how to work together and she reassured him about the doctors he would be working with and treated by. However, she felt uncertain about whether this would be the case with all hospital staff. She decided to raise this in a team meeting and found that others in the team had similar concerns. They brainstormed the kinds of issues that had arisen both with patients but also in more general conversations about difference, particular religious differences. When the team raised this with their manager, he was surprised that there wasn't already cultural diversity training which would be congruent with the hospital's stated values. What emerged was that the current training didn't include religious diversity, as it was assumed that cultural diversity would cover this. The training team agreed this needed to change at a policy level and to have spiritual and religious diversity included in the training. The team also agreed to offer this outside the hospital given that the doctors in the region all sent patients there. They advocated successfully that users of the hospital's services or other community members representing different religious traditions would be asked to participate in providing the training.

9 Socially just spirituality – engaging ethically

I suspect part of what makes including spirituality challenging is the expectation of ethical dilemmas. If you think back to social work history, becoming more secular was partly in reaction to some workers imposing their religious values on those they worked with. Clearly this is an ethical issue, one that social workers have to engage with constantly: being aware enough of where you are coming from not to impose this consciously or unconsciously on others across many ways of being. However, this has contributed to another ethical issue: excluding from practice an aspect of people's lives that is an integral aspect of who they are. Gilbert (2009, p. 7) for example raises concerns that social work is "promoting a position of providing the illusion of inclusion while excluding many of the most vulnerable, particularly those who do not share Western liberal beliefs or Christian traditions."

Part of the ethical imperative for engaging with religion and spirituality is recognising that

> these are possible areas of harm for those we work with ... some women stay in violent relationships on the basis of their religious beliefs often influenced by the religious leaders they engage with. Those who are not heterosexual can feel judged by their religious communities. (Crisp, 2020, p. 972)

Kvarfordt (2010) identifies eight forms of religious or spiritual abuse for children and young people. Some are more perhaps what you might expect such as abuse by someone with religious authority, misuse of religious teachings to frighten children or spiritual wellbeing shaken by violence. Given the human right of children to have their own form of spirituality, she also includes the lack of inclusion of spirituality in modern culture and the impact of intolerance to spirituality in the community. Not including a socially just expectation can also be an ethical issue. Gray (2016, p. 162) suggests that problematic for social work practice are forms of spirituality which are "geared to self-development and creating meaning for our isolated individual senses of self" but in doing so "may mollify and placate people rather than help liberate them from oppression."

DOI: 10.4324/9781003132677-13

Social work codes of ethics related to religion and spirituality

Spirituality and religion are now generally included in social work codes of ethics usually alongside respecting other ways that people may be perceived as different from each other. How exactly this is named depends on context, including whether spirituality and religion are named. Crisp and Dinham (2020) compared 16 codes of ethics for social work practice and found all but two mentioned religion and belief, but few explained what these meant and there was significant variation in whether they named knowledge or skills. The British Association of Social Workers (2021, p7) says

> Social workers have a responsibility to challenge oppression on any basis, including (but not limited to) age, capacity, civil status, class, culture, disability, ethnicity, family structure, gender, gender identity, language, nationality (or lack of), political beliefs, poverty, race, relationship status, religion, sex, sexual orientation or spiritual beliefs.

Similarly, the South Korean Social work code of ethics also names the importance of challenging discrimination, but here religion is first: "Social workers should never be discriminatory of clients for their religion, race, gender, nationality, marital condition, sexual orientation, economic status, political faith, mental or physical disability, and other individual preferences, features, or status (Korea Association of Social Workers). In Australia both are named "Social workers respect others' beliefs, religious or spiritual world views, values, culture, goals, needs and desires, as well as kinship and communal bonds, within a framework of social justice and human rights (AASW, 2020, p. 6). Crisp and Dinham (2020) assert that it is ethically essential that social workers can engage with religion and belief and that codes of ethics have the potential to contribute to much needed religious literacy.

While codes of ethics are context specific to some degree, they do also have shared themes and values, which reflect some of those explored in Chapter 4. Respecting the dignity and intrinsic value of the person and their community is fundamental to social work ethics, working in ways that increase wellbeing and avoid harm, acting in accord with human rights, actively working towards a socially just society as well as maintaining confidentiality and caring for the self as a worker. However, codes of ethics cannot always provide answers, partly because acting ethically is not a totally rational process. The implication can be that there is one clear answer, but often the way forward may be about what is least harmful. I like here the story of the two monks who were to cross a river swollen by spring rain. A woman was hesitating on the bank worried she would be swept away, so one of the monks carried her over. Several hours later, the other monk said to him, brother you know our vows mean we can't touch women. The other monk said: ah you are still carrying her, I put her down hours ago. Similarly, Gray (2016, p165) suggests "we are going the wrong way when we treat values, ethics, spirituality, the environment, and traditional knowledge for that matter, solely as a rational scientific project—seeking concrete explanations—without embracing a truly holistic understanding." Essentially, acting ethically is about living and working in tune with your fundamental values. Ideally as a social worker these are congruent with social work values, integrated into your way of being and in interacting with your environment. Banks (2016, p35) for example, talks about ethics work as "part of everyday practice" that is part of working in a relational way and understanding the broader context."

Personal and professional beliefs and ethics

However, even when you are clear about values and what you think is an ethical approach to life, particular experiences of your own and those you work with will inevitably throw up ethical challenges. Acting ethically may be seen as meaning a conflict between personal and professional values and beliefs. Judd (2013, p. 186) suggests that social work and religious traditions both want social justice, even though they may not always agree what that means, but because of social work's move away from the inclusion of religious beliefs, the expectation is that "when conflicts between personal and professional values develop social workers must suspend their personal values with a duty to uphold professional values or violate social work's mission and code of ethics." For example, Fenton (2019 p. 455) points out that Sheffield University expelled a social work student for saying on social media that, as a Christian, he didn't agree with same sex marriage and asks "Do privately held discriminatory beliefs always mean discriminatory behaviour?" In principle, they need not, but workers then need to be aware of the potential issues and complexities for themselves and for their clients, particularly now given social media means the personal or private often becomes public.

Being able to act ethically or in accord with your values and beliefs is named across professions as central to work satisfaction, so this can be a significant issue (Ulrich and Grady, 2018). How being ethical is explored and named varies considerably in social work and related professions including moral conscience, moral distress, professional integrity, conscience or professional disjunctions. One of the common themes here is the distress or frustration that comes from not acting in ways that fit with values. Notice what could be seen as religious language here, the morality of a particular action, the question of conscience or an internal sense of making ethical judgements. What is meant by morality is acting in ways that feel 'right' according to values and professional ethics. It's important to recognise how undermining not doing this can be over time. Epstein and Delgado (2010, p. 9) from nursing, say moral distress relates to making decisions contrary to values leaving a 'moral residue'; the "sum of the nicks in one's moral integrity and self-punishment inflicted when one does not do the right thing." They link this to burnout, withdrawal or conscientious objection. What is needed is a sense of being "active moral agents in a political context of challengeable framings, norms, rules and policies about social justice, social responsibility and societal compassion" (Banks, 2016, p. 46).

Influence of context

Ethical issues are then also context specific, first in the organisational context: Barlem and Ramos (2015, p. 612) say moral distress "plays out in the 'micro spaces' of professional practice, where there is inevitably moral uncertainty given the nature of the work and interactions between morality and power differences." Like Banks, they suggest the organisation and policy environment is influential here. Sometimes workers ask: who am I accountable to? The organisation or those I work with? A common experience for workers is when someone needs a service offered in a way that their organisation is not able or willing to do. It might be as simple as having a waiting list because too many people need a service. Workers might then ask: is it ethically better to work well with each person before taking on more? Or is it better to work with more people even if it means that each have less time and energy from their worker? Awareness of the demand can be ethically challenging and emotionally exhausting. Workers can end up frustrated with their agency and/ or taking on more work than is realistic. However, the broader context of how the agency is funded is also relevant here. In one agency I worked in, staff agreed reluctantly to a waiting list because they felt it was the only way to register the need with the funding body. In another the agency decided everyone would be seen for a longer than usual initial interview, then put on the waiting list so that people whose issues could be resolved at least to some degree in an individual session could then move on.

Banks (2013) suggests that it is more helpful to see these worker and organisational differences as complementary and explore how to negotiate the balance. Similarly, Musto and Rodney (2018, p. 16) point out that structures such as sociopolitical and economic policies will influence how organisations deliver health care, suggesting 'moral agency' is a way of moving "past the view of constraints resting either within the individual or with the organization pointing to the idea of reciprocity between structure and agency." From this relational perspective, both individuals and organisations can constantly influence each other. Questions might include: how do we encourage organisations and communities to allow each other to spiritually celebrate in their own way including balancing rights and responsibilities? What are the ethical dilemmas of this? How do we seek to change exclusion and oppression in society generally and in communities and organisations in relation to spirituality and religion? How could organisations support their workers to engage with what they experience as ethical issues given conflicts between personal and professional values?

Framing ethical approaches

In balancing the principles of codes of ethics with how to integrate being ethical, some writers are more explicit about the values or attitudes that contribute to an ethical stance. Sneed (2010, p. 180) for example, as a black, gay Christian argues for what he calls an 'ethics of openness.' He sees this as a way of reflecting on moral choices "that relies on a deep appreciation of human worth, value and action, is religious in that it draws on those categories of human experience that humans hold sacred and of deep and abiding value and meaning." The key questions then become what will foster human flourishing, human happiness and fulfilment in the world as well as in individuals. Central to this is "treating people as we would wish to be treated, we become open to difference, for it requires a vulnerability, an openness to others" (Sneed, 2010, p. 192).

A number of other writers advocate for the 'ethics of care.' For Béres (2014, p. 127) this fits with learning from Benedictine monks about hospitality as well as a feminist ethics of care, moving "towards a connected relationship based practice, resulting in cooperation, explorations of possibilities, expectations of possible change, stronger bonds and personal renewal." We can think about how to be a good host in welcoming people, but also good guests when home visiting. Similarly, Gilbert (2009, p7) also advocates for an ethics of care focusing on "the reciprocal and relational aspects of caring relationships" and including the "Ethics of Emotion…the rational and deliberate use of emotion, in particular compassion, to promote caring relationships and provide a balance to abstract ethical concepts drawn from liberal ethics." Reinforcing a green perspective, he also includes an 'ethics of life' that addressed the importance of all systems that sustain life. Finally, he includes postmodern approaches that "explore the relationship between social interaction, language and meaning" where "values of human dignity, worth, and social justice can be accommodated as each promotes a political imperative capable of social change."

Banks (2013, 2016) is helpfully specific about ways of being ethical in organisations: firstly, she names **framing work** as key: identifying what the key ethics aspects of a situation are and seeing how these are influenced by the political and social context.

> It is essential that the work of framing a situation includes elements of personal engagement and professional accountability, that the social worker sees her/himself in the picture and sees her/his professional self as having agency (that is, she/he does not frame her/himself as victim of bureaucracy or an innocent bystander, for example). (Banks, 2013, p. 600).

For example, this might include not simply standing by when racist comments are made about a colleague at work or assuming change is impossible when the agency is not providing services well.

Secondly, she suggests identifying the **role work** related to the ethical situation: asking what is my role here, being prepared to negotiate and change roles as needed. For example, being an advocate in some situations, a more impartial mediator in others. Third it is important to name and put effort into **emotion work** naming and showing emotions such as being compassionate and empathic when appropriate and not showing emotions that would be unhelpful such as fear or disgust. She suggests that working "on creating emotions is in the realm of personal engagement, but in professional work they are 'managed' within a framework of professional accountability (we may strive for a 'detached closeness' or 'caring fairness', for example)" (Banks, 2013, p. 600). This might include working with people who have acted in ways you feel justifiably uncomfortable about, for example people's whose spiritual expression is abusive in some way, but also those acting in ways you don't personally feel comfortable with such as someone wanting to talk about their fear of dying without religious absolution. This may mean needing to do what she calls **identity work** asking what is means for you to have an identity as an ethically good professional part of which is negotiating your personal and professional selves. This needs to include **reason work** working to understand all the perspectives of a particular situation and being able to make ethical judgements based on these. Finally, **performance work** related to how to carry out ethical actions, how to communicate and act.

To give an example of how you might use these: when I worked in a Catholic agency providing relationship counselling, I saw a woman I will call Dora, who had decided she could no longer remain in her marriage. She and her husband, Patrick, had three children, the youngest had left home a year ago and she felt stifled in her relationship with Patrick. Dora described Patrick as well-meaning, but stuck in a rut, not able to change or see why anyone would want a different life from his and not able to allow her to change either. She gave many examples of how she had tried to change their relationship, including suggesting joint counselling and described herself as worn out by trying. As a Catholic, she was well aware of what this meant for her and her family, but could see no other way. She wanted to talk this over with someone not involved in her life and as she talked she became even clearer about what she wanted and how to manage separating. She went home, told Patrick she had seen me and that she was leaving. A week later Patrick came in essentially to say that as a worker in a Catholic auspiced agency, I had to tell Dora that she had to stay in the marriage with him. Initially I was taken aback by Patrick's perception of how the Church's teachings would play out in my role in the agency, but I could see that it made sense from his perspective. I struggled to maintain what I felt was an ethical stance towards Patrick. The issue was not whether to agree with Patrick, but how to maintain an attitude of respect for him while affirming Dora's right to make her decision. Implicit in this was the desire to open up life-enhancing possibilities for all concerned, if possible. This example also highlighted for me the ethical complications of working in a faith based organisation. The agency did not support Patrick's perception, but I realised that it complicated his expectations and might influence how the agency is seen generally – and me as a worker in it.

From the position of **framing work,** the agency's religious auspice was clearly important in terms of how I was seen by both Dora and Patrick. They expected me to understand the implications for them as Catholics seeking separation and divorce. I also needed to be aware of and ensure Dora was aware of what this might mean for her given structural norms, what she could expect of the legal and social systems. The social context in terms of gender expectations also felt relevant. It soon became clear that Dora had thought through issues related to the church and while she was anxious about losing what was an important community for her, my **role work**, what she wanted from me, was to be a thoughtful and neutral sounding board. Patrick on the other hand, wanted me to be an advocate for him. I needed to be explicit about how I saw my role as impartial, but also supporting Dora's right to make her own decision. This meant managing my **identity** self: as a woman who was not Catholic, I also had to work at not imposing my personal assumption about Dora's right to simply make choices, but to see that given her context this was a more challenging decision than for someone from a non-religious background. I also needed to be careful of my underlying assumption that Dora had done the hard work and it was Patrick's turn to own the need to change. Part of the challenge ethically then was the **emotion work**. I was conscious that to work effectively and respectfully with them both, I had to be able to demonstrate compassion and empathy for how each was feeling. I had to work harder to accept that Patrick's perspective was reasonable from his point of view and to use **reason work** to manage this. Once I was able to truly feel compassion for Patrick's pain at the ending of the relationship, **performance work** became possible: we could communicate about opportunities for change Patrick could now see he had missed, how to separate constructively and the possibilities for future relationships to be different.

How then do you work on ethical practice related to spiritual and religious issues?

If you look back through this book, you will find much that will help with exploring an ethical attitude to including spirituality and religion in practice. First, is the assumption that it is important to include spirituality and religion and to understand that how these are identified and perceived is infinitely variable. The theoretical framework outline in Chapter 3 provides a basis for thinking about this: to recognise how spirituality and religion are expressed now is partly context specific and influenced by history. Inevitably there are significant differences in how these are expressed and how they are perceived ethically. "Given the religious, philosophical and cultural pluralism characteristic of modern liberal democracies, we cannot assume a common understanding of how moral and non-moral considerations should be distinguished, or of the sense in which a moral judgement can be "sound"

(Vokey and Kerr, 2011, p. 64). This is where the relationship building is key; social workers need to be courageous about naming the ethical issues and being prepared to explore these: "to be grounded in an ethics that is capable of holding together the debates between moral duties, consequences, virtues, care, the natural world and other ethical approaches" (Hugman, 2012, p. 144).

There are many skills and capacities that are part of social work practice that facilitate being ethical in this area as in all other areas of practice. The qualities explored in Chapter 4 make these explicit. Including a socially just attitude is a key aspect of this. As well as listening, being deeply respectful of difference, an ethical stance requires asking is everyone's view being heard? Is anyone being abused in any way? Is one person's right to express themselves undermining someone else's?

The critically reflective approach explored in Chapter 5 provides a process for engaging with ethical issues. This can prompt identifying questions you need to ask of yourself as well as those you are working with. Am I working in ways that ensure all voices are heard? Are there some ways in which I am not open to hearing what is nurturing for others even if alien to me? Understanding the influence of your own values and beliefs, your own sense of the spiritual and/or religious is central here. Carrington (2017, p. 297) suggests that conscious or critically reflective practice "allows for the exploration and management of tensions and ethical issues." Engaging in critically reflective practice with others can further enable you to determine why you might be reacting in a particular way to an ethical issue or feeling ethically torn. Being able to put yourself in the position of the other and seeing the situation from their perspective opens up the complexity of how issues may be seen differently. Similarly, exploring your own experience of a spiritual and/or religious journey may sharpen your awareness of how your history has influenced what you are open to hearing and anything that you may want to discourage.

Taking time to discern is an important aspect of being and acting ethically. The idea of discernment from religious traditions is to focus on a particular issue, often something that needs a decision. The aim is to allow time to sit with whatever the issue is and to allow feelings and thoughts to emerge, gradually to sense a direction for the decision that fits with fundamental values, but also acknowledges the issues in the broader context and for others involved. In some ways this is similar to critical reflection when you seek to understand in a deeper way what is influencing you. The idea of discernment from a religious perspective is that you hold the issue in a transcendent space, seeing the issue in a different light because it is in the context of what really matters overall. This in some ways is also like the narrative process of externalising: being able to see the issue as separate from yourself can mean it is possible to understand that there are many ways that the issue could be seen. Implicit in this, is the ability to wait and allow the process of discerning to happen. You could link this to the Garraba idea of waiting a little way identified in Chapter 4 meaning that you might need to wait before a decision is made for another source of wisdom or knowledge to appear which might be through Elders or dreams. This waiting and discerning can feel contradictory to the organisational pressure to make decisions, but surprisingly often decisions can wait until the discernment is clear.

Case studies

Case Study One: Right to choose religion

Karen works in a women's refuge and has started a group for the women who are living in the refuge. It started as a mutual support group and has become a place where women share their stories, fears and hopes. Karen is now struggling with the group because three of the women currently in it have strong religious beliefs, though from totally different backgrounds: Mandy is Christian, Ria is Muslim and Tara is Buddhist. As they talk with each other, they articulate their new understanding that being abused was not the essence of their religion, but their husbands had used it to justify themselves. The other two women in the group Peta and Sally initially said they didn't believe in anything, but as the other women have talked about their beliefs, they have started to name what they see as spiritual values. What all the women have in common is that they were experiencing violence in their relationships with a partner, four of them with a male partner and one with a woman. They all believed that they had to 'put up with this' for the sake of the relationship.

Karen identifies as having no religious background. She struggles to understand how the three women can be positive about their religion when it seems to have supported their husbands to be violent towards them. From an ethical perspective she feels torn, on the one hand, she wants to respect their preferences and encourage them to make their own decisions. On the other hand, from a social justice perspective she needs to be explicit that violence is not acceptable and that using religious teachings to justify it is a form of abuse. She is also challenged by Sally's response to the women, she just can't understand their religious beliefs and will say in the group, *this is just stupid to believe all this, look where it's got you.* While personally part of Karen agrees with this, she feels strongly that this is not congruent with her social work values.

She decides to use her next supervision session with her supervisor to critically reflect on this experience hoping for some direction. She uses the experience of Sally's comment in the group and feeling stuck about how to respond. When Cate her supervisor asked her to say more about how she felt, she responded stuck, ethically challenged, uncomfortable, then she said honestly, I think I feel revulsion at these religions that can make people stay and be abused. I just feel like saying to them exactly what Sally said. I know I can't and I shouldn't want to. She and Cate explored what her competing assumptions might be:

People should leave whatever is contributing to their abuse.

Religion is a contributor to abuse.

I should respect other people's views and what's important to them.

Next, Cate asked where Karen thought Sally was coming from. After naming similar feelings of frustration, she articulated assumptions:

Religion is out of date

You should leave your past behind you and start a new life.

If other people are being stupid, you should tell them.

Because Karen had been identifying with what Sally said, she found these particularly challenging and suggested going with where Mandy might be coming from. Because Karen struggled with this, together they came up with possible assumptions for Mandy:

My religion is more than what my husband or church says

My religion has a lot of meaning for me about how to live

My faith in God keeps me going through this hard time.

It really helps to be with others who are also religious and understand what it means.

Putting these together, Karen could see that she had been operating from assumptions like Sally's. While in theory she believed she should respect other views, in practice her assumption was you should reject these beliefs and leave your religion. She suspected that she was conveying that message at least non-verbally and that the three women were providing each other with more support than she was. Ethically, she felt in retrospect she was being disrespectful. In Bank's terms she needed to do more reason work: see other points of view and emotion work: to empathise genuinely with the pain of change and to respect what was still important. She could also see how this had meant she didn't call on clergy or other spiritual mentors in the community who might provide ongoing support.

Case Study Two: Choice re prayer

Peter supervises Jane, both social workers, who work in a large city hospital. Peter is contacted by a family member, Jess, who is concerned that when she arrived unexpectedly to visit her father, Ron, she found Jane praying with him. Jess describes her father as a committed atheist who is extremely uncomfortable with being prayed for, but who would feel 'rude' to tell a social worker to go away or stop. When Jess arrived, Jane left saying she would leave them to have time together. Ron asked Jess to see if she could stop him being prayed for and asked why this was happening in a large government run hospital.

This was not the first time something like this had happened. Previously Jane suggested to a patient that they would die more happily if they renewed their childhood faith. The patient and family had felt this was pushing her own faith values and asked to have a different social worker. Peter had thought he and Jane had reached agreement that it was not ethically appropriate to 'evangelise' i.e. that she could ask open questions about whether people had a religious or spiritual belief they wanted to express, but not to suggest her own, unless asked. He raised the issue of Ron's reaction in supervision and was frustrated that Jane was unable to understand his concern. She said that she hadn't been evangelising, she had just said that she would pray for Ron and he hadn't objected. Peter asked how would you feel if someone prayed for you and you hadn't asked and Jane answered she would really appreciate it. Peter was tempted to express his own frustration with this answer, but suggested instead they use critical reflection to explore where Jane and Ron were coming from.

Jane was easily able to express her own values and beliefs:

It is better to have a religious faith to bring you comfort when dying.

She found it harder to express where Ron might be coming from and initially her assumptions got in the way:

I will appreciate Jane cares for me in this way.

Peter suggested he contribute ideas about Ron's perspective and that given that Ron had asked his daughter to stop Jane praying for him, Jane's assumption didn't work. Together they reached:

I do not believe in the power of prayer

If you impose prayer on me, I will react negatively to it.

I don't want prayer imposed on me, it should be my choice

This is violating my way of being, is disrespectful to my life choices.

Peter was conscious after he contributed the final assumption that his own emotions and values were being expressed. When he asked Jane how she was reacting to these, she said she felt really uncomfortable about the word violated and asked him to explain that. Peter explained that being prayed for, if he hadn't asked for that, would feel intrusive, deeply disrespectful and disempowering; that the other person was assuming he couldn't do that for himself if he wanted prayer. If he was a patient, already feeling somewhat disempowered by the hospital system, it would feel even worse.

Jane was taken aback by this, saying she never imagined that her praying would be experienced in this way. Because Peter could speak from his own reaction, she could somehow hear this more clearly. They were able to move to exploring what was and wasn't ethical. This included how to ensure people who wanted to engage with religious and spiritual could do so in ways that suited them.

Case Study Three: Treating people respectfully

Leslie, a social worker providing external supervision to hospital staff, was asked to go and see the Human Resources Manager Felicity in her hospital. Because of funding cuts, the hospital was making several staff redundant. Leslie was surprised to be asked to sit in on interviews with these staff and to offer them counselling. The expectation was that the staff members would leave that day. Felicity apologised for the short notice, but said that the team had been advised Leslie's involvement would be part of their duty of care. Reluctantly Leslie sat in on three interviews. Only one person, Rob, asked for a counselling session. He explained that he was feeling so upset that he didn't want to go home till he had a chance to debrief with someone. He lived with his mother who was significantly disabled and he didn't want to distress her.

Afterwards, Leslie felt very disturbed by this including her accepting this role. From an ethical stance, she felt she had implicitly condoned the orga-nisation working in a way that was unnecessarily disrespectful and under-mining. While she could understand the political context and the organisational need to save money, she could not understand or accept the process as it was. She was also aware that her own area of responsibility: the social work team in the major department of the hospital would also be under threat and potentially her own role. If she questioned the process, it might be tempting to move her up the list of people to be made redundant.

After wrestling with this for some time, Leslie felt she couldn't remain silent about it. She raised it with her own line manager, who didn't feel it was their role to 'rock the boat' about the issue. He thought it would be more prudent to work on making sure their team was seen as important. Leslie decided to go and sit in the hospital chapel as a quiet space where she wouldn't be inter-rupted to see whether any clarity emerged for her. As she sat what came from her own childhood experience was do unto others as you would have them do unto you. This felt like an inner truth for her. She went to see the human resources manager and outlined how she was feeling. Felicity was initially taken aback, but agreed it was a tough process. Her view had been let's do it quickly. As they discussed it more, both could affirm that the person being made redundant needed the same kind of valuing as anyone who left, the offer of public appreciation of their work, the opportunity for mutual farewells and time to accept the change. Felicity was unsure how much she could influence this but committed to raising it with her own manager. Leslie left feeling that at least she had acted with her own sense of integrity intact and that there was an openness for other ways.

Conclusion

The essential message of this book is simply the value of embedding spirituality and religion as an essential aspect of social work practice. Paying attention to the spiritual encourages asking about meaning, what it is at a fundamental level that nurtures, restores, fulfils or inspires us. Including a sense of the transcendent, that which is greater than and part of who we are encourages interconnectedness, depth and an ability to act in a grounded way. The aim here is to make explicit that just as this is important for those we work with, it is also important for our own personal and professional well-being. Our effectiveness is greater if we care for ourselves by nurturing our own spirituality.

Given that the spiritual – and for many this is expressed in religion – is consciously or unconsciously part of who we are, it is integral to holistic practice. We need to understand what influence the spiritual has in how people live and what that means for them individually, for their families and communities. While there are connecting themes across spiritual and religious traditions of seeking hope, love and peace, inevitably, there are also differences. If we can name and celebrate these, they can add richness to communities, provided each of us can allow for the different expressions of the other.

The first part of the book set the background exploring the diverse ways we understand the spiritual and religious and the common themes of meaning, transformation, transcendence, and celebrating diversity. Outlining the history of the changing nature of social work's relationship with spirituality and religion made explicit the past and continuing concerns about imposing values and assumptions on others. However, it is important to understand these within the context of the complex ways in which spirituality and religion are now perceived and particularly the desire of those using social work services to have these be part of holistic practice.

The critical spirituality framework provides a set of theories that provide an integrating structure that reinforces understanding this complexity, identifying key themes of interconnectedness of all beings, understanding the self in the context of social structures, the influence of history, the value of relatedness and community and the importance of socially just action. These combine with key qualities or capacities such as openness, the ability to wait and deep listening and the processes of critical reflection and working with spiritual

DOI: 10.4324/9781003132677-14

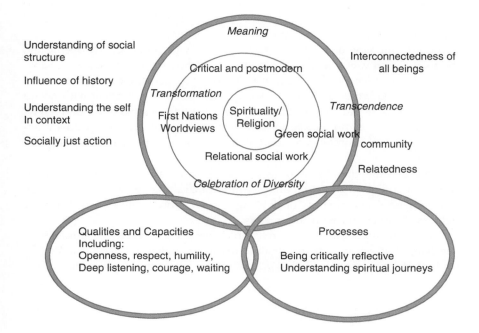

Understanding of social structure

Influence of history

Understanding the self In context

Socially just action

Meaning

Critical and postmodern

Transformation

First Nations Worldviews

Spirituality/ Religion

Green social work

Relational social work

Celebration of Diversity

Interconnectedness of all beings

Transcendence

community

Relatedness

Qualities and Capacities Including:
Openness, respect, humility,
Deep listening, courage, waiting

Processes

Being critically reflective
Understanding spiritual journeys

Figure 10.1 Putting it all together: embedding spirituality and religion in social work practice.

journeys. Integrating these fosters embedding spirituality and religion in social work practice.

You can see in Figure 10.1 how these come together overlapping to re-inforce each other. So what does this mean for how you practice?

Let's return to Tessa. What she needs from you is:

First, a holistic understanding of who she is and that her religious and spiritual experiences are important to her, an essential part of who she is and how she lives her life. What she means by this is both her individual experience of the spiritual, but also her religious tradition's expectations about how that is expressed individually and in her community.

Second, she wants you to understand how the broader structures and the historical context have impacted on her: the difference in being a Muslim in a country where this is the norm compared to one where this is the exception. She also would like you to understand how this interacts with issues of race, culture, the global pressures on refugees and asylum seekers and the in-stitutionalised expectations of where she now lives and what this means for her subjectively and individually as well as for her family.

Third, she would like you to have done your own work: to recognise what is meaningful for you, your own beliefs and values, your understanding of the spiritual and how that might have changed over time. She would like you to have processes that mean you ensure you don't make assumptions that are unhelpful about her and her spiritual way of being.

Fourth, she would like you to relate to her by listening deeply, openly and respectfully, to wait when she is unsure what to say or how to say it, to allow her to be uncertain and to be honest in your engagement with her.

Fifth, Tessa would like you to work sensitively and creatively with her to change what she can – to challenge her own assumptions and to act differently, but also to name and engage in advocacy organisationally and in policy development and community action when that is what is needed for socially just change.

The challenge then for all of us is to work at holding all of this together. If we are focusing on the interconnectedness of all things, as well as celebrating the uniqueness and diversity of all beings, we are more likely to be in harmony with each other and with the universe.

Ideally, adding spirituality and religion to our practice will foster more deeply satisfying, holistic, socially just practice that is grounded in what is meaningful and transformative for individuals, communities and our environment.

Appendix: Further reading about religious and spiritual traditions

Canda, E.R., Furman, L.D. and Canda, H. (2020) *Spiritual diversity in social work practice the heart of helping*. 3rd edn. New York: Oxford University Press, particularly chapters 5 and 6.

Crisp, B.R. (2017) *The Routledge handbook of religion, spirituality and social work*. London: Routledge, particularly Section Three.

Deming, W. (2015) *Understanding the religions of the world: an introduction*. Chichester: John Wiley and Sons.

Gale, F., Bohan, N. and McRae-McMahon, D (eds.). (2007) *Spirited practices spirituality and the helping professions*. NSW: Allen & Unwin Crows Nest.

Loue, S. (2017) *Handbook of religion and spirituality in social work practice and research*. New York: Springer.

Sorajjakool, Carr, M.F. and Nam, J.J. (2010) *World religions for healthcare professionals*. New York and London: Routledge.

References

Admirand, P. (2018) 'Why liberation theology should be taught in Catholic secondary schools', *International Studies in Catholic Education*, 102, pp. 156–169.

Alston, M., Hargreaves, D. and Hazeleger, T. (2018) 'Post disaster social work: reflections on the nature of place and loss', *Australian Social Work*, 714, pp. 405–416.

Australian Association of Social Workers (2020) *Code of ethics.* https://www.aasw.asn.au/document/item/13400 (Accessed: 10 May 2021).

Bacchi, C. (2009) *Analysing policy: what's the problem represented to be?* Frenchs Forest Australia: Pearson Education.

Baird, J. (2019) *Phosphorescence.* Australia: Harper Collins.

Banks, S. (2013) 'Negotiating personal engagement and professional accountability: professional wisdom and ethics work', *European Journal of Social Work*, 16(5), pp. 587–604.

Banks, S. (2016) 'Everyday ethics in professional life: social work as ethics work', *Ethics and Social Welfare*, 101, pp. 35–52.

Barlem, E.L.D. and Ramos, F.R.S. (2015) 'Constructing a theoretical model of moral distress', *Nursing Ethics*, 22(5), pp. 608–615.

Bennett, Z. (2007) 'Action is the life of all": the praxis-based epistemology of liberation theology' in *The Cambridge companion to liberation theology*. Cambridge: Cambridge University Press, pp. 39–54.

Béres, L. (2012) 'A thin place: narratives of space and place, celtic spirituality and meaning', *Journal of Religion & Spirituality in Social Work: Social Thought*, 31(4), pp. 394–413, DOI: 10.1080/15426432.2012.716297.

Béres, L. (2014) *The narrative practitioner.* U.K.: MacMillan Education.

Bessarab, D., Green, S., Jones, V., Stratton, K., Young, S. and Zubrzycki, J. (2014) *Getting it Right Creating Partnerships for Change. Integrating Aboriginal and Torres Strait Islander knowledges in social work education and practice. Teaching and Learning Framework 2,* Retrieved from Sydney: Australian Government Office for Learning and Teaching.

Besthorn, F.H. (2012) 'Radical equalitarian ecological justice a social work call to action' in Gray, M., Coates, J., and Hetherington, T. (eds.) *Environmental social work.* Taylor and Francis, pp. 31–45.

Bhagwan, R. (2017) 'The sacred in traditional African spirituality creating synergies with social work practice' in Crisp, B.R. (ed.) *The Routledge handbook of religion, spirituality and social work.* London: Routledge, pp. 64–72.

Bien, T. (2008) 'The four immeasurable minds preparing to be present in psychotherapy' in Hick, S.F. and Bien, T. (eds.) *Mindfulness and the therapeutic relationship.* London: The Guilford Press, pp. 37–54.

Bisno, H. (1952) *The philosophy of social work.* Washington: Public Affairs Press.

Bodhi, S.R. (2011) 'Professional social work education in India, a critical view from the periphery, discussion note 3', *The Indian Journal of Social Work*, 72(2), 289–300.

Bowpitt, G. (1998) 'Evangelical Christianity, secular humanism, and the genesis of British Social Work', *British Journal of Social Work*, 285, pp. 675–693.

Brett, L. (2001) *New York*. Sydney: Picador.

Brickell, M. (2011) 'Melissa Brickell' in Gardner, F. (ed.) *Critical spirituality*. Farnham: Ashgate, pp. 167–178.

British Association of Social Workers (2021) *Code of Ethics*. Available at: https://www.basw.co.uk/system/files/resources/basw_code_of_ethics_-_2021.pdf (Accessed: 16 August 2021)

Brookfield, S.D. (2011) *Teaching for critical thinking tools and techniques to help students question their assumptions*. San Francisco: Jossey Bass.

Brookfield, S.D. (2017) *Becoming a critically reflective teacher*. 2nd edn. John Wiley and Sons.

Brunn, S.D. (2015) 'Changing world religion map: status, literature and challenges' in Brunn, S.D. (ed.) *The changing world religion map sacred places, identities, practices and politics*. New York: Springer, pp. 3–9.

Calman, S. (2019) *Sunny side up: a story of kindness and joy*. London: John Murray Press.

Canda, E.R. and Furman, L.D. (1999) *Spiritual diversity in social work practice the heart of helping*. New York: The Free Press.

Canda, E.R. and Furman, L.D. (2010) *Spiritual diversity in social work practice the heart of helping*. 2nd edn. Oxford: Oxford University Press.

Canda, E.R., Furman, L.D. and Canda, H. (2020) *Spiritual diversity in social work practice the heart of helping*. 3rd edn. New York: Oxford University Press.

Carey, L.B., Swinton, J. and Grossoehme, D.H. (2018) 'Chaplaincy and spiritual care' in Carey, L.B. and Mathisen, B. (eds.) *Spiritual care for allied health practice a person-centered approach*. London: Jessica Kingsley Publishers, pp. 229–257.

Carrington, A.M. (2017) 'A spiritual approach to social work practice' in Crisp, B.R. (ed.) *The Routledge handbook of religion, spirituality and social work*. London: Routledge, pp. 291–299.

Carroll, B. and Landry, K. (2010) 'Logging on and letting out: using online social networks to grieve and to mourn', *Bulletin of Science, Technology & Society, SAGE*, 305, pp. 341–349.

Catholic Welfare Services (2021) *Mission statement*. Available at: https://www.catholicwelfare.org.sg/about.html (Accessed: 12 April 2021).

Cobb, M., Rumbold, B. and Puchalski, C. (2012) 'The future of spirituality and healthcare' in Cobb, M., Puchalski, C.M. and Rumbold, B. (eds.) *Spirituality in healthcare*. Oxford: Oxford University Press.

Costello, T. (2016) *Faith: embracing life in all its uncertainty*. Richmond: Hardie Grant Books.

Cox, D. (1987) *Migration and welfare: an Australian perspective*. New York: Prentice-Hall.

Cree, V.E. and Phillips, R. (2019) 'Feminist contributions to critical social work' in Webb, S.A. (ed.) *The Routledge handbook of critical social work*. London: Routledge, pp. 126–136.

Crisp, B. (2014) *Social work and faith-based organizations*. Abingdon: Routledge.

Crisp, B.R. (2017) *The Routledge handbook of religion, spirituality and social work*. London: Routledge.

Crisp, B. (2020) 'Charting the development of spirituality in social work in the second decade of the 21st century: a critical commentary', *British Journal of Social Work*, 50(3), pp. 961–978.

Crisp, B. and Dinham, A. (2020) 'Are codes of ethics promoting religious literacy for social work practice?' *Australian Social Work*, 73(2), pp. 204–216. DOI: 10.1080/0312407X.2 019.1698628

Danso, R. (2018) 'Cultural competence and cultural humility: a critical reflection on key cultural diversity concepts', *Journal of Social Work*, 18(4), pp. 410–430.

Deepak, A.C. (2019) 'Postcolonial feminist social work' in Webb, S.A. (ed.) *The Routledge handbook of critical social work*. London: Routledge, pp. 182–193.

Document on Human Fraternity for World Peace and Living Together (2019) *L'Osservatore Romano*, 4–5 February, p. 6.

Dominelli, L. (2012) *Green social work from environmental crises to environmental justice*. Cambridge: Polity.

Dominelli, L., Nikku, B.R., and Ku, H.B. (2018) 'Introduction Why green social work?' in Dominelli, L., Nikku, B.R. and Ku, H.B. (eds.) *The Routledge handbook of green social work*, Routledge International Handbooks, Taylor & Francis, pp. 1–6.

Dominelli, L. (2018) 'Green social work in theory and practice: A new environmental paradigm in the profession' in Dominelli, L., Nikku, B.R. and Ku, H.B. (eds.) *The Routledge handbook of green social work*. Routledge International Handbooks, Taylor & Francis, pp. 9–20.

Dominelli, L. (2019) 'Green social work, political ecology and environmental justice' in Webb, S.A. (ed.) *The Routledge handbook of critical social work*. London: Routledge.

Drummond, A. (2020) 'Embodied Indigenous knowledges protecting and privileging Indigenous peoples' ways of knowing, being and doing in undergraduate nursing education', *The Australian Journal of Indigenous Education*, pp. 1–8. DOI: 10.1017/jie.2020.16

Dulmus, C.N. and Sowers, K.M. (eds.) (2012). *The profession of social work guided by history, led by evidence*. New Jersey: John Wiley and Sons.

Duncan, G. (2015) 'Celtic spirituality and the environment', *HTS Teologiese Studies/ Theological Studies*, 71(1), pp. 1–10.

Dylan, A. and Coates, J. (2012) 'The spirituality of justice: bringing together the eco and the social', *Journal of Religion and Spirituality in Social Work: Social Thought*, 31(1–2), pp. 128–149.

Dylan, A. and Smallboy, B. (2017) 'The constructed 'Indian' and Indigenous sovereignty Social work practice in Indigenous peoples' in Crisp, B.R. (ed.) *The Routledge handbook of religion, spirituality and social work*. London: Routledge.

Editorial (2021) The Guardian view of liberal Christianity: is this their moment? 2nd January. https://www.theguardian.com/commentisfree/2021/jan/01/the-guardian-view-on-liberal-christians-is-this-their-moment

Ellis, L.M., Napan, K. and O'Donoghue, K. (2018) 'Greening social work education in Aotearoa/New Zealand' in Dominelli, L., Nikku, B.R. and Ku, H.B. (eds.) *The Routledge handbook of green social work*. London: Routledge, pp. 535–546.

Epstein, E.G. and Delgado, S. (2010) 'Understanding and addressing moral distress', *The Online Journal of Issues in Nursing*, 15(3), pp. 1–12.

Eyadat, Z. (2013) 'Islamic feminist: roots, development and policies', *Global Policy*, 44, pp. 359–368.

Fenton, J. (2019) 'Social work education and neoliberal hegemony' in Webb, S.A. (ed.) *The Routledge handbook of critical social work*. Abingdon: Routledge.

Ferreira, S.B. (2010) 'Eco-spiritual social work as a precondition for social development', *Ethics and Social Welfare*, 4(1), pp. 3–23.

Finch, J. and McKendrick, D. (2019) 'Securitising social work: counter terrorism, extremism, and radicalization' in Webb, S.A. (ed.) *The Routledge handbook of critical social work*. London: Routledge, pp 244–255.

Firth, S. (1999) 'Spirituality and Ageing in British Hindus, Sikhs and Muslims' in Jewell, A (ed.) *Spirituality and ageing*. London: Jessica Kingsley, pp. 158–174.

Folgheraiter, F. and Raineri, M.L. (2012) 'A critical analysis of the social work definition according to the relational paradigm', *International Social Work*, 55(4), pp. 473–487.

Fook, J. and Gardner, F. (2007) *Practising critical reflection: a resource handbook*. Maidenhead: Open University Press.

Fook, J. (2016) *A critical approach to practice*. 3rd edn. London: Sage.

Fook, J. (2017) 'Finding fundamental meaning through critical reflection' in Béres, L. (ed.) Practising Spirituality. London: Palgrave, pp. 17–29.

Ford, D.F. (2003) 'Holy spirit and Christian spirituality' in Vanhoozer, K.J. (ed.) *The Cambridge companion to postmodern theology*. Cambridge: Cambridge University Press, pp. 269–290.

Forman, R. (2004) *Grassroots spirituality*. Exeter: Imprint Academic.

Fowler, J.W. (1981) *Stages of faith the psychology of human development and the quest for meaning*. San Francisco: Harper and Row.

Fox, M. (1983) *Original blessing*. Santa Fe, New Mexico: Bear & Company.

Furman, L.D., Benson, P.W. and Canda, E.R. (2011) 'Christian social workers' attitudes on the role of religion and spirituality in U.S. social work practice and education', *Social Work & Christianity*, 38(2), pp. 175–200.

Gale, F., Bohan, N., and McRae-McMahon, D. (eds.) (2007) *Spirited practices spirituality and the helping professions*. NSW: Allen & Unwin Crows Nest.

Gardner, F. (2011) *Critical spirituality: a holistic approach to contemporary practice*. Farnham: Ashgate.

Gardner, F. (2012) 'Training and formation a case study' in Cobb, M., Puchalski, C. and Rumbold B. (eds.) *Oxford textbook of spirituality in healthcare*. Oxford: Oxford University Press, pp. 451–458.

Gardner, F. (2014) *Being critically reflective*. Houndmills Basingstoke: Palgrave.

Gardner, F. (2016) *Working with human service organisations*. 2nd edn. South Melbourne: Oxford University Press.

Gardner F. and Béres, L. (2018) 'Social Work and Spiritual Care' in Carey, L.B. and Mathisen, B. (eds.) *Spiritual care for allied health practice a person-centered approach*. London: Jessica Kingsley Publishers, pp. 94–112.

Gardner, F., Tan, H., and Rumbold, B. (2020) 'What spirituality means for patients and families in health care', *Journal of Religion and Health*, 59(1), pp. 195–203. DOI: 10.1007/s10943-018-0716-x

Gardner, F. (2020) 'Social work and spirituality: reflecting on the last 20 years', *Journal for the Study of Spirituality*, 10(1), pp. 72–83. DOI: 10.1080/20440243.2020.1726054

Garth, M. (1994) *Sunshine more meditations for children*. North Blackburn: Collins Dove.

Gilbert, T. (2009) 'Ethics in social work: a comparison of the international statement of principles in social work with the code of ethics for British social workers', *Journal of Social Work Values and Ethics*, 6(2), https://jswve.org/download/2009-2/JSWVE-Summer-2009-Complete.pdf

Gilligan, P. and Furness, S. (2006) 'The role of religion and spirituality in social work practice: views and experiences of social workers and students', *British Journal of Social Work* 36(4), pp. 617–637.

Goodman, H. (2014) 'Relational therapy: constructivist principles to guide diversity practice' in Rosenberger, J. (ed.) *Relational social work with diverse populations*. New York: Springer, pp. 31–53.

Graham, J.R. and Shier, M. (2009) 'Religion and social work: an analysis of faith traditions, themes and Global North/South authorship', *Journal of Religion and Spirituality in Social Work and Social Thought*, 28, pp. 215–233.

Graham, M. (2008) 'Some thoughts about the philosophical underpinnings of Aboriginal world views', *Australian Humanities Review*, 45, pp. 181–194.

Granter, E. (2019) 'Critical theory and critical social work' in Webb S.A. (ed.) *The Routledge handbook of critical social work*. London: Routledge, pp. 3–14.

Gray, M., Coates, J. and Yellow Bird, M. (2008) 'Introduction' in Gray, M., Coates, J., and Yellow Bird, M. (eds.) *Indigenous social work around the world towards culturally relevant education and practice*. Farnham: Ashgate, pp. 1–10.

Gray, M., Coates, J. and Hetherington, T. (2012) 'Introduction overview of the last ten years and typology of ESW' in Gray, M., Coates J. and Hetherington T. (eds.) *Environmental social work*. London: Taylor and Francis, Routledge, pp. 1–28.

Gray, M. and Coates, J. (2015) 'Changing gears: shifting to an environmental perspective in social work education', *Social Work Education*, 34(5), pp. 502–512.

Gray, M. (2016) 'More than science: reflections on science, spirit, tradition, and environment', *Journal for the Study of Spirituality*, 6(2), pp. 155–167.

Grenz, S.J. and Franke, J.R. (2001) *Beyond foundationalism: shaping theology in a postmodern context*. Louisville: John Knox Press.

Grieves, V. (2006) *Indigenous well-being: a framework for Governments' aboriginal cultural heritage activities*. Sydney: NSW Department of Environment and Conservation. Available at: http://www.nationalparks.nsw.gov.au/npws.nsf/Content/Indigenous+wellbeing+framework

Grieves, V. (2009) *Aboriginal spirituality: aboriginal philosophy the basis of aboriginal social and emotional wellbeing*, Discussion Paper No 9. Darwin: Cooperative Research Centre for Aboriginal Health.

Hamerton, H., Hunt, S., Smith, K., and Sargisson, R. (2018) 'Community resistance and resilience following an environmental disaster in Aotearoa/New Zealand' in Dominelli, L., Nikku, B.R. and Ku, H.B. (eds.) *The Routledge handbook of green social work*. London: Routledge, pp. 420–430.

Hanh, T.N. (1976) *The miracle of mindfulness*. Boston: Deacon Press.

Harms, L. (2010) *Understanding human development: a multidimensional approach*. Melbourne: Oxford University Press.

Harms, L. (2015) *Working with people: communication skills for reflective practice*. South Melbourne: Oxford University Press.

Harms, L. and Connolly, M. (2019) *Social work from theory to practice*. 3rd edn. Cambridge: Cambridge University Press.

Healy, K. (2014) *Social work theories in context: creating frameworks for practice*. 2nd edn. Basingstoke: Palgrave Macmillan.

Heelas, P. and Woodhead, L. (2005) *The spiritual revolution why religion is giving way to spirituality*. Oxford: Blackwell Publishing.

Hick, S.F. (2008) 'Cultivating therapeutic relationships the role of mindfulness' in Hick, S.F. and Bien, T. (eds.) *Mindfulness and the therapeutic relationship*. London: The Guilford Press, pp. 5–13.

Hick, S.F. and Bien, T. (2008) (eds.) *Mindfulness and the therapeutic relationship*. London: The Guilford Press.

Hicks, S. (2008) 'Thinking through sexuality', *Journal of Social Work*, 8(1), pp. 65–82.

Ho, R.T.H., Sing, C.Y. and Wong, V.P.Y. (2016) 'Addressing holistic health and work empowerment through a body-mind-spirit intervention program among help-ing professionals in continuous education: A pilot study', *Social Work in Health Care*, 55(10), pp. 779–793.

Hodge, D. (2001) 'Spiritual assessment: a review of major qualitative methods and a new framework for assessing spirituality', *Social Work*, 46(3), pp. 203–214.

Hodge, D. (2012) 'Social justice, international human rights, and religious persecution: the status of the marginalized human right-religious freedom', *Social Work and Christianity*, 39(1), pp. 3–26.

Hodge, D.R. (2015) 'Spirituality and religion among the general public: implications for social work discourse', *Social Work*, 60(3), pp. 219–227.

Holloway, M. (2007) 'Spiritual need and the core business of social work', *British Journal of Social Work*. 37(2), pp. 265–280.

Hugman, R. (2012) *Culture, values and ethics in social work: embracing diversity*. Hoboken: Taylor and Francis.

Hunt C. (2011) 'Editorial', *Journal for the Study of Spirituality*, 1(1), pp. 5–9.

Hunt, C. (2016) 'Spiritual creatures? Exploring an interface between critical reflective practice and spirituality' in Fook, J., Collington, V., Ross, F., Ruch, G. and West, L. (eds.) *Researching critical reflection multidisciplinary perspectives*. London: Routledge, pp. 34–47.

Hunt, C. (2021) *Criticalreflection, spirituality and professional practice*. Switzerland: Palgrave Macmillan.

Hurley, D.J., Martin, L. and Hallberg, R. (2013) 'Resilience in child welfare: a social work perspective', *International Journal of Child, Youth and Family Studies*, 4(2), pp. 259–273.

Ilanbey, S. (2021) What are the proposed laws on gay conversion therapy?, The Age Newspaper: https://www.theage.com.au/politics/victoria/what-are-the-proposed-laws-on-gay-conversion-therapy-20210203-p56z93.html (Accessed: 12 April 2021).

Innovative Resources. https://innovativeresources.org/ (Accessed: 15 August 2021).

Jewish Care (2021), 'Mission statement' https://www.jewishcare.org.au/icms_docs/285188_transforming-for-our-future-strategic-plan-2018-2020.pdf (Accessed: 12 April 2021).

Johnson, R. (1986) *Inner work*. San Francisco: Harper and Row.

Judd, R.G. (2013) 'Social justice: a shared paradigm for social work & religion?', *Journal of Religion and Spirituality in Social Work: Social Thought*, 32, pp. 177–193. DOI: 10.1 080/15426432.2013.779187

Jung, C.G. (1959) *The archetypes and the collective unconscious*. New York: Bollingen Foundation Princeton University Press.

Kavanagh, J. (2007) *The world is our cloister a guide to the modern religious life*. Winchester, UK: O Books, John Hunt Publishing.

Kennedy, E. (2018) 'Historical trends in calls to action' in Dominelli, L., Nikku, B.R. and Ku, H.B. (eds.) *The Routledge handbook of green social work*. London: Routledge, pp. 409–419.

Korea Assocation of Social Workers (2012) 'Code of ethics' https://www.ifsw.org/wp-content/uploads/2018/01/Code-of-Ethics-of-the-KASW.pdf, retrieved: 7 May 2021.

Kossak, M.S. (2009) 'Therapeutic attunement: a transpersonal view of expressive arts therapy', *The Arts in Psychotherapy*, 36(1), pp. 13–18. DOI: 10.1016/j.aip.2008.09.003

Kraus, B. (2019) 'Relational constructivism and relational social work' in Webb, S.A. (ed.) *The Routledge handbook of critical social work*. Abingdon: Routledge, pp. 93–104.

Kvarfordt, C.L. (2010) 'Spiritual abuse and neglect of youth: Reconceptualizing what is known through an investigation of practitioners' experiences', *Journal of Religion & Spirituality in Social Work: Social Thought*, 29(2), pp. 143–164.

Lartey, E.Y. (2003) *In living color an intercultural approach to pastoral care and counseling*. 2nd edn. London and Philadelphia: Jessica Kingsley Publishers.

Lawson, D. (2021) *Poem*. Personal communication.

Leary, M.R. and Banker, C.C. (2019) 'A Critical Examination and Reconceptualization of Humility' in Wright, J.C. (ed.) *Humility*. Oxford Scholarship Online, pp. 64–91. DOI: 10.1093/oso/9780190864873.001.0001

Leighninger, L. (2012) 'The history of social work and social welfare' in Dulmus, C.N. and Sowers K.M. (eds.) *The profession of social work guided by history, led by evidence*. New Jersey: John Wiley and Sons, pp. 1–34.

Lindsay, R. (2002) *Recognizing spirituality the interface between faith and social work*. Crawley, Australia: University of Western Australia Press.

Loch, C.S. (1904) 'The development of charity organisation', *Charity Organisation Review. New Series*, 15(86), pp. 63–83.

Loring, P. (1997) *Listening spirituality – Volume 1: Personal spiritual practices among friends*. Woodchester, UK: Openings Press.

McGarrigle, T. and Walsh, C.A. (2011) 'Mindfulness, self-care, and wellness in social work: effects of contemplative training', *Journal of Religion & Spirituality in Social Work: Social Thought*, 30(3), pp. 212–233.

McMahon, M. (2017) *Lotjpa-nhanuk: Indigenous Australian child-rearing discourses*. PhD Thesis. Melbourne: La Trobe University.

McMahon, M. and McMahon, J. (2019) Yorta Yorta Sisters First Nations Relational Worldviews & Principles Informing Acknowledgement of Country. https://drive.google.com/file/d/1stS60kIAwCOFcftELkUFveERwKzQTZQ3/view?usp=sharing (Accessed: 31 August 2021).

Maddrell, A. (2013) 'Moving and being moved: More-than-walking and talking on pilgrimage walks in the Manx landscape', *Culture and Religion*, 14, pp. 162–177. DOI: 10.1080/14755610.2012.756409

Martin, S. (2009) 'Illness of the mind or illness of the spirit? Mental health-related conceptualization and practices of older iranian immigrants', *Health and Social Work*, 34(2), pp. 117–126.

Mathews, I. (2009) *Social work and spirituality*. Exeter: Learning Matters Ltd.

May, T. and Perry, B. (2017) *Reflexivity: the essential guide*. London: SAGE Publications.

Michener, R. (2007) *Engaging deconstructive theology*. Aldershot: Ashgate.

Mila, K. (2017) 'Mana Moana Healing the Vā, developing spiritually and culturally embedded practices' in Béres, L. (ed.) *Practising Spirituality*. London: Palgrave.

Miller, A. (2020) *Max*. Crows Nest, NSW: Allen & Unwin.

Mistry, H. (2021) Critical Spirituality in Leadership, Podcast Transcript, pp. 1-3 https://www.yorku.ca/edu/unleading/podcast-episodes/critical-spirituality.docx.pdf

Morinis, A. (2019) 'Occupying your rightful space' in J C Wright (ed.), *Humility*. Oxford Scholarship Online, pp. 25–40.

Morley, C. (2014) *Practising critical reflection to develop emancipatory change challenging the legal response to sexual assault.* Farnham: Ashgate.

Morley, C., Macfarlane, S. and Ablett, P. (2014) *Engaging with social work a critical introduction. Port Melbourne.* Melbourne: Cambridge University Press.

Musto, L. and Rodney, P. (2018) 'What we know about moral distress' in Ulrich, C.M. and Grady, C. (eds.) *Moral distress in the health profession.* ebook, Springer, pp. 9–20.

Nadkarni, V.V. and Joseph, S. (2014) 'Envisioning a professional identity: charting pathways through social work education in India' in Noble, C., Strauss, H. and Littlechild, B. (eds.) *Global social work: crossing borders, blurring boundaries.* Sydney: Sydney University Press, pp. 71–83.

Nagai, C. (2010) 'Space for cultural and spiritual experiences in social work education and clinical training journal of teaching' in *Social work,* 30, pp. 435–449.

Narvaez, D. (2019) 'Humility in four forms intrapersonal, interpersonal, community and ecological' in Wright, J.C. (ed.) *Humility.* Oxford Scholarship Online, pp. 117–145. DOI: 10.1093/oso/9780190864873.001.0001

Neff, K.D. (2003) 'Self-compassion: an alternative conceptualization of a healthy attitude toward oneself', *Self and Identity,* 2, pp. 85–102.

Neff, K. and Germer, C. (2017) 'Self-compassion and psychological well-being' in Seppala, E., Simon-Thomas, E., Brown, S.L., Worline, M.C., Cameron, C.D. and Doty, J.R. (eds.) *The Oxford handbook of compassion science.* Oxford Univresity Press, Online, pp. 371–398. DOI: 10.1093/oxfordhb/9780190464684.001.0001

Ni Raghallaigh, M. (2011) 'Religion in the lives of unaccompanied minors: an available and compelling coping resource', *British Journal of Social Work,* 41(3), pp. 539–556.

Nipperess, S. and Boddy, J. (2018) 'Greening Australian social work practice and education' in Dominelli, L., Nikku, B.R. and Ku, H.B. (eds.) *The Routledge handbook of green social work.* London: Routledge, pp. 547–557.

O'Brien, L. and Watson, I. (2014) 'In conversation with Uncle Lewis Bushfires, weather-makers, collective management', *AlterNative,* 10(5), pp. 450–461.

O'Donohue, J. (1999) *Anam Cara: spiritual wisdom from the Celticworld.* Sydney: Bantam Books.

Ontario Human Rights Commission (2013) Human rights and Creed Research and consultation report. http://www3.ohrc.on.ca/sites/default/files/consultation%20report_creed%20human%20rights%20research%20and%20consultation%20report.pdf (Accessed: 25 August 2021), p. 34.

Paine, D.R. (2017) 'Psychology, faith, and training: humility and mature alterity for graduate study', *Journal of Psychology and Christianity,* 36(2), pp. 110–120.

Palmer, P. (2000) *Let your life speak: listening to the voice of vocation.* San Francisco. John Wiley and Sons.

Parsloe, P. (1999) 'Some spiritual and ethical issues in community care for frail elderly people a social work view' in Jewell, A (ed.) *Spirituality and ageing.* London: Jessica Kingsley Publishers, pp. 136–145.

Pascoe, B. (2018) *Dark emu.* Broome: Magabala Books.

Payne, M. (2011) *Humanistic social work core principles in practice.* Chicago: Lyceum Books Inc.

Perera, Y. (2018) 'Sowing the seeds a green social work project in Sri Lanka' in Dominelli, L., Nikku, B.R. and Ku, H.B. (eds.) *The Routledge handbook of green social work.* London: Routledge, pp. 325–339.

Petrella, I. (2017) 'Liberation theology undercover', *Political Theology,* 18(4), pp. 325–339.

Pew Research Center (2012) https://www.pewforum.org/2012/12/18/global-religious-landscape-exec/ (Accessed 18 December 2020).

Pierson, J. (2011) *Understanding social work history and context.* Maidenhead: McGraw-Hill Education.

Puchalksi, C.M.A. and McSkimming, S. (2006) 'Creating healing environments', *Health Progress*, 87(3), pp. 30–33.

Puchalski, C.M., Vitillo, R., Hull, S.K., and Reller, N. (2014) 'Improving the spiritual dimension of whole person care: reaching national and international consensus', *Journal of Palliative Medicine*, 17(6), pp. 642–656.

Ragsdale, J.R. (2018) 'Transforming chaplaincy requires transforming clinical pastoral education', *Journal of Pastoral Care and Counselling*, 72(1), pp. 58–62.

Rahman, A. (2021) 'My 'Christmas' – Eid-ul-Fitr- matters as well', *The Age, Education Section*, p. 16.

Randall, W. (2020) 'Strengthening our stories in the second half of life: narrative resilience through narrative care' in McNamee, S., Gergen, M.M., Camargo-Borges, C. and Rasera E.F. (eds.), *The SAGE handbook of social constructionist practice*. London: SAGE Publications, pp. 444–554.

Rego, A. and Pina e Cunha, M. (2008) 'Workplace spirituality and organisational commitment: an empirical study', *Journal of Organisational Change Management*, 21(1), pp. 53–75.

Rock, L.F., Joseph, D. and Harper, A.O. (2018) 'Dominica - tropical storm Erika and its impacts' in Dominelli, L., Nikku, B.R. and Ku, H.B. (eds.) *The Routledge handbook of green social work*. London: Routledge, pp. 144–155.

Rogers, H. and Maytan, M. (2012) *Mindfulness for the next generation*. Oxford: Oxford University Press.

Rosenberger, B. (2014) 'Orientation to and validation of relational diversity practice' in Rosenberger, J (ed.), *Relational social work practice with diverse populations*. New York: Springer, pp. 13–29.

Rowkith, S. and Bhagwan, R. (2020) 'Honoring tribal spirituality in india: an exploratory study of their beliefs, rituals and healing practices', *Religions, Basel, Switzerland*, 11, 549–565, DOI: 10.3390/rel11110549

Rowson, J. (2017) Spiritualise. https://www.thersa.org/globalassets/pdfs/reports/spiritualise-2nd-edition-report.pdf

Ruch, G. (2012) 'Where have all the feelings gone?', *British Journal of Social Work'*, 42, pp. 1315–1332.

Ruch, G. (2016) 'Relational practice in critical reflection the role of communication and containment' in Fook, J., Collington, V., Ross, F., Ruch, G. and West, L. (eds.) *Researching critical reflection*. Abingdon: Routledge, pp. 23–33.

Rumbold, B. (2007) 'A review of spiritual assessment in health care practice', *Medical Journal of Australia*, 18(6), S60–S62.

Saleebey, D. (2009) *The strengths perspective in social work practice*. 5th edn. Boston: Pearson/Allyn and Bacon.

Schneider, K. (2014) 'Enchanted agnosticism, awe and existential-integrative therapy', *Spirituality in Clinical Practice*, 1(1), pp. 71–73.

Schon, D.A. (1983) *The reflective practitioner: how professionals think in action*. USA: Basic Books, Perseus Books Group.

Shah, V. (2021) 'Welcome to unleading a call to reclaim and redefine leadership', https://www.yorku.ca/edu/unleading/ (Accessed: 25 May 2021).

Sneed, R.A. (2010) *Representations of homosexuality black liberation theology and cultural criticism*. New York: Palgrave Macmillan.

Sorajjakool, S. Carr, M.F. and Nam, J.J. (2010) *World religions for healthcare professionals*. London and New York: Routledge.

Starnino, V.R. and Canda, E.R. (2014) 'The spiritual development process', *Journal of Spirituality and Religion*, 33(3–4), pp. 274–299.

Steere, D. (2000) 'To listen another's soul into a condition of disclosure', *Gleanings,* XIII (3), https://friendsofsilence.net/quote/source/gleanings

Stirling, B., Furman, L.D., Benson, P.W., Canda, E.R. and Grimwood, C. (2010) 'A comparative survey of Aotearoa New Zealand and UK social workers on the role of religion and spirituality in practice', *British Journal of Social Work*, 40(2), pp. 602–621.

Streets, F.J. (2014) 'Relational Social Work and Religious Diversity' in Rosenberger, J. (ed.) *Relational social work with diverse populations*. New York: Springer, pp. 67–78.

Swinton, J. (2014) 'Spirituality-in-healthcare: just because it may be "made up" does not mean that it is not real and does not matter', *Journal for the Study of Spirituality*, 4(2), pp. 162–173.

Tacey, D. (2003) *The spirituality revolution*. Sydney: HarperCollins.

Taylor, B. (2010) *Dark green religion: nature, spirituality and the planetary future*. Berkeley: University of California Press.

Taylor, S.A. (2018) 'Intersectionality in health pandemics' in Dominelli, L., Nikku, B.R. and Ku, H.B. (eds.) *The Routledge handbook of green social work*. London: Routledge, pp. 335–346.

Trelfa, J. (2005) 'Faith in Reflective Practice', *Reflective Practice*, 6(2), pp. 205–212.

Townsend, A. and McMahon, M. (2021) COVID-19 and BLM: humanitarian contexts necessitating principles from first nations world views in an intercultural social work curriculum, *British Journal of Social Work*, 51, pp. 1820–1838.

Ulrich, C.M. and Grady, C. (2018) (eds.) *Moral distress in the health professions*. e-Book, Springer.

Ungunmerr-Baumann, R. (1988) 'Dadirri: Inner Deep Listening', https://www.miriamrosefoundation.org.au/images/Dadirri (Accessed: 8 August 2021).

Veylanswami, S.B. (2009) 'The Three Stages of Faith', *Hinduism Today*, Retrieved from https://www.hinduismtoday.com/modules/smartsection/item.php?itemid=5033

Vernon, M. (2007) *After atheism science, religion and the meaning of life*. Houndmills: Palgrave, Macmillan.

Vernon, M. (2011) *How to be an agnostic*. London: Palgrave.

Victorian Department of Families, Fairness and Housing (2021) https://www.vic.gov.au/department-families-fairness-and-housing (Accessed 25 May 2021).

Vince, R. and Mazen, A. (2014) 'Violent innocent: a contradiction at the heart of leadership', *Organization Studies*, 35(2), pp. 189–207.

Vokey, D. and Kerr, J. (2011) 'Intuition and Professional wisdom can we teach moral discernment?' in Bondi, L., Carr, D., Clark, C. and Clegg, C. (eds.) *Towards professional wisdom*. Farnham: Ashgate, pp. 63–80.

Wang, W. (2020) *Chinese*. Palgrave Macmillan, Curriculum Studies Worldwide.

Waterson, J. (2021) 'Choose a better future for all, Justin Welby tells UK in Easter sermon', *The Guardian*: https://www.theguardian.com/uk-news/2021/apr/04/justin-welby-uk-easter-sermon-covid, retrieved: 11 April 2021.

Watson, I. (2014) 'Re-centring first nations knowledge and places in a terra nullus space', *AlterNative*, 10, 508–520.

Wielenberg, E.J. (2019) 'Secular humility' in Wright, J.C. (ed.) *Humility*. Oxford Scholarship Online.

Wilber, K. (1997) *The eye of spirit*. Boston: Shambhala Publications.

Wilson, S. (1996) *This we can say*. Queensland: Australia Yearly Meeting, p. 10.

Wilson, S. (2014) Bird, https://australianfriend.org/three-poems-2/

Witt, J. (2015) 'Dark green religion: advocating for the sacredness of nature in a changing world' in Brunn, S.D. (ed.) *The changing world religion map sacred places, identities, practices and politics*. New York: Springer Macmillan, pp. 381–388.

Wood, J. and Schuck, C. (2011) *Inspiring creative supervision*. London: Jessica Kinglsey Publishers.

Wooden, C. (2020) 'Pope Francis' new encyclical: Fratelli Tutti', Catholicweekly.com.au, October 5th, https://www.catholicweekly.com.au/pope-francis-new-encyclical-fratelli-tutti/ (Accessed: 10 November 2020).

Yin, A. (2019) 'Media Statement: Australian Social Worker welcome the Victorian Government plan to ban 'conversion therapy', https://www.aasw.asn.au/news-media/2019-2/australian-social-workers-welcome-the-victorian-governments-plan-to-ban-conversion-therapy (Accessed 10 April 2021).

Zapf, M.K. (2010) 'Social work and the environment: understanding people and place', *Critical Social Work*, 11(3), pp. 30–46.

Index

Page numbers in *italics* refer to figures.

history of relationship with social work 33; liberation theology 53

Kauma language 47
knowledges: First Nations 47–51; indigenous 46, 49, 57, 86–87; 'not knowing' 67–69

language: communication 116–117; First Nations knowledges 47; including religion and spirituality 120–121; neutrality 136–137; postmodernism 55, 82
LGBTIQ+: conflict with religious communities 32, 103; families and individuals 113–114; organisational context 140; policy context 137–139; religion and social work 35; social media case study 151
liberation theology 53, 81–82
life stages 98–99; *see also* spiritual journeys
listening as social workers 116–117
listening deeply 69–70, 164

management: relational perspectives 59; social work practice 134–135
meditation 26–27, 38, 72, 78, 121, 125, 143–144
mental illness 100–101
mindfulness 72–73, 74, 125, 142
money 77–78
moral distress 151–152
morality: considerations of 155–156; personal and professional beliefs and ethics 151–152; religion and social work 35; *see also* ethics
music 127
Muslims *see* Islam

narrative approaches 115–116
natural world/nature 56–58, 68–69, 76–77, 91–92
neutrality 136–137
not knowing 67–68, 79

openness 69, 153
organisational practice 134, 139–144, 152

performance work 154, 155
persecution 73–74
personal crises 1–2

personal meaning making 81, 85–95, 130–131, 163–164
place 75–78
policy context 134, 135–139
political framing 153
the Pope 145
postmodernism: critical reflection 82; language 55, 82; societal thinking 41–42; theoretical framework 51–56
power: critical social workers 52–53; respect 116
practice *see* social work practice
prayer 19–20, 106, 121, 123, 125, 142–143, 158–160

Quaker beliefs 4–5

reason work 154, 155
reflection *see* critical reflection
reflective learning 81
reflective questioning 104
reflexivity 83–84
refugees 73–74; Muslim refugee case study 62–63, 117–119, 121–122, 123, 145–146, 163–164
relational perspectives 59–60; attunement to the other 71; Indigenous Relational ontology 46; reflective practice 84–85
relationships counselling 131–133, 154
religion: attitudes about 31–32, 37–42, 81; as distinct from spirituality 17–24; embedding in social work practice 65–66, 111, 113–117, 162–164, *163*; ethics and social work 35, 155–161; history of relationship with social work 33–36; identifying as religious 26–28; and social work practice 2–6, 28–30, 31–33; theoretical framework 61, 62, *61, 62*; traditions and expression of 19–23, 27–28
religious abuse 149
religious celebrations 141–142
religious dialogue 13
religious leaders 145
respect 116, 154–155, 160–161
rituals 128–129, 131
role work 154, 155

sacred texts 19, 104
school community case study 146–147
sectarianism 35
secularism: ethical dilemmas 149;

identifying as not spiritual or religious 24–25; in social work 2–3, 5; and spirituality 22–24
self-awareness 65–66; *see also* critical reflection
self-care 124
self-compassion 71–72
self-development 149
service user perspectives 38–39
Sikhism 147–148
silence 126
social context 73–74, 80, 153
social justice: courage 78; liberation theology 81–82; personal and professional beliefs and ethics 151–152; Quaker beliefs 4–5; religion and social work 34; social work practice 134–135
social media 151
social work assessment 40–41
social work education 5, 31, 36, 40, 42, 47–48
social work practice 8–9; as an art or a science 34–35, 46; beliefs and ethics 151–152; changing attitudes 36–44; codes of ethics 150–151; community context 144–148; critical reflection in 80–81; embedding spirituality and religion 65–66, 111, 113–117, 162–164, *163*; with families and individuals 115–128, 130–133; history of relationship with spirituality and religion 33–36; limitations 129; narrative and strengths approaches 115–116; organisational practice 134, 139–144; policy context 134, 135–139; rituals 128–129; social justice 134–135; spiritual practices 123–129; spirituality and religion 2–6, 28–30, 31–33
South Korean Social work code of ethics 150
space/spaciousness 75–78
spiritual abuse 149
spiritual directors 129
spiritual growth 100–101
spiritual interest screening tool 120–121
spiritual journeys 8, 96–97; case studies 106–108, 109–110; changing aspects of 97–101, *102*; stages in 98–99; ways of being 99–100, 101–105; your own spiritual journey 108–109

spiritual practices 123–129
spiritual resilience 124
spiritual self: approaches to 16–17; identification of 25–26; in social work 2–6
spirituality: aspects of *29*, 29–30; attitudes about 37–42; as distinct from religion 17–24; embedding in social work practice 65–66, 111, 113–117, 162–164, *163*; as experience of the transcendent 15–17; history of relationship with social work 33–36; identifying as spiritual 25–27; meaning of 14–15, 17; and secularism 22–24; and social work practice 2–6, 28–30, 31–33; theoretical framework 61, 62,*61*,*62*; *see also* critical spirituality
spirituality assessment tools 120–121
storylistening 115
strengths approaches 115–116

Tarot cards case study 92–95
terrorism 52, 74, 144
transcendence: postmodernism 54; relational perspectives 59; religious values 22; spiritual journeys 105; spirituality 22, 61, 62
transformation *29*, 30

uncertainty 68–69, 84–85, 98
universal transcendence 105
universal truth 41–42
usefulness 67–68

values: family influences 113–114; personal and professional beliefs and ethics 151–152; personal meaning making 81, 85–95, 130–131, 163–164; self-awareness 65; spiritual journeys 102, 103–104; spirituality and religion 4; unearthing assumptions 84–85; your own spiritual journey 108–109
vocation, work as 128
vulnerability 69

'waiting' 72–73, 156–157
wellbeing policies 141–142
Western worldview 46